U-BOAT HUNTERS

DURING THE GREAT WAR

ROY R. MANSTAN

THE LISTENERS

WESLEYAN UNIVERSITY PRESS

MIDDLETOWN, CONNECTICUT

Wesleyan University Press
Middletown CT 06459
www.wesleyan.edu/wespress
© 2018 Roy R. Manstan
All rights reserved
Manufactured in the United States of America

5 4 3 2 1

Typeset in Charter and Clarendon by
Nord Compo

Library of Congress Cataloging-in-Publication Data

Names: Manstan, Roy R., author.
Title: The listeners : U-boat hunters during the Great War / Roy R. Manstan.
Other titles: U-boat hunters during the Great War
Description: Middletown CT : Wesleyan University Press, [2018] | Series:
   Garnet books | Includes bibliographical references and index. |
   Identifiers: LCCN 2018017912 (print) | LCCN 2018020180 (ebook) | ISBN
   9780819578372 (ebook) | ISBN 9780819578358 (cloth)
Subjects: LCSH: World War, 1914–1918—Naval operations—Submarine. |
   Anti-submarine warfare—United States—History—20th century. | United
   States Naval Engineering Experiment Station—History. | World War,
   1914–1918—Connecticut—NewLondon. | Hydrophone—History—20thcentury. |
   Submarines (Ships)—Germany—History—20th century. | World War,
   1914–1918—Aerial operations. | World War, 1914–1918—Campaigns—
   Atlantic Ocean.
Classification: LCC D590 (ebook) | LCC D590.M36 2018 (print) | DDC
   940.4/5160973—dc23
LC record available at https://lccn.loc.gov/2018017912

CONTENTS

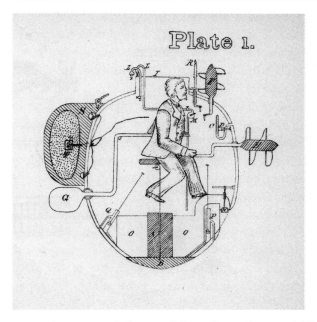

Nineteenth-century illustration of David Bushnell's submarine Turtle *used during the Revolutionary War in an attempt to sink the British flagship HMS* Eagle, *September 7, 1776. (Barber, 1875)*

The external shape of the sub-marine vessel bore some resemblance to two upper tortoise shells of equal size, joined together; the place of entrance into the vessel being represented by the opening made by the swell of the shells, at the head of the animal. The inside was capable of containing the operator, and air, sufficient to support him thirty minutes . . .

—David Bushnell, "General Principles and Construction
of a Sub-marine Vessel," 1799[1]

Writing after the war from his home in Stamford, Connecticut, David Bushnell sent a lengthy letter to Thomas Jefferson on October 13, 1787, describing the "sub-marine vessel" used eleven years earlier in an attempt to sink the British flagship HMS *Eagle*, anchored in New York Harbor. The underwater attack was unsuccessful, as were two later attempts against British warships in the Hudson River. The history of Bushnell's submarine and the creation and testing of a working replica can be found in the book by Roy R. Manstan and Frederic J. Frese, *TURTLE: David Bushnell's Revolutionary Vessel* (2010), which includes a facsimile of Bushnell's letter to Jefferson as published in the *Transactions of the American Philosophical Society* (1799).[2]

The concept of submarine warfare has a long history, evolving in concert with the emergence of science and technology during the Age of Enlightenment of the seventeenth and early eighteenth centuries. In 1648, the Reverend John Wilkins, tutor and member of the Anglican clergy, published *Mathematical Magick: or the Wonders that may be Performed by Mechanical Geometry*. Wilkins' goal was to show, by example, the application of mechanical principles to the many ideas that arose during the seventeenth century. He included a lengthy chapter: "Concerning the possibility of framing an Ark for submarine Navigation," arguing "that such a contrivance is feasible, is beyond all question, because it hath been already experimented here in England by Cornelius Dreble [sic]."[3]

Wilkins suggested several commercial and scientific applications, but made particular note of its military uses. "It may be of great advantage against a Navy of enemies, who by this means may be undermined in the water, and blown up. It may be of special use for the relief of any place that is besieged by water, to convey unto them invisible supplies. . ." then suggesting the possibility of clandestine operations: ". . . and so likewise the surprisal of any place that is accessible by water."

Wilkins was familiar with the vessel Cornelius Drebbel submerged in the Thames in 1623, with the intent to sell the concept to King James I. Although his idea never found favor within the English Admiralty, Drebbel did eventually receive funds from King Charles I to develop an underwater mine that he referred to as a "water petard," used, albeit unsuccessfully, against the French in 1627.[4] It is likely that Bushnell was familiar with Wilkins' *Mathematical Magick*. Wilkins was a founding member of the Royal Society of London, and all of the publications of that society were available at Yale College when Bushnell entered as a freshman in the fall of 1771. Yet the submarine vessels Bushnell may have read about were fanciful concepts with little practical value.

The story of submarine warfare, therefore, began in Connecticut at the onset of the Revolutionary War when David Bushnell conceived, built, launched, tested his submarine, and trained the vessel's operators. The *Turtle*, a name bestowed by his friend Colonel David Humphreys[5], was the world's first undersea vessel designed and used specifically as a naval combatant.

Bushnell lived during a time when inventive minds were being influenced by the expanding knowledge of science, then referred to as natural philosophy, being taught in universities throughout Europe and America. The "Principles" Bushnell was referring to in his letter to Jefferson—the "General Principles and Construction of a Sub-marine Vessel"—were based on the natural philosophy he soon became associated with when he entered Yale.

> When Nehemiah Strong (Yale, 1755) was hired to teach mathematics and natural philosophy in 1770, the college had made a commitment to provide students with the ability to concentrate their studies on subjects leading to careers other than the ministry. It was good timing for Bushnell whose interests were definitely secular.[6]

War with England was almost a certainty, and Bushnell was determined to use his creative mind rather than a musket to support the revolutionary spirit growing in America. The library at Yale was filled with books by those natural philosophers—Isaac Newton, Robert Hooke, Robert Boyle, Edmund Halley and many more—their ideas appearing in the *Transactions of the Royal Society*, every volume of which could be found on the library shelves.

In his letter to Jefferson, Bushnell referred to his propulsion system: "An oar, formed upon the principal of the screw, was fixed in the forepart of the vessel; its axis entered the vessel, and being turned one way, rowed the vessel forward, but being turned the other way rowed it backward; it was made to be turned by hand or foot."[7] An eye witness described it as: "a pair of oars fixed like the opposite arms of a windmill."[8] One of Bushnell's textbooks, the *Philosophia Britannica* by Benjamin Martin (1747), devoted a section to windmill design, a significant power generation technology in the eighteenth century, and may have been the inspiration leading to Bushnell's propeller.[9] After the war, in 1785, Yale College president Ezra Stiles included Bushnell's "Submarine Navigation by the Power of the Screw" in a list of notable inventions along with Benjamin Franklin's "Electrical Pointed Rods."[10] What Stiles described as the power of the screw was Bushnell having created the first use of what is now referred to as a screw propeller—keeping in mind that the word "propeller" did not exist in 1776.

Without any hope of an American navy capable of facing the world's most formidable naval force, which was expected to soon arrive from over the horizon, Bushnell's goal was to find another way to destroy a fearsome British man-of-war. The most vulnerable location of a ship's hull was its nearly flat underbelly. Bushnell understood that because of the incompressibility of water, the destructive force of an explosion would be directed upward and into the flexible wooden planking. How to place a sufficient amount of gunpowder into a waterproof container; then covertly attach the container under a ship's hull; and finally detonate the explosive charge were only a few of the technical problems Bushnell faced. Each of these goals was solved only with a combination of scientific knowledge, mechanical instincts and intuition, and a team of innovative and patriotic individuals.

Bushnell experimented with explosives while at Yale and enlisted others in New Haven for help designing and building the parts for his submarine. Construction of the *Turtle* began at the family farm in Saybrook, partly in the hands of his brother, Ezra. The project was eventually moved to Ayers Point on the Connecticut River, where the Bushnell brothers, helped by artisans in the area, finished and tested his submarine, and where Ezra trained as its operator. Ready for action by the summer of 1776, the *Turtle* was carried down Long Island Sound and brought across land to the Hudson River. On September 6, the little wooden submarine was afloat at the southernmost tip of Manhattan, within sight of HMS *Eagle*.[11]

Although unsuccessful at sending *Eagle* to the bottom, Bushnell's *Turtle* performed the rudimentary functions required of a submarine vessel. His ideas were a product of the age of enlightenment, yet it would take an industrial revolution to solve the inherent difficulties associated with propulsion, with underwater navigation, with providing an adequate air supply, and with placing an explosive device near, on, or into the targeted ship. The nineteenth century saw several attempts, most notably the sinking of the steam sloop USS *Housatonic* by the Confederate submarine *Hunley* in 1864. The *Hunley*, however, was also lost as a consequence of the attack. Technology had simply not advanced sufficiently by the Civil War to solve those same problems Bushnell faced, but it would not take long before that would happen.

A hundred years after Bushnell launched his *Turtle*, Lieutenant Francis Barber, an instructor at the Navy Torpedo Station in Newport, Rhode Island, predicted the following: "The science of submarine navigation is likely to be one of great importance in connection with torpedo operations of future wars, both for attacking vessels and for entering harbors . . ."[12] Within a generation, "the science of submarine navigation" became a reality, as did Barber's "future wars."

THE TWENTIETH CENTURY

Warfare soon took a devastating turn, with unprecedented destruction and loss of life on the battlefields of Europe. Aircraft added to the lethality associated with technologies introduced to the world at the onset of the twentieth century. Naval warfare, it would soon be discovered, would be dominated by the submarine. The devastation of World War I, known as The Great War, began with Germany's advance through Belgium in August, 1914, to face the opposing army of France. At sea, the German submarine *U-9* encountered a squadron of British cruisers operating in the North Sea on September 22. Within an hour, *U-9* torpedoed and sank the *Aboukir, Cressy,* and *Hogue*—to the surprise of both the British and the Germans.

Germany, which had initially considered the submarine only useful for coastal defense, soon embraced this vessel as an effective naval combatant. During the early years of the war, the Allies could do little to disrupt the *Unterseeboote*, Germany's infamous U-boat.

Although America remained neutral for two-and-a-half years, preparations were underway for what many considered an inevitable entry into the war. A submarine fleet was being organized, and the Atlantic flotilla soon found a home along the Thames River in Groton, Connecticut. Scientific and industrial leaders had been attempting to convince President Woodrow Wilson and Secretary of the Navy Josephus Daniels that a solution to the submarine problem—a contemporary understatement—which was having a devastating effect on the war, could be found if resources were allocated to put those civilian minds to work. Almost immediately after the United States declared war on April 6, 1917, antisubmarine efforts were underway at experimental stations at Nahant, Massachusetts, and at Fort Trumbull in New London, Connecticut. The monumental efforts of these civilian scientists and engineers supported by naval personnel at home and abroad would rein in U-boat predation on the high seas and hasten the end to a brutal war.

After Armistice, the Naval Experimental Station at New London continued its work until August, 1919, when it was closed. Two decades later, as Germany's submarines descended into the Atlantic, and Japan's patrolled the Pacific during World War II, scientists returned to Fort Trumbull. The New London Laboratory of the Columbia University Division of War Research was established to create the next generation of antisubmarine devices. Additional submarine detection technologies were being developed at the Harvard Underwater Sound Laboratory in Cambridge, Massachusetts. Soon after Japan surrendered in a formal ceremony aboard the USS *Missouri* on September 2, 1945, the Soviet Union emerged as the next great threat. The Cold War had begun. Experimental work that had been underway in New London and Cambridge throughout World War II was consolidated at Fort Trumbull and continued when the Navy-supported university research transitioned directly into the Navy Department—now officially titled the U.S. Navy Underwater Sound Laboratory, USN/USL. For two World Wars, the focus had been submarine detection; this would remain the mission of the "Sound Lab" in New London with a succession of name changes, for the next half-century.[13]

I joined the USN/USL staff in 1967, when the world was under threat of a nuclear confrontation. Soviet submarines patrolled the oceans, carrying weapons far beyond the imaginations of those who went before us. The "listening devices" of 1918 had also improved, but the goal was the same: detect, track, and, if the Cold War became a hot war, destroy the enemy. I can remember the nervous anticipation of everyone on board USS *Pargo* (SSN 650) in 1970 when we detected and then tracked a Charlie-class Soviet submarine. We were using an experimental, passive "listening" sonar system, which would eventually be installed on every U.S. attack submarine.[14] All of us on board *Pargo* felt the same urgency to provide an effective deterrent to an enemy submarine, as did those who preceded us a half century earlier.

This book tells the story, often through the voices of those who were there, of the emergence of the submarine in 1914, when no one, including the Imperial German Navy, anticipated the impact these sleek, submersible vessels would have on the war. By Armistice on November 11, 1918, after a four-year effort to put an end to this efficient predator, the "listeners" had gained the upper hand. In the words of Admiral William Sowden Sims, then commander of all U.S. naval forces in Europe: "A listening device placed on board ship, which would reveal to practiced ears the noise of a submarine at a reasonable distance, and which would give its direction, would come near to solving the most serious problem presented by the German tactics."[15]

After the war, Ernst Hashagen, captain of *U-62*, and someone very familiar with those "German tactics," described the effect antisubmarine technologies had on German submarine crews:

> The last year of the War is the worst. For three long years we have allowed our enemies time to study the nature of the submarine, to pry into its most intimate secrets. They pursue and fight us on the surface, through fog and storm, from the air and in the depths of the sea, on the coasts and in the open. . . . They listen-in for us, to hear the distant beat of our screws; and feel for us with electric fingers along the sea-bed.[16]

THE LISTENERS

L-class submarines on station at Bantry Bay, Ireland. The "A" has been added to distinguish the American submarines from British L-class boats. Forward of each sail is the barrel of a stowed 3-in/23 caliber retractable deck gun. Visible on AL-10 are three vertical struts on which are mounted hydrophones in a K-tube arrangement. (Naval History and Heritage Command (NHHC) NH 60252)

They bear, in place of classic names,
Letters and numbers on their skin.
They play their grisly blindfold games
In little boxes made of tin.

—Rudyard Kipling, *Sea Warfare*, 1916.[1]

I n 1915 and 1916, Rudyard Kipling published a series of articles in British and American newspapers describing the early progress of the naval war, writing of the U-boat as a hidden predator. "One class of German submarines meant for murder off the coasts may use a winding and rabbit-like track between shoals . . ." while others are sent "off for deep sea assassinations."[2] His writings evoked a sense of the violence and desperation of a war that had taken his eighteen-year-old son along the Western Front on September 27, 1915.

As far as the world was concerned, this had become a global conflict as countries aligned with either the Central Powers (primarily Germany, Austria-Hungary, Bulgaria, and the Ottoman Empire), or with the allied countries referred to as the Triple Entente (Russia, France, and the United Kingdom of Britain and Ireland). Most contemporary authors referred to it as "The Great War," although the phrase "The War to End All Wars" became popular after H. G. Wells published *The War that will End War* in 1914.

By the end of 1914, Britain had begun a blockade of the North Sea, yet presumably allowing neutral shipping with cargoes consisting of non-military goods bound for Germany to pass. It was argued by Germany, however, that shipments intended for civilian use were being confiscated, providing an excuse for Germany to retaliate. On February 4, 1915, Admiral Hugo Von Pohl, Chief of the Admiralty Staff, announced: "The waters round Great Britain and Ireland, including the English Channel, are hereby proclaimed a war region," and that: "On and after February 18th every enemy merchant vessel found in this region will be destroyed, without its always being possible to warn the crews or passengers of the dangers threatening." Von Pohl added that "incidents [are] inevitable in sea warfare, attacks intended for hostile ships may affect neutral ships also."[3]

There was nothing ambiguous about this. The Imperial German Navy was about to embark on what everyone understood would be a massive assault on merchant shipping: a U-boat campaign to restrict the flow of food and fuel to Britain, starving them into submission. This policy resulted in the sinking of the Cunard Line *Lusitania* on May 7, 1915. As more lives were lost at sea, angry protests by America and other neutral countries resulted in a reduction in the aggressiveness of U-boat attacks during 1916. Yet, with the ground war in a stalemate and Germany willing to risk America's entry into the war, a policy of unrestricted submarine warfare was announced to commence on February 1, 1917. No longer would warnings be given to ships encountered; no longer would ships be boarded to inspect cargoes; no longer would the "prize laws" be followed—there would be no attempt to recover survivors; they would be on their own. The message to all merchant ships, neutral or not, would be *sail at your own risk*!

What Germany hoped would end the war was the U-boat. The ground war had slogged into a lethal stalemate along the Western Front, and it had become apparent that a decisive battle—by either side—would not be possible. German scientists and engineers had developed an efficient predator in their U-boat, which had evolved from a small vessel designed for coastal defense to large cruisers capable of lengthy missions far from Germany, including the east coast of the United States. Twentieth-century technology created this new form of naval warfare; it would take twentieth-century technology to provide effective tools for the U-boat hunters. Some of those tools came from a unique organization established at the behest of President Woodrow Wilson—the Naval Experimental Station in New London, Connecticut. Formed soon after America joined the war, the station was staffed by civilian scientists and engineers supported by naval personnel—their mission: solve "the submarine problem."

To Catch a Ghost

> Allied warfare upon the submarine was still largely a game of blind man's buff. . . We were constantly attempting to destroy an enemy we could not see. So far as this offensive at sea was concerned, the Allies found themselves in the position of a man who has suddenly gone blind. . . Deprived of sight, he is forced to form his contacts with the external world by using his other senses, especially those of touch and hearing.[4]

Once submerged, as Admiral William S. Sims understood, the elusive submarine became invisible. Offensive action against Germany's fleet of submarines had depended on observations from ships and aircraft attempting to intercept a U-boat which had surfaced while on patrol. On rare occasions, an observer might see the wake of a U-boat periscope, or the track of a torpedo launched against some unwary vessel. The chase was on. A destroyer would track back along the path of the torpedo or to the last location given by an observer, hoping to ram the submarine before it was able to submerge to a depth below the destroyer, an approach proposed by Admiral George W. Melville, USN, as early as 1902:

> There are . . . experts who believe that fast running boats will be able to run the submarine down. . . [Thus] with the submarine—being slow in action, and deficient in maneuvering qualities, the picket boat would have an opportunity to run over them before the submarine could disappear . . ."[5]

Destroyers also dropped depth charges, yet without knowing its target's precise location, the submarine could easily maneuver beyond the area and avoid the force of the explosions. While troublesome, a random depth charge attack may have had little effect on a U-boat's operation. The perceived invisibility of the U-boat, and the initial lack of an effective deterrent, led to an increased reliance by Germany on undersea warfare.

At the beginning of the war, Germany had twenty-eight submarines. Between August 1914 and November 1918, an additional 346 were produced. When Germany declared the waters around the British Isles a war zone in February, 1915, only thirty-seven submarines were available. As construction continued, and with losses sustained during the 1915 offensive, Germany's submarine fleet had increased to sixty-four by December. Monthly commissioning rates increased in 1916, and on February 1, 1917, when Germany instituted her policy of unrestricted submarine warfare leading to America's entry into the war, the fleet had increased to 152. At no time did the German submarine fleet exceed 180.[6] While some of the large cruiser-sized submarines carried a compliment of around sixty, most U-boat crews numbered forty or less.[7] By the end of the war, a total of 178 submarines were lost due to mines, depth charges, allied submarine torpedoes, and a variety of combat-related causes, including that brute force method of ramming a U-boat, which couldn't escape the bow of a destroyer.[8]

Early in the war, it became evident that sounds produced by a submarine when submerged and underway could betray its location. For two years the British had attempted to exploit this vulnerability, but the expertise and tools available were rudimentary and the results were less effective than hoped for. Immediately after America entered the war, the scientists in New London and the Navy's other experimental facilities worked in concert with their European counterparts to perfect a technology with which U-boat hunters could detect these sounds—then pursue, locate, and destroy the predator.

Much of the Navy's antisubmarine development work occurred on, above, and under Long Island Sound, just beyond the harbor at New London. Under the guidance of the newly created Special Board on Antisubmarine Devices, with headquarters at the nearby submarine base, many of the technologies created by civilian scientists and their naval colleagues were soon on their way to the war. Well-trained "listeners" were anxious to hear their adversary attempting to slip away undetected. By 1918, now able to locate a U-boat with some precision, it became difficult for the submarine to evade an attack by a barrage of depth charges. If the U-boat avoided damage, crew morale did not. Without the listeners and their hydrophones, The War to End All Wars may have ended badly for the Allies.

"Periscope showing again on the sta'board bow!" the crow's-nest lookout was roaring. Yes, there she goes—conning tower awash, and a feather of foam streaking behind her periscope as she races toward the north. It must be a mine-laying sub, surprised while laying her eggs off the entrance to Corfu. . . Just then she dives.[9]

In his memoir, *The Splinter Fleet of the Otranto Barrage* (1936), Ray Millholland described this encounter between a U-boat and a hunting group of American subchasers stationed at the Greek island of Corfu. As chief engineer on board *SC-124*, Millholland was on barrage duty along the passage between the Adriatic and Mediterranean, known as the Straits of Otranto. There was an abundance of secrecy associated with the subchasers and their activities, and Millholland carried those concerns into his memoir, only referring to his vessel as "1X4." He used a fictitious name for his commanding officer, referring to him as the "skipper, Dorgan . . . a bull-necked, red-headed Irishman." The actual commanding officer of *SC-124* was a red-headed Irishman, Lieutenant Junior Grade (LTJG) "Red" Kelly, although history doesn't confirm the size of his neck. Millholland's story continues:

> The big red hunting flag breaks out from our yardarm, signaling chasers A and C that we have sighted a submarine. Then the *Stand By* signal bangs out its warning on the alarm gong. Dorgan is getting set for a depth-bomb attack.
>
> The engine-room deck plates bounce under our feet, and old 1X4 shudders in every frame. Dorgan has just kicked over his first depth bomb. Three more follow in rapid succession. Then comes the signal to stop all engines for a listening period.

Early in 1918, the first subchasers designed and equipped specifically for hunting Germany's relentless underwater predators left New London, Connecticut, heading for the war zone. Over the next nine months, over one hundred of these fast, maneuverable 110-foot-long wooden-hulled vessels hunted day and night in the waters around Britain, France, and throughout the Mediterranean. The subchasers carried a new technology on board, which, when lowered beneath the surface, enabled well-trained sailors to hear the distinct sounds of a U-boat.

During the "listening period" Millholland referred to, an inverted T-shaped device known as an "SC-tube" was lowered from a housing near the keel. A sound sensor was mounted at each end of the horizontal section of pipe forming the "T," with the vertical portion of the "T" passing through a watertight seal in the hull. Within the pipe, copper tubes connected each sound sensor to one of the listener's ears through a stethoscope. As he rotated the "T," the sound in each ear would be of the same intensity when the source of the sound—a U-boat—was perpendicular to the "T," a process referred to as "binaural listening." The same effect occurs when a person rotates his head to determine the direction of a sound in air. The SC-tube, however, could not be used when the vessel was underway; hence the vessel had to stop during the listening period.

Three subchasers, operating a distance apart but abreast, comprised a hunting group, where the central, or flagship, subchaser directed the pursuit: *SC-124*, in this case. All three had to stop for each listening period to obtain a bearing to the target. The flagship, which was in contact with the port and starboard wing chasers, plotted the three bearings; where they crossed was the approximate location of the sub at that time. Then from the captain of *SC-124*:

> "Up tubes and away!" roars Dorgan on deck. *Full speed ahead!* . . . Port and starboard engines roar wide open.

Once the location of the U-boat was determined, the listeners raised their SC-tube up and into its protective housing. The hunting group tactic to pursue, stop, listen, and pursue was a process often repeated several times—an operation for which *SC-124* had received ample training while at New London. U-boat captains, also well trained, had many options when attempting to escape the hunters, and the ears of the listeners. Millholland:

> Dorgan had stopped and listened for the fleet mine-laying submarine, sufficiently to plot its general course and lay plans for a quick dash ahead for a final bombing attack. But the rain also cut down visibility to a point where a low object in the water, like a submarine, could not be seen at more than a half-mile away. We had stopped to get one last "fix" on the sub when the listener suddenly reported "Sub has broached to the surface. She's running away on her Diesels, sir!"

Once again, it was "Up tubes and away!" and "Full speed ahead!" The other subchasers, which had been listening to the U-boat on their SC-tubes to provide that "fix" on its position, followed *SC-124* through the rain. As the trio passed out of the squall, the crow's nest lookout shouted, "Sub-mar-reen! Dead ahead on the surface!" The subchaser gun crews had prepared to engage the U-boat, but the pursuit ended suddenly. The U-boat had escaped to its base along the Albanian coast and to the protection of Austrian destroyers.

Not all U-boats were as fortunate as the one *SC-124* chased into the Adriatic. As the months of 1918 went by, however, morale deteriorated among many of the crews of U-boats which did survive. American subchasers maintained their relentless pursuit, with their listeners constantly on duty. As Admiral William S. Sims recalled, "Who would ever have thought that a little wooden vessel, displacing only sixty tons, measuring 110 feet from bow to stern . . . proved one of the formidable enemies of the submarine?"[10]

The technologies used by the listeners during the Great War had their origins in the minds of dedicated civilians on both sides of the Atlantic. Motivated by a sense of urgency, everyone worked in a successful collaboration with men like Ray Millholland and the crew of *SC-124* to create effective deterrents to the notorious U-boat. By the end of the war, the staff of the Naval Experimental Station at Fort Trumbull in New London, Connecticut, consisted of thirty-two scientists and engineers from several universities supported by nearly 700 naval officers and enlisted men.[11]

The Great War had been referred to as "The War to End All Wars," an unrealized hope when only two decades later, the Second World War saw submarines return to the waters of the Atlantic, the Mediterranean, and the distant Pacific. Once again, a new generation of civilian scientists and engineers assembled at Fort Trumbull to resume the development of what became known as SONAR, an acronym for SOund Navigation And Ranging. Their work continued after the surrender of Germany and Japan when the Soviet Union rose from the ashes to become the next adversary to democracy. Submarine and antisubmarine warfare soon became a major component of Cold War strategy; once again, the "listeners" played a major role.

PART I

1914-1916

At 7:47 P.M. on August 4 we received the message, "Prepare for war with England."

—Admiral Reinhard Scheer, *Germany's High Sea Fleet*, 1920[1]

After massing her troops along the Belgian border on the 3rd of August, 1914, Germany declared war on France. An ultimatum that Germany respect Belgian neutrality and withdraw was immediately sent by Britain, and summarily rejected. The British ambassador to Berlin, Sir Edward Goschen, was recalled and at 11:00 p.m. on the 4th, Britain declared war. With an efficiency brought by a newly-mechanized twentieth century, German invasion forces rapidly crossed into Belgium and soon established a front along the northern border of France. When Admiral Reinhard Scheer received the message to prepare for war with England, the Imperial German Navy, the *Kaiserliche Marine*, was ready.

Earlier that day on the 4th, the auxiliary minelayer *Königin Luise*, already at sea, received the wireless message: "Make for sea in Thames direction at top speed. Lay mines near as possible the English coasts . . ."[2] It was on August 5, the day after Britain declared war, that the minelayer completed her mission, but had been discovered by British destroyers; after a brief chase *Königin Luise* was sent to the bottom. In less than twenty-four hours, however, the mines had done their work when one of them was struck by HMS *Amphion*, which soon shared the minelayer's fate. War had arrived off the British Isles.

Throughout Europe, Germany had been perceived as a military powerhouse after her swift victory during the Franco-Prussian War in 1871. For three decades, Germany's High Seas Fleet had been gathering strength and was anxious to prove itself against what the British unabashedly referred to as The Grand Fleet. Unprepared for the scale of aggression brought by their belligerent neighbor on the continent, the British Admiralty scrambled to meet what was obvious to everyone—that this war would quickly expand beyond the battlefields of Europe and onto the surrounding seas.

What was less obvious was that the war would also slip beneath the surface of the ocean.

Admiral Reinhard Scheer, who became Commander in Chief of the High Seas Fleet in January, 1916, and later Chief of the Admiralty Staff, noted in his memoir: "[A] decision was taken which was extremely important for the further course of the war . . . for the U-boats received orders to proceed on August 6 [1914] against English battleships, the presence of which was suspected in the North Sea."[3] These orders would set the stage for additional forays into the waters between Britain and Germany. On the morning of September 22, Otto Weddigen, in command of *U-9* with a crew of four officers and twenty-five enlisted, sent torpedoes into the sides of three British armored cruisers, *Aboukir, Cressy,* and *Hogue,* all three sinking within an hour with a loss of over 1400 officers and crew.

The success of a single submarine, and a nearly obsolete one at that, had surprised not only the British, but Germany as well. Maybe the Grand Fleet was not so grand after all. Construction of bigger, faster, better armed submarines would become a priority at Krupp-Germania and other German shipyards. No longer just a vessel designed for coastal defense, the U-boat fleet soon had the capability to spend weeks—even months—at sea, covering thousands of miles. They could now lay mine fields across harbors, undetected. They carried large caliber guns mounted on deck which could engage Allied shipping on the surface, saving their torpedoes for higher value, higher tonnage targets.

A massive engagement between the Grand Fleet and the High Seas Fleet was inevitable, where dreadnaughts, battleships, cruisers, and destroyers on both sides pummeled each other with their massive firepower. This confrontation occurred over two days, May 31 to June 1, 1916, at the Battle of Jutland—known in Germany as the Battle of the Skagerrak. Both sides claimed victory, but ended any further major engagements between the surface fleets of Britain and Germany; future naval operations during the Great War would be defined beneath the sea.[4]

Britain had depended on the Grand Fleet to deal with warfare on the open ocean, and the Admiralty's first priority was to mobilize all of its resources—old ships reconditioned; new ships designed and built; manpower recruited. Submarines and the deadly torpedoes they carried, however, soon defined the realities of the twentieth-century, and antisubmarine warfare would also have to become a priority. Yet in 1914, no one really understood the complexity of the submarine problem nor the technology that would be needed to counter the threat.

I endeavoured for many years to get torpedoes introduced into practice in France, and in England; which, though unsuccessful, gave me the opportunity of making numerous very interesting experiments on a large scale . . ."[5]

Robert Fulton published his pamphlet "Torpedo War and Submarine Explosions" in 1810 as another war with England seemed inevitable. Fulton was attempting to convince Congress that his device could be "so arranged as to blow up a vessel which should run against it . . ."[6] He had already been unsuccessful in selling his concept of a submarine, his *Nautilus,* to the French and English, and had turned to other methods of using underwater explosives. The word "torpedo" was apparently coined by Fulton during the first decade of the nineteenth century. In a September 6, 1807 letter from British Commodore E. W. C. R. Owen, distributed among the Admiralty, Owen included a "Description of the Machine invented by Mr. Robert Fulton for exploding under Ship's Bottoms and by him called the Torpedo."[7] The term, however, was in reference to what is now referred to as a tethered subsurface mine. The following extracts are from the September 9, 1807 edition of the *Connecticut Current*:

[T]hese aquatic incendiaries have come forward at the present alarming juncture, and announced a most potent discovery, which is to guarantee our port from the visit of any foreign marauders . . . a cunning machine shrewdly y'clep'd a *Torpedo*, by which the stoutest line of battle ship . . . may be caught napping, and *decomposed* in a twinkling.[8]

The War of 1812 was primarily a naval war. There were stories of a submarine built by Silas Clowden Halsey, reportedly used in 1814 against a British warship anchored at the harbor of New London, Connecticut. Hartford's Samuel Colt, who had proposed the use of electrically triggered underwater mines in the 1840s, drew a sketch of the vessel.[9] The American Civil War brought on a flurry of submarine designs, few of which had any impact on naval warfare at the time other than the Confederate submarine *Hunley*.[10] Floating and sub-surface mines, however, became a common defensive technology used by the Confederacy.[11] The *Hunley* carried a device referred to as a "spar torpedo," an explosive device held at the end of a long pole or spar. That system became a common weapon used on small surface vessels called torpedo-boats.

A self-propelled torpedo would not appear until after the Civil War, initiated during the late 1860s by an English engineer, Robert Whitehead, based on a concept by an Austrian naval officer, Giovanni Luppis. Several countries purchased Whitehead torpedoes, or the manufacturing rights, in the 1870s. By 1875, designs were being considered within the U.S. Navy, specifically at the Naval Torpedo Station in Newport, Rhode Island.

Introductory remarks to a publication titled "Notes on Movable Torpedoes" produced between 1874 and 1875 at the torpedo station defined the prevailing opinion regarding these new weapons. Submarine mines, or what were called "stationary torpedoes," which proliferated during the Civil War, were considered primarily "for defense of channels against the entry of fleets." Yet by the decade of the 1870s, these new "Movable or Locomotive Torpedoes to assail ships on the high seas" were becoming a reality.[12] In this same publication was an 1873 article by an Austrian officer, Lieutenant J. Lehnert, titled "Torpedo Vessels in Naval Engagements," in which he predicted the interest, and dread, this new weapon was about to bring to the world:

> The gradual and probable introduction of Torpedo vessels into fleets, the general emotion which the appearance of these terrible engines has created, the attention with which seamen of all countries watch the progress of this new arm, now an offensive power, and finally the complete revolution which they will probably produce in naval tactics are sufficient reasons for rendering the study of Torpedoes not only necessary, but attractive to officers of all navies.
>
> Torpedoes carried by vessels constructed for that purpose, and which, discharged in a given direction, retain under water a motion which is inherent in them and thus reach the enemy at considerable distances. This system is known under the name of Whitehead-Lupis [or Fish] Torpedoes.[13]

Lieutenant Francis M. Barber, instructor at the torpedo station, wrote his "Lecture on the Whitehead Torpedo," a thorough description of what was known about the torpedo in 1874.[14] At that time, the U.S. Navy was considering production of its own torpedo, which Barber described in a section titled "Plans for Fish Torpedo Submitted to Board of Ordnance, June 1st, 1874." Barber mentioned that the "general idea which was originally intended to control the construction of this proposed fish was to approximate as closely as possible to what was supposed to be the plan of the Whitehead . . ."[15] Barber then added a copy of a letter to Commodore Wm. Jeffers, Chief of the Bureau of Ordnance, from Lieutenant Commander W.M. Folger, a naval observer at the Whitehead factory in Fiume, Austria, January 6, 1875. Folger had arrived at the factory two days earlier and met with Whitehead. The worldwide interest was becoming obvious:

> The German government has ordered from the Messrs. Whitehead & Co. 100 of the latest improved torpedoes, and had advanced funds for the establishment of a regular torpedo factory. . . .The French government has ordered 50. . . In addition to those already known to the Bureau, the subject is being considered by the Governments of Russia, Denmark, and Belgium.[16]

It was still premature to see these "fish" torpedoes launched from a submarine, but by the end of the century, John Holland was ready to provide the U.S. Navy with this capability. Other nations were also anxious to enter the new century with at least a small fleet of submarines outfitted with Whitehead torpedoes, and the Holland Torpedo Boat Company had a major influence on these early efforts. The Navy's first submarine, the USS *Holland* (SS-1), commissioned in 1900, had a single torpedo tube and carried three torpedoes.[17] As Germany quietly prepared for war, the next decade saw major changes in submarine designs and operational capabilities, along with improvements in torpedoes. This became the weapon that brought the U-boat its fame—and infamy.

AFTER WHITEHEAD, THEN SCHWARTZKOPFF AND BLISS-LEAVITT

> At the beginning of the war the torpedo factory at Friedrichsort had been the only place where our torpedoes were manufactured; but during the war the engineering works (formerly L. Schwartzkopff) in Berlin, which in earlier years had also manufactured torpedoes, was converted into a torpedo factory, as were other works as well.[18]

Admiral Scheer continued: "Under the direction of the Chief of the Torpedo Factories, Rear-Admiral Hering, the enormously increased demand for the manufacture of torpedoes was fully satisfied . . ."[19] By 1917, German submarines were being sent to sea fully anticipating the use of their increased capacity to carry torpedoes (see next page). Prior to 1917, however, much of the destruction of commercial vessels was accomplished when the U-boat had surfaced and fired on the unarmed vessels with deck-mounted guns, leaving their expensive torpedoes for larger, high-value prey. Britain's Admiral John Rushworth Jellicoe recognized that "before the days of the unre-

Schwartzkopff torpedoes captured during the Spanish-American War and held at the Naval Torpedo Station, Newport, Rhode Island. (NHHC *NH 84471*) Inset: *Detonator on one of the remaining examples of the Schwartzkopff torpedo.* (Courtesy Naval Undersea Warfare Center; Richard Allen)

stricted submarine campaign, and although ships were frequently torpedoed, very large numbers were still being sunk by gun-fire."[20]

In the United States, torpedo development was centered at the Naval Torpedo Station in Newport, Rhode Island, beginning in 1869. In 1920, a pamphlet produced at the torpedo station outlined its five decade history.[21] By the end of the nineteenth century, several hundred torpedoes of various designs had been purchased for testing in Narragansett Bay—the Hall, Lay, Howell, and the wire-guided Patrick torpedoes, for example—but the most popular was the Whitehead. During the Spanish American War, however, even the German Schwartzkopff torpedo was among the station's inventory, where a "tube was mounted for experimental purposes, and twelve torpedoes were purchased and sent to the station." After the war, the torpedo station received sixteen of these torpedoes recovered from Spanish ships. Many were so badly damaged, however, that "[the] shells of these torpedoes are still in use [in 1920] at the Station as light posts." In 1900, the Navy's first submarine, the USS *Holland*, arrived in Narragansett Bay, armed with three Whitehead Mark II torpedoes. During sea trials, the *Holland* demonstrated the ability to approach the battleship *Kearsarge* undetected.[22]

In 1904, the U.S. Navy contracted the E.W. Bliss Company to produce a torpedo similar to the Whitehead, based on designs by Frank M. Leavitt. A factory to accommodate an anticipated need for increased production was built at the station in 1907. The following are excerpts from the torpedo station pamphlet:

> In September 1912 an order was received for ninety Mark VII Mod 2 Bliss-Leavitt Torpedoes. . . . By 1915 the effect of the European War, which threatened to involve the armament of the world, was being anticipated in America and the preparedness which was being talked about throughout the country was being actively practiced at the Torpedo Station. . . . Early in 1917 an open break with Germany was obvious and preparations were made at the Station to meet the emergency. . . . Station activities were further increased and the [civilian] working force enlarged to three thousand two hundred employees. . . . Navy personnel during the war numbered about thirteen hundred.[23]

Torpedoes, fired from surface ships as well as submarines during the Great War, were about to define the weaponry of twentieth-century naval warfare. A reminder is appropriate here: Soviet submarines dispatched to North American waters during the Cuban Missile Crisis in 1962 carried nuclear-tipped torpedoes.

ADMIRAL REINHARD SCHEER—PREDATOR

> When the U-boat campaign was opened on February 1, 1917, there were 57 boats already in the North Sea. The officer commanding the Baltic district had eight assigned to him, the Naval Corps in Flanders had at its disposal 38, and the stations in the Mediterranean 31 boats of different types. . . . With this fleet of U-boats the Navy was well equipped to do justice to the task assigned to it, although England had used the whole of 1916 to develop her defense.[24]

Admiral Scheer, convinced of the predatory efficiency of Germany's fleet of U-boats, became a proponent of a renewed dependency on submarine warfare early in 1917, in spite of the likely entry of the United States into the war (chapter 9). The two visits of Germany's mercantile submarine

Deutschland to American ports in 1916 (chapter 10) had provided credible evidence to Admiral Scheer that long-range operations were possible:

> When they could no longer be used for trade purposes the commercial U-boats were taken over by the Navy and altered for use as warships. They were fitted with two guns of 15 cm. caliber and two torpedo tubes, and could carry about 30 torpedoes in accordance with the extended period during which they could be used on cruises . . .[25]

With significant firepower when on the surface or while submerged, the U-boat predators controlled the oceans. The images on pages 68 and 92 are examples of Germany's cruiser submarines adopted after the successful trips of *Deutschland*. In response, drastic measures had to be put into place by the Admiralty—and quickly. Admiral Jellicoe devoted a chapter in his book *The Grand Fleet, 1914-1916* to Britain's early actions against German submarines.[26]

Referring to operations during 1915, Jellicoe expressed concern over the relative lack of success by the vessels Britain was using at the time, primarily destroyers. By that summer, several depth charge designs were being developed and carried by destroyers.

> On July 1st the *Hampshire* reported that a torpedo had been fired at her in the Moray Firth. Twelve destroyers were sent to endeavour to locate and sink the submarine. . . .The boats exploded a large number of charges on the bottom in the hope of forcing any submarine to the surface.[27]

While there was no evidence that the above account resulted in the destruction of that U-boat, the prevailing strategy, besides ramming a surfaced submarine or dropping depth charges at its suspected location, was "to keep the submarine down long enough to cause her to exhaust her battery power, a period of some 48 hours."[28] There had also been accounts of British submarines finding and sinking a surfaced U-boat with a torpedo.[29] Once submerged and free to maneuver at will, however, German submarines continued to be an elusive target.[30]

The solution was the hydrophone, though it would take more than two-and-a-half years, and America's entry into the war, before this technology began to become a U-boat deterrent. Even by the end of 1916, according to Admiral Jellicoe, "[the] hydrophone had been in the experimental stage and under trial for a considerable period, but it had not so far developed into an effective instrument for locating submarines. . ."[31] adding that . . . "all devices for use afloat suffered from the disadvantage that it was not possible to use them whilst the ship carrying them was moving . . . [the ship], when stopped, an easy target for the submarine's torpedo."[32]

Of all the weapons used in the anti-submarine war the two most important were the *hydrophone* and the *depth charge*. They were employed in conjunction with each other and comprised the surface warship's principal means of offense against submarines operating beneath the surface.[33]

This assessment by Charles Domville-Fife, who commanded a British hydrophone flotilla during the Great War, underscored the significance of hydrophone detection, which would lead to a targeted location for the depth charges. Without the ability to provide a precise location of a submerged U-boat, however, dropping a barrage of depth charges was just a hit-or-miss attack. Perfecting the hydrophone would take time and resources. Early efforts within the British and French Admiralties were aided by their scientists and engineers who searched for ways to exploit the physics of underwater sound. Domville-Fife emphasized the importance of the hydrophone, which "enables the surface ship to discover, first, the presence of the submarine . . . and, secondly, its approximate location. . . When a surface ship is hot on the track of a moving submarine she endeavours to attain a position directly over the top of her quarry, or even a little ahead, and then releases one or more depth charges according to whether the chance of a hit is good or only poor."[34]

The story of *The Listeners* begins with a single British officer assigned to a naval base in Scotland's Firth of Forth. With a background in radio communication, Commander C. P. Ryan began experimenting with crude devices comprised of microphones housed in home-made, watertight containers. Ryan was soon able to hear, and distinguish from other vessels, the sound of a submarine. The technology continued to improve with significant advances occurring after America entered the war. The hunters, armed with an ample supply of depth charges, would soon have the tools they needed to detect, pursue, and destroy a German submarine—Admiral Scheer's predators would become the prey.

> In January, 1915, Commander Ryan assembled a working party, the personnel of which consisted of half a dozen able seamen, and himself, with the result that the first authorized hydrophone was laid from Granton harbor [Edinburgh], from a small open boat. From this small beginning did the hydrophone service grow.
>
> —Lieutenant H. W. Wilson, *Hush*, 1920[1]

To supplement the current active duty naval forces, and in particular the need for officers and enlisted to deal with the submarine problem, the Admiralty relied on recalling its reserve forces and the return to service of the many officers who had recently resigned or retired. One of these retirees was Commander C. P. Ryan. He would initiate the first British efforts to investigate the use of underwater listening devices and create operational systems to detect submerged submarines, as described in a 1920 memoir by a member of his staff, Lieutenant H. W. Wilson, Royal Navy Volunteer Reserves (RNVR).

Beginning as a young midshipman in the 1890s, much of Ryan's career during the early years of the twentieth century occurred in the Mediterranean, where he had become recognized for his "inventive genius" while commander of the destroyer HMS *Zealous*. Ryan recognized the military advantages brought to the fleet by Marconi's wireless telegraphy, and in 1903 had submitted suggestions for improvements to the system, for which he received a commendation from the Admiralty. Ryan continued to pursue his interests in wireless technology, yet his peace-time service was uneventful, including his time on patrol in his home waters as commanding officer of the armored cruiser HMS *Euryalus*. After realizing that further advancements would not be forthcoming, Ryan retired in June, 1911, and joined the Marconi Company. Three years later, Ryan's technological know-how would serve him well.[2]

Returning to naval service in August, 1914, Commander Ryan's first assignment was the naval base on the Scottish island of Inchkeith in the

Commander C. P. Ryan was promoted to Acting Captain, October 1, 1916, shown here on one of the vessels used to support his antisubmarine research in the Firth of Forth. (Wilson, 1920)

Firth of Forth. He brought with him his in-depth understanding of wireless telegraphy and a pragmatic and tenacious determination to apply that "inventive genius," which the Admiralty had acknowledged only a decade earlier. It was soon understood, however, that the threat to British naval superiority would not come from German dreadnaughts, but from their rapidly increasing submarine fleet, and the Admiralty would look for solutions among the country's (and their navy's) many inventive geniuses.

Commander Ryan was at his station when *U-21* quietly entered the Firth of Forth on September 4, 1914, passing Inchkeith and venturing nearly as far as the Rosyth naval base. Having been spotted and fired on from shore batteries, *U-21* made its escape from the Forth at night. The following day, the scout cruiser HMS *Pathfinder* was seen through *U-21*'s periscope southeast of the Isle of May, just beyond the entrance to the Forth; by four o'clock that afternoon, a single torpedo sent the British cruiser to the bottom. By the end of September, the loss of *Pathfinder, Aboukir, Cressy,* and *Hogue* would dispel any doubts about the efficacy of the U-boat. Asymmetric warfare in the twentieth century had arrived in the form of what war correspondent Lowell Thomas referred to as *Raiders of the Deep* (1928), which "came within an ace of bringing the combined forces of twenty nations to their knees with their new form of warfare—warfare under the sea."[3] To stop these raiders of the deep, an entirely new concept of antisubmarine warfare would be needed, and that would require another new technology—the hydrophone.

In 1914, a device that could convert sound energy, in particular a human voice, into electrical energy was relatively new; the microphone had been developed independently during the 1870s in England by David E. Hughes and in America by Emile Berliner and Thomas Edison. At the beginning of the war, any device that could be submerged and generate an electrical signal from underwater sounds was referred to as a hydrophone, consisting of one of a variety of microphone-like devices available at the time, held within a watertight housing. The term "hydrophone" became a generic term for these devices; their efficiencies as submarine detectors, however, varied considerably.

Some contemporary authors preferred to refer to these devices as "sound receivers," as did Dr. Harvey C. Hayes (see also chapter 12), writing for the American Philosophical Society in 1920. He distinguished a difference between resonant and non-resonant receivers, important here because, as Hayes pointed out, the "Germans have made use of [resonant receivers] in the listening gear installed on U-boats as have the British in much of their earlier work."[4] The resonant receivers were very sensitive to sounds which were of the frequency at which the receiver vibrated most efficiently, but were not sensitive to sounds at other frequencies, making it difficult for a listener to distinguish a submarine from other underwater sounds. According to Hayes, the only advantage of a resonant receiver was that it could detect that specific sound at a much further range than a non-resonant receiver, "providing the submarine gives out sound of the same frequency to which the receiver is tuned . . ." Hayes then added: "An analysis of the sound emitted by a submarine shows a continuous sound spectrum throughout the range of the audible. No characteristic frequency is emitted."[5] Soon, microphone-based non-resonant receivers, including those Commander Ryan began using as he continued his work in the Firth of Forth, became the preferred device, improving as hydrophone development continued. Eventually, as more was learned about the sounds generated by a U-boat, electronic filtering was added "to allow all sounds above a certain definite frequency to pass but eliminate almost entirely the lower frequencies [not associated with a submarine]."[6]

In spite of the loss of *Pathfinder* and other naval vessels in 1914, the Admiralty was slow to initiate a serious effort into the detection of a submerged U-boat. The early work by Ryan had not yet received official recognition. He initially relied on any hydrophones available in 1914, which were built similar to those produced by the Submarine Signal Company[7] for ship to ship (or submarine) communications. Others were cobbled together by Ryan with whatever he could find, including microphones that he installed in housings of his own design. With at least some success that fall, the Admiralty finally recognized the potential of Ryan's work, and in February, 1915, authorized him to begin formal experiments with his latest device.[8] Ryan was encouraged to move forward with his ideas, but it was a slow process, while U-boats continued to strike mercantile targets with impunity

UK SCIENCE AND THE BOARD OF INVENTION AND RESEARCH

> We have produced no counter stroke at all to the enemy's submarine and no efficient protection against his improved torpedo. . . we have not produced any novelty at all except in the field of recruiting posters.[9]

It was June, 1915, when popular science fiction writer H. G. Wells echoed the nation's concern with the new forms of warfare brought onto the battlefields of Europe and under the seas. *The Times* enabled Wells' voice to be heard by individuals within the Government and the Admiralty. Throughout Britain, it had become painfully obvious that Germany had prepared for war, not just through its decades-long development of a strong military, but had engaged that country's scientific minds in expanding her war-fighting technology. Wells understood the urgent need to match the technological superiority of the enemy. In a letter to *The Times*, published June 11 and titled "Mobilisation of Invention," he called for the Government to organize the "scientifically and technically competent men for this highly specialized task."[10]

Wells was not the only voice that appeared in *The Times* that June. British scientist Professor J. A. Fleming, referring in particular to the navy, emphasized to *The Times* readers that there "is no want of ability, but there is an entire absence of external directing power . . . [and that] . . . steps have been taken to inhibit scientific activity in directions which might assist the Navy," lamenting the fact that he had not received "one word of request to serve any committee, co-operate in any experimental work, nor place expert knowledge at the disposal of the Crown." Sir Phillip Magnus, an educator and Member of Parliament during the war, was insistent, proclaiming that "our scientific men are in no way inferior to those of Germany," and recommended the creation of a committee of scientists who could provide a critical look at German weaponry, which the allies were facing.[11] Parliament would soon take the advice of the scientist and the science fiction writer.

At the beginning of 1915, when Germany declared the waters around Britain a war zone, U-boats expanded their predatory attacks on commercial shipping. Public outcries against this deadly aggression were heard loud and clear throughout the government. Submarine warfare dominated the suggestions submitted by well-intentioned citizens, who continued to flood the Admiralty with ideas throughout the war. But good intentions were not enough—technology would have to be based on science. The Admiralty staff, however, was preoccupied with strategic planning and day to day decision-making. There was simply no organization tasked to separate ideas with potential from a vast collection of well-meaning but fanciful inventions. Yet, by the spring of 1915, Parliament, as well as the Admiralty, was acutely aware that matching what Germany's scientific minds had devised required an appropriate response . . . and quickly.

The solution came from Arthur James Balfour who was named First Lord of the Admiralty on May 25, 1915, a member of Prime Minister Asquith's Cabinet, replacing Winston Churchill. On July 5, through Lord Balfour's urging, two scientific boards were created, one attached directly to the War Office. The other would focus specifically on naval technology—the Board of Invention and Research (BIR). Oversight of the BIR was assigned to Balfour, who fully understood the Admiralty's urgent need to enlist scientific minds from both industry and academia. His insistence that the Board be free of administrative control by the Admiralty enabled the civilian scientists the flexibility to operate independently.[12]

Although the BIR would exist outside of direct naval control, the Board's chairmanship would be best served by a man with extensive naval experience. Balfour then offered former First Sea Lord, Admiral Sir John Fisher, that position. The now retired Fisher, who eagerly accepted the offer, would have to deal with skepticism within the Admiralty, whose members recalled the loss of one of their first submarines. While engaged in fleet maneuvers in 1904, the *A-1* was accidentally rammed by a steamer and sank with all hands. It would take another six years before the Admiralty once again considered the potential use of submarines as significant elements in naval engagements; there was, at that time, no thought of submarines as a threat to commerce. In 1913, as Germany's intentions were beginning to be felt throughout Europe, Fisher had cautioned the Admiralty that the U-boat would likely be used against commercial shipping, but the idea was dismissed as utterly repugnant by the then First Lord of the Admiralty, Sir Winston Churchill.[13]

Fisher was also known as a vocal proponent of modernization, and had alienated some of his peers who were deeply entrenched in centuries-old naval traditions . . . modernization was not always embraced. But the potential blockade of Britain by a "modernized" fleet of U-boats became a reality in February 1915 when Kaiser Wilhelm's Chief of the Naval Staff, Admiral Hugo von Pohl, announced that the waters around Great Britain and Ireland, including the English Channel, were considered a war zone, and that as of February 18, mercantile shipping encountered in this area would be sunk, and without warning. Submarine warfare would now be directed primarily against commercial vessels, affecting Britain's lifeline—just as Fisher had forewarned nearly a year prior to the war.[14]

Lord Balfour was ready to put the BIR to work. A former First Sea Lord with a reputation of having a forceful personality had accepted the chairmanship. In his acceptance letter, Fisher replied that "German mines and submarines have walked ahead of us by leaps and bounds."[15] Fisher emphasized that among the most pressing issues were submarines and antisubmarine devices; Balfour was anxious to place the BIR in Fisher's hands. On September 14, 1915, the primary goals Balfour envisioned for the BIR were provided to Fisher:

1. To concentrate expert scientific enquiry to certain scientific problems the solution of which is of urgent importance to the naval service;
2. To encourage research in a number of directions in which it is probable that results of value to the Navy might be obtained by organized scientific effort, and to consider schemes and suggestions put forward by inventors and other members of the general public.[16]

The BIR was organized into six sections: airships and general aeronautics; submarines and wireless telegraphy; naval construction; anti-aircraft equipment; ordnance and ammunition; armament of aircraft, bombs, and bomb sights. Committees and sub-committees were formed, and, it was hoped, Britain could match Germany's technological advantages, which that country had benefitted through connections between their academic researchers and the military.[17]

Now with Admiral Sir John Fisher at the helm, a team of prestigious scientists were selected to serve on the board's various committees, including Nobel Laureate Sir Ernest Rutherford. A colleague of Rutherford, physicist Henry Moseley, would have been an ideal candidate for membership, but had joined the Royal Engineers as a communications officer. Moseley was killed by a sniper on August 10 during the disastrous Gallipoli campaign. There was an obvious need to provide an avenue for Britain's scientists to serve their country, not in the trenches, but in the laboratories. Another BIR member, Professor William H. Bragg, more than his colleagues, understood the urgency to work toward a rapid conclusion to this devastating war. His youngest son, Robert, also died in August at Gallipoli, while his other son was an officer serving in France.[18]

MEANWHILE, BACK AT THE FORTH

A noteworthy occurrence . . . was the removal of the entire establishment, or what remained of it, from Granton to Hawkcraig, and in December, 1915, the Service was first known as H.M. Experimental Station, Hawkcraig.[19]

As Lieutenant Wilson from Commander Ryan's staff pointed out, the Admiralty took notice of the hydrophone work Ryan had accomplished, resulting

A commercial vessel known as a "drifter" was commissioned HMS Tarlair *and provided to then Commander Ryan for his experimental work in the fall of 1914. (Wilson, 1920)*

in the establishment of an official experimental station. As early as February, 1915, the Admiralty had provided Ryan with the *Tarlair*, from a class of vessels known as "drifters," to support his off shore experiments.[20] Commander Ryan, who had been working initially at Inchkeith, now had what he wanted—recognition of his hydrophone work by the Admiralty and a vessel to expand his ability to conduct realistic operations in the Forth. At the beginning of 1915, Ryan, headquartered in a small building on Edinburgh's Granton Pier, had a staff of six Royal Navy Volunteer Reserve (RNVR) officers and twenty chief petty officers.[21] There was a lot of activity in the Firth of Forth during the winter of 1915.

The Admiralty's first priority was to use the hydrophone as a defensive technology, and Ryan was their primary hope. Beginning in February, Ryan had tested his concept of mounting a hydrophone on a tripod set on the sea bottom, connected by cable to shore. By March the first hydrophone station was operating at Oxcars, a small island in the Forth, just south of Hawkcraig Point. This station was soon replaced by two other experimental shore-based stations in the Forth: one on the island of Inchcolm, the other at Elieness along the north shore near the entrance to the Forth.[22]

The Admiralty, of course, was delighted with Ryan's rapid progress with this stationary submarine detection system, and the decision was made to expand his research, beyond what could be accomplished at Edinburgh's Granton Pier. He must have been pleased when Hawkcraig Point was selected, as it provided access to an underwater environment much more appropriate for his submarine detection system development. Located along the northern coast of the Forth off the small fishing village of Aberdour, the water between Hawkcraig Point and Inchkeith Island allowed testing his ideas under conditions similar to where German ships and submarines might be operating.[23] In modern terms, Ryan could perform the technical evaluation (TECHEVAL) and operational evaluation (OPEVAL) of any system he might devise, and Ryan's creativity led to many such systems.

The Admiralty authorized the construction of a small building at Hawk-craig, known as "the Number One hut," which was completed by the summer of 1915, and by the end of the year, the Hawkcraig Admiralty Experimental Station was born (see page 41). Lieutenant H. W. Wilson (RNVR), who served on Ryan's staff throughout the war, recalled this new facility:

> As a direct consequence of the erection of this hut, from this time afterwards, most experimental work was carried on from the north side of the Forth, and as the star of Hawkcraig waxed, so that of Granton, as a hydrophone base, waned. . . It was [in Number One hut] that the Captain's marvels might be viewed, [which] drew hosts of distinguished visitors to our base, whether British or foreign, and it was certainly possible to detect a mystified awe on the countenance of the illustrious stranger, as he issued from Number One . . .[24]

The first step necessary was a considerable increase in the instructional facilities for training listeners both for the increased number of shore stations and for the large number of vessels that were fitted for hydrophone work . . .

—Admiral John Rushworth Jellicoe,
The Crisis of the Naval War, 1921[1]

Britain's First Sea Lord, Admiral John R. Jellicoe, was confident in the work being carried out at the Admiralty Experimental Station at Hawkcraig, but understood the need for the listeners to be properly trained. That would eventually happen, but from his now fully functioning and staffed station at Hawkcraig, Ryan continued with operational trials of his shore-based hydrophone listening stations throughout 1916, monitoring the sounds of passing vessels. The goal, however, was not just any vessel—rather a submerged, hostile submarine attempting to infiltrate a river, harbor, or when approaching any strategic waterfront infrastructure. The Admiralty, anxious to exploit the potential of this new technology, had been increasing the scope of Ryan's work to include the use of hydrophones on surface ships.

The summer marked the growth of the shore hydrophone policy, and an ambitious and far-reaching programme commenced . . . So full of promise did the principal of the hydrophone appear to be in the detection of the submarine that, during the autumn and winter of 1916, a policy of offence was inaugurated.[2]

Listening stations served as an effective defensive measure, but throughout 1915, U-boats had turned to aggressive attacks on mercantile shipping. An equally aggressive antisubmarine policy became an Admiralty priority, and that priority was passed to Hawkcraig. Submarine hunting on the open seas required the ability to detect a U-boat as it transited toward the shipping lanes and certainly long before the predator could maneuver into

British listener on board a trawler. He is rotating a directional hydrophone suspended from the end of the boom. (Courtesy Marist College; Lowell Thomas Archive)

a torpedo firing position. The vessels assigned to Ryan would now head beyond the Firth of Forth with this new mission.

Once again, Ryan began with a single, non-directional hydrophone. Although intended to provide mobility, the vessel, initially *Tarlair*, later joined by the drifter *Couronne*, had to stop while the hydrophone was lowered over the side. The vessel's machinery would have masked any sounds coming from a distant target, and this early hydrophone was not designed to be towed far enough astern to eliminate the vessel's own noise. The sophistication of these single hydrophone drifter systems would improve with time, but the practical-minded Ryan had an immediate need—detect the U-boat—and he would use what was available.

LISTENER TRAINING BECOMES A PRIORITY

But the concept of submarine detection depended on two things—the hydrophone and the listener's ear. There were, however, uncertainties within the hydrophone service as to the quality of both. Lt. H. W. Wilson, RNVR, serving under Ryan, described, with a bit of naval irony, the medical exam given to those seeking membership in a service dependent on a sailor's ears:

[I]t will not surprise you to hear that we were subjected to a rigorous medical examination on joining. All the organic equipment with which man is born into this world, including the vermiform appendix, was scrutinized and tested. Everything came under a punishing medical survey except only—the hearing![3]

It would not be an easy job, that of the listener. The oceans resonated with the sounds of whales and other marine mammals, of the chatter from many species of fish and invertebrates, of storms that churn the ocean surface, and of waves crashing against the shore. But it was the ships, large and small, commercial and naval, that filled the depths of the oceans with sound. And then there was that new vessel—the submarine—whose characteristic sounds depended on whether it was patrolling on the surface with its diesel engines, or submerged and running on electric motors. Even the rotating propellers of ships and submarines created their own list of distinct rhythmic sounds. Ryan's hydrophones were capable of "hearing" it all. It was a technology not well understood by those in the hydrophone service; yet with training, it became, according to Lt. Wilson, a trusted and valued tool:

All I can tell you is that a hydrophone is a piece of gear assuming various forms, containing a microphone, . . . [where] the flow of electrical current, results [in] the translation of the engine sounds of ships in the vicinity, and any other neighboring subaqueous tremors, such as the sighs of a lovesick mermaid. All this medley of sound is reproduced by telephone receivers connected by cable with the hydrophone, and the classification is left to the listener.[4]

Was it a submarine or a lovesick mermaid? With experience a listener could learn to distinguish many natural and man-made sounds. But it was the ability to classify specific sounds as being from a U-boat which would enable the hydrophone-equipped hunters to carry out an attack. Training was the key to success, and that became yet another mission for Ryan and his Hawkcraig staff. Candidates for the hydrophone service would learn to recognize the rhythmic sounds from a submarine's rotating propellers and machinery.[5] The "sighs of a lovesick mermaid" would be classified among the sounds not characteristically rhythmic, though why the poor girl shouldn't sigh rhythmically I don't know.

Thus, at Hawkcraig, "an organized system of training of officers and ratings was instituted, an instructional staff appointed, and lecture-halls, workshops, *ad hoc genus mone* [and that sort of thing], put up."[6] Ryan's students had access to the Firth of Forth shore stations where vessels from

One of the British B-class submarines commissioned during the first decade of the twentieth century. Considered obsolete by the beginning of the war, they still performed important missions, including support of Captain Ryan's experimental work in the Firth of Forth. (Library of Congress (LOC) LC-F81-2000)

the British 6th Battle Squadron (Admiral Beatty) at Rosyth provided opportunities to hear large and small surface vessels, essential for distinguishing them from a submarine. But . . . that required the student listeners to have heard what a submarine sounded like.

Among the vessels provided for the ever-resourceful Ryan was the aging HM Submarine *B-3*, which, in 1916, had been outfitted at Leith, on the southern coast of the Firth of Forth, with one of Ryan's experimental hydrophone systems. Throughout the remaining years of the war, *B-3* was stationed at Rosyth for use by the training staff at Hawkcraig. Lieutenant Wilson, however, lamented the use of an inappropriate submarine for their listener training: "Why an obsolescent submarine of our own, and that, too, only occasionally? Why not a U-boat captured from the enemy, and run daily for our benefit?"[7] These were questions for which Wilson had no answer. He was, however, certainly justified to ask them. During the summer of 1916, a captured German submarine in the hands of the French Ministry of Invention was being thoroughly investigated, and was found to have its own acoustic system.[8]

Because *B-3* was not always available, "the actual movements of a submarine under water at varying distances from a hydrophone were recorded by a phonograph, and records made so that the sounds might be reproduced at will for the education of the ear."[9] Recordings of submarines and other underwater sounds became a common practice, both in Britain and eventually the United States, where the Victor Talking Machine Company in Camden, New Jersey, provided the phonograph recording technology.[10]

Listener training soon expanded beyond the Firth of Forth. Instructor teams were assembled and dispatched from Hawkcraig to listening stations and hydrophone schools that were being established in 1917 and operated throughout the war. "At Malta an experimental station, with a hydrophone training school, was started in the autumn of 1917, and good work was done both there and at a hydrophone station established southward of Otranto at about the same time, as well as a hydrophone training school started at Gallipoli at the end of the war."[11]

The success of Ryan's training program can be measured by the recognition of this effort by Britain's Admiral John R. Jellicoe: "The greater part of this training took place at the establishment at Hawkcraig, near Rosyth, at which Captain Ryan, R.N., carried out so much exceedingly valuable work during the war. . . . I am not able to give exact figures of the number of officers and men who were instructed in hydrophone work either at Hawkcraig or at other stations by instructors sent from Hawkcraig, but the total was certainly upwards of 1,000 officers and 2,000 men."[12]

Jellicoe was close. According to Lieutenant Wilson, based on his service under Captain Ryan at Hawkcraig, "1090 officers, including Base hydrophone officers, submarine officers, and Royal Marine submarine mining officers, and 2731 ratings had either attended Hawkcraig for courses, or had received instruction from *Tarlair* travelling parties."[13]

While the successes of Commander Ryan and his Hawkcraig staff brought praise from the Admiralty, as far back as 1915 there had been growing interest in the need to incorporate science into the development of listening devices. Ryan had his first encounter with a scientist that summer when a retired professor, Alexander Crichton Mitchell, arrived at Granton Pier with an idea to detect submarines with a non-acoustic technology. Ryan, who was skeptical of the civilian scientist at first, soon found Mitchell's ideas worthy of further investigation and supported the experimental work in the Firth of Forth (chapter 4). Mitchell's ideas were independent of the Admiralty, and there continued to be a cooperative effort between the officer and the civilian.

The Board of Invention and Research was created by Lord Balfour, First Lord of the Admiralty, in July as a way to insert scientific insights into the development of antisubmarine technologies by integrating teams of scientists and engineers into the various experimental stations under Admiralty control. Because the submarine had became a problem of national significance as more and more ships were sent to the bottom, victims of U-boat torpedoes, the BIR was given submarine detection as a high priority. The next step was to assign BIR staff members to the Admiralty Experimental Station at Hawkcraig. They arrived in November, while Commander Ryan was still in the midst of moving from Granton Pier at Edinburgh to this (his) new experimental station. It soon became evident that Ryan was less than enthusiastic about the influx of civilians and what he likely perceived as a disruption in his own approach to solving the submarine detection problem.

A CRITICAL LACK OF COOPERATION

[A]t the time of our arrival at Hawkcraig the state of our knowledge of underwater sound propagation in the sea was very primitive. . . . It became immediately apparent, however, that this early work was essentially empirical, and that the serving officers at the station were not greatly interested in the physical properties involved.[14]

These comments by Albert B. Wood, a research assistant from Liverpool University, now on the BIR staff at Hawkcraig, summarized the different approach that would be taken by the BIR over that of Commander Ryan and his naval staff. By the time Wood and his colleagues arrived, Ryan had been demonstrating successful submarine detection with his hydrophones to his Admiralty bosses, who were already authorizing shore-based listening stations using Ryan's designs.[15]

There was never a true spirit of cooperation between Ryan's staff and the BIR, and by the spring of 1916, complaints began to arrive on the desk of BIR chairman, Admiral Fisher. Professor William H. Bragg, from the University College in London and in charge of the BIR efforts at Hawkcraig, wrote to Fisher complaining about the lack of ability to build the various apparatus his team needed for their experimental work. "What holds us back is the lack of instrument fitters and workshops. . . . It is quite exasperating that so much should turn on getting hold of the instrument makers."[16]

Not only was it difficult to have equipment built, the scientists also experienced frustrations having access to test vessels, one of the most important being the British submarine, *B-3*. In March, Albert Wood wrote to Sir Ernest Rutherford, a principal civilian scientist serving on the BIR in London:

The usual difficulties in obtaining a second ship or submarine still exist. Commander Ryan informs that we have no right to demand two ships and we are only allowed to have them when he considers it convenient . . . With regard to submarine B-3 . . . he said that it was to be used by both of us (Navy and BIR). He could not tell us, however, when we could have it for our own use; indicating that it would be possible for us to have it only on those occasions when he did not require it himself—which occasions from our previous experience will probably be rare.[17]

Rutherford continued to receive negative reports from Hawkcraig, revealing the lack of cooperation between his scientists and naval interests; he also sensed similar attitudes from members of the Admiralty. Rutherford reportedly "attacked the view taken by 'certain parties' in the Admiralty which appeared to suggest that research and development of listening apparatus was useless and irrelevant."[18] With pressure being put on the Admiralty, some improvements were made in the operations at Hawkcraig after April, but by the end of summer, rivalries continued to exist. In November, Admiral John Rushworth Jellicoe was appointed Britain's First Sea Lord; a month later, in response to the growing U-boat threat, he created the Admiralty's Anti-Submarine Division (ASD). The effect was to re-emphasize the importance of attacking the submarine problem with both research and development, stressing the immediate tactical needs at sea.

One impact was the transfer of the Hawkcraig scientists to the Admiralty Experimental Station at Parkeston Quay, Harwich, where there was access to test ships and laboratory facilities. Ryan would be left to his resourcefulness and his own staff at Hawkcraig. The year 1916 had come to an end, and the United States would soon enter the war. When Rutherford joined other colleagues from Britain and France during a scientific mission to America at the end of May, 1917, the submarine problem was a principal topic (chapter 12). Among the technical discussions, however, it was likely that the friction between British scientists and the military, which had seriously hampered the rapid development of submarine detection devices, was included. To avoid a similar lack of cooperation, U.S. Secretary of the Navy Josephus Daniels, who was aware of British technological developments, created the Special Board on Antisubmarine Devices (chapter 11), which was instrumental in the rapid integration of science and technology into wartime naval requirements.

A FISH, AN EEL, AND A PORPOISE

> All such praise the Nash's fish
> Are frankly forced to own,
> It's nothing near as swish
> As the porpoise hydrophone[19]

British P-class vessels were designed primarily for antisubmarine warfare. P-33 is shown here supporting U-boat hunting operations along the northeast shore of Scotland. (Wilson, 1920)

These lines are from a song sung on board a British submarine hunting vessel, *P-33*, operating off the northern coast of Scotland. By 1918, in addition to destroyers, British antisubmarine work was carried on by motor launches, trawlers, and drifters, as well as larger P-class vessels used in convoy work and capable of twenty-five knots. Hundreds of these various vessels patrolled the waters around the British Isles and into the North Sea, each carrying one or more of the many hydrophone designs available, including those provided by American designers. Lieutenant Wilson, in addition to his work at Hawkcraig with Ryan, also served on *P-33*. Wilson described the friendly competition between the listeners on his ship and those on the destroyer HMS *Dee*:

> The Nash fish was the rival form, fitted on the Peterhead trawlers, with which *Dee* and P.33 hunted. When we were ashore, the Club was often the scene of fierce arguments as to the rival merits of Nash's fish and the porpoise.[20]

Spring of 1917 had brought about the development of new directional listening devices, but the most important improvement in their capability was providing a streamlined housing, which could be towed behind the hunting vessel. Prior to this, hunting groups had to stop and then deploy their hydrophones for a listening period. When in pursuit, continuous listening while underway was the goal. With the BIR scientists working from the Parkeston experimental station, the Admiralty also encouraged universities

Left: *A variety of Nash Fish towed listening devices.* Below Left: *A British assembly and test facility.* (Courtesy George Malcolmson)

and industries to tackle the submarine detection problem. A very promising device was that created by George H. Nash, chief engineer of Western Electric Company's British subsidiary. Nash began his work with hydrophones early in 1917. His first trials occurred in June, with final acceptance by the Admiralty four months later. His device was comprised of a free-flooding, one-foot diameter cylinder approximately five feet long with conical ends (several versions were built, see top image above). The fish held two hydrophones—one bi-directional, which provided a measure of the direction to the source; and one uni-directional, which the operator could rotate with an electric motor to provide a more precise bearing. All of this was accomplished while the ship was underway.[21]

When the BIR scientists moved from Hawkcraig, Commander Ryan continued his hydrophone development unencumbered by the civilian

Porpoise towed listening devices developed by Captain Ryan at the Hawkcraig Experimental Station.
(Wilson, 1920)

scientists. His inventive mind, however, was also able to tackle the underway pursuit problem. Ryan had designed two systems that could be towed aft of a ship; one referred to as the "porpoise", the other his "rubber eel."

> We now reach the era of the rubber 'eel' and 'porpoise' hydrophones. . . . Both these instruments spelt a new departure. They could be towed from the stern of a vessel under way—a marked advance—and furthermore the latter instrument was a direction finder.[22]

The rubber eel was available by 1918, with 463 being issued to a variety of vessels, including trawlers and P-class ships. The device was a free-flooding, three-inch diameter rubber cylinder, eighteen inches long—the sensor consisting of a two-inch diameter button microphone with a phosphor-bronze diaphragm. When towed at speeds up to eight knots, the listener could detect a submarine at ranges up to four miles. Because the microphone was non-directional, two eels were often towed and the operator relied on binaural listening to obtain a target bearing.[23]

Ryan's most effective device, the porpoise, was not available until September, 1918. The porpoise was similar to the Nash fish, but only carried a single, improved uni-directional hydrophone, also rotated by an electric motor. In comparison trials with the Nash fish, the porpoise had a longer range to detection, performing well at speeds up to six knots. By Armistice, only thirty-one of the one hundred units ordered by Admiral Jellicoe's Anti-Submarine Division were in operation.[24] Nonetheless, the British hydrophone service was glad to have them.

> A new school of porpoise instruction was started at Elie for training personnel in its use; and hunting flotillas, using the porpoise, commenced operations in the summer, and carried on until Armistice . . ."[25]

Whether hunting at sea or from shore, it was hoped that with all the new technology available, including American listening devices being installed on destroyers and other British submarine hunting vessels, neither a U-boat nor a lovesick mermaid could avoid detection.

CHAPTER 4 HUNTING SUBMARINES FROM SHORE

> For the detection of submarines at certain congested lanes near the coast, and at entrances of harbors and bays, the British rather early in the war developed a tripod, with a microphone mounted upon it, which was lowered to the bottom and a listening station established on shore with connection by cable to the tripod.
>
> —Admiral Robert S. Griffin, *History of the Bureau of Engineering*, 1922[1]

Admiral Griffin, Chief of the U.S. Navy's Bureau of Engineering, recognized the work of the British early in the war to use shore-based listening stations. During the spring of 1915, Commander Ryan, initially at his station on Inchkeith Island and then at Edinburgh's Granton Pier, had demonstrated to an anxious Admiralty the application of hydrophones for submarine detection and, in particular, for creating a shore station listening post. Between March and August, 1915, hydrophone stations were established within the Firth of Forth at Oxcars, Inchcolm, and Elieness.

Ryan's success led to the rapid expansion of his shore station operations with installations to the north at Cromarty and to the south at Lowestoft near the entrance to the English Channel. Because the hydrophones used for these listening stations were non-directional, several units were installed in a line, where the listener could switch to each individual hydrophone in sequence. Where the sound was loudest indicated the position of an approaching submarine. The shore station listener was in contact with anti-submarine patrols assigned to the area, the submarine's position transmitted via wireless telegraphy. The vessels would then speed to the location, dropping their depth charges.

Installing these stations required running cables along the bottom, connecting the listeners to their offshore hydrophones. Three cable-laying drifters, *Vanguard, Couronne,* and *Eros,* were added to Ryan's small fleet.[2] Now with listening stations fully operational and a staff that would increase to twenty officers and eighty enlisted, he was able to deal with station

Hawkcraig Admiralty Experimental Station, along the north shore of the Firth of Forth. (Wilson, 1920)

logistics, maintenance, and listener training. Ryan was no longer confined to the Firth of Forth; he also continued to expand his hydrophone development beyond shore stations.

Once accepted by the Admiralty as an effective U-boat counter-measure and with the creation of the Anti-Submarine Division (ASD) in December 1916, multiple shore stations were rapidly established, covering strategic locations along the English Channel; across choke points at the northern and southern entrances to the Irish Sea; and as far north as the Orkney Islands. Stations were also established in the Mediterranean at the Malta hydrophone school and at locations in Italy associated with the Otranto Straits, through which U-boats stationed in the Adriatic had to pass when entering the Mediterranean. Another shore station was installed at Cap Griz Nez south of Calais as part of the mine fields that stretched between England and France at the Dover Straits.[3]

Mine fields across areas transited by U-boats were referred to as "mine barrages." The Dover Mine Barrage was a major deterrent that discouraged U-boats stationed at Zeebrugge and Ostend in Belgium from passing down the Channel, forcing them to transit past the north coast of Scotland in order to access their hunting grounds in the Atlantic.[4] This route, and passage beyond the Shetland Islands, however, was also defended by aggressive antisubmarine patrols and the extensive mine fields known as the North Sea Mine Barrage, much of which had been created by mine laying ships from the U.S. working with the British between the Orkneys and Norway.[5] As the reliability of the mines, as well as their numbers, increased, their effect on U-boat operations became a major concern of submarine commanders, including Ernst Hashagen, captain of *U-62*:

> The danger of the mines mounted from year to year throughout the war. There was no effective defense against them. We could only try to avoid the mines whenever possible, and, if there was no other way, we had to pass over them or dive through them. But they were dangerous foes, because they were always invisible and took us unawares by stealth.[6]
>
> At the beginning of 1918 the British succeeded too, at last, in blocking effectively the Straits of Dover. Between Folkstone and Griz Nez they had laid a wall of mines, ten deep, hermetically sealing the passage under water. Should a submarine be reported in the neighborhood, a row of buoys would light up, at a signal, with bright magnesium flares, turning night into dazzling brilliance. The submarine, forced to dive, was almost certainly destroyed upon the walls of mines. In the net lurked many a spider, ready for its victims. This barrage had indeed become a 'barrier of death.' Its completion spelt the end of the U-boat base at Zeebrugge, on the Belgian coast. When one U-boat after another had left it, never to return, it had to be abandoned."[7]

Shore stations installed in the vicinity of coast and harbor defense mine fields were sometimes equipped with the ability to remotely detonate the mines. When a listener was sufficiently certain that a U-boat was in close proximity to the mines, he could trigger them electronically. On May 4, 1918, *U-59* was heard on hydrophones at Cap Griz Nez, only two weeks after the shore station was installed. The listener triggered the mines, severely damaging the sub, which barely managed to return to her base at Ostend. It is thought that *UC-78* may have been destroyed at this same location. While the majority of the U-boats lost passing through the Dover Straits were from direct contact with a mine, U-boat commanders were very aware of the listeners on shore.[8] Ernst Hashagen:

> [By 1918] the British concentrated their mines in areas constantly traversed by German submarines, such as the English Channel. Between the mines were 'listening-buoys,' electrically connected with the nearest lookout post on shore. From far away, the electric cable could carry the faint hum and beat of propellers to the diaphragm of a telephone. Then a feverish switching to and fro would commence, an eager listening, as the enemy sought to trace the course [of the

U-boat]. At the right moment, when it had led directly to a group of mines, an electric button would be pressed and it would be silenced forever.[9]

Hashagen had described what he and his colleagues understood about the lethal capability of shore stations. He may have been confused by what he referred to as "listening-buoys." There were buoys on the surface that supported submarine nets, which also held mines. When a U-boat ran into the net, the violent tug could trigger a mine, or the motion of the buoy might catch the attention of a destroyer on a U-boat hunt. However, Hashagen may have also been aware of another submarine detection system connected electrically to a shore station, and which the station operators could use to then detonate nearby mines.

MAGNETIC INDICATOR LOOPS

The existence of this very valuable device was due to the work of certain distinguished scientists, and experiments were carried out in 1917. It was brought to perfection in late autumn, and orders were given to fit it in certain localities. . . . [T]he work was well in hand by the end of the year, and quickly proved its value.[10]

One of the "distinguished scientists" Admiral Jellicoe referred to was a retired professor, Alexander Crichton Mitchell. Families were desperate to shorten the war and bring their sons home. A Scottish family offered the Royal Society of Edinburgh £300 to find "better methods for detecting and locating the presence of submarines."[11] In June, 1915, responding to their pleas for action, the Royal Society contacted Professor Mitchell to put his mind to the problem of submarine detection. For this family, however, the war would not end in time; one son was killed at Gallipoli, another in France.

Mitchell's past interests included the physics behind magnetic fields, and he was intrigued by the electrical current generated in a loop of wire when crossed by a steel object—a phenomenon known as "electromagnetic induction." He immediately traveled to the Edinburgh waterfront, and by the first of August, Mitchell began his initial experiments at the end of West Pier at Leith where he lowered a wire loop and waited for a vessel to pass. After trying a few modifications in the design and orientation of the loop, all giving encouraging results, Mitchell was ready to apply his ideas to the ultimate prize—detecting a submerged submarine.[12]

On August 20, a visitor arrived on Granton Pier and approached Commander Ryan with a new idea. Professor Mitchell had been gathering data with his electromagnetic induction loop tests only a half mile away. At this time, Ryan was moving to a better location across the Firth of Forth at Hawkcraig Point, Aberdour (see page 41). Ryan was well entrenched in his experimental work with shore station installations within this estuary of Scotland's River Forth,[13] but he seemed interested in what the professor was suggesting. This civilian scientist, who had completed a significant amount of experimental work in three weeks, must have impressed Ryan, a hard-nosed, make-it-happen naval officer. The following day, Mitchell and Ryan installed operational indicator loops in the channel, possibly working from Ryan's new facility at Hawkcraig Point. Over the next few weeks, Mitchell monitored the galvanometer, recording the comings and goings of the naval squadron based at Rosyth. His overwhelming success was reported to the Royal Society, which had funded the work, the results soon forwarded to the Admiralty Board of Invention and Research.[14]

The response of the BIR, whose mission included reviewing ideas submitted by British citizens, was not at all encouraging. The report was probably given only a cursory review, as it was only one of thousands of suggestions being submitted to the BIR. The decision makers who reviewed these suggestions, including Professor Mitchell's report, often relied on estimates by scientists at the National Physics Lab in London who had already discounted the viability of electromagnetics as a method of submarine detection. One member of the BIR, physicist William Henry Bragg, began to reconsider Mitchell's experimental results, and, although it wasn't until November, 1916, renewed the effort to develop the loop idea. During the following year, indicator loop experiments conducted at the Parkeston Quay Experimental Station at Harwich led to operational "Bragg Loop" submarine detection systems being deployed at shore stations during 1918. That same year, a similar indicator loop technology was developed in the U.S. at the Naval Experimental Station and installed at the entrance to Chesapeake Bay.[15]

The war was almost over when a U-boat made an attempt to attack the British Grand Fleet, thought to be at anchor in Scapa Flow. Unfortunately for the U-boat, the fleet had left the Orkneys—but the Stanger Head hydrophone station at the entrance to Scapa Flow was still operating. To make entry even more perilous, a dozen Bragg indicator loops had been installed along the mine barrage. While the well-trained petty officers with their headphones listened intently for the distinctive sounds of a transiting U-boat, another member of the shore station crew kept watch on the dozen galvanometers, each with a known location near specific groups of mines. The listener tracked the approximate location and direction of the submarine based on the intensity of the sound from each of the line of five bottom-mounted hydrophones. As the invader approached and crossed one of the indicator loops, a member of the six-man crew, with his finger on the button, was ready to detonate the nearest mines.[16]

> UB 116 . . . set off with a volunteer crew of officers, bent on a gallant attempt to penetrate into Scapa Flow and there sink the British flagship. The forlorn venture was sadly misdirected, since the Grand Fleet was at that time in the Firth of Forth. On October 28 [1918], the submarine was located on the screen connected with electrical detectors of the outer Hoxa defenses [at the entrance to Scapa Flow]. When she was well over the field of controlled mines, the circuit was closed.[17]

The Scottish family who provided the funds to the Royal Society of Edinburgh which led to the development of "electrical detectors," later losing two sons in the war, may have gained some satisfaction if they learned these systems had contributed to the sinking of at least one U-boat. While the technology—hydrophones and magnetic loops—in the hands of the naval personnel who manned the listening posts had to be operating at peak efficiency, so did the sailors. For them, success against Germany's "Raiders of the Deep" depended on training, not luck.

CHAPTER 5 A GAME OF HIDE AND SEEK

> [V]essels were formed into special hydrophone flotillas, whose duties consisted of listening in long lines for submarines and when a discovery was made attacking them in the most approved tactical formation, with the aid of depth charges. . .Nearly all U-boats were fitted with a number of hydrophones and therefore were as well able to receive timely warning of an approaching surface ship as the surface ship was of the presence of the submarine. . .[allowing] a game of hide and seek to be played between a hunting vessel and a hunted submarine.
>
> —Charles Domville-Fife, *Submarine Warfare of Today*, 1920.[1]

In his 1920 book *Submarine Warfare of To-Day*, Charles Domville-Fife related his experiences as commander of a British hydrophone flotilla engaged in antisubmarine operations. German submarines had enjoyed the ability to disappear beneath the sea after an attack on an unarmed merchant ship, becoming nearly undetectable once they submerged. It would be more than a year before the Royal Navy would have a vessel designed specifically for submarine hunting—fast, maneuverable, and capable of operating far off shore. Success as an antisubmarine asset, however, was dependent on the hydrophone and the listeners on board.

During the first two years of the war, as Commander Ryan, who had been promoted to Captain, continued to develop hydrophones for shore-based listening posts, the only vessels available in any significant numbers for submarine patrols around the British Isles were commercial trawlers and what were referred to as "drifters" because of the drift nets used for fishing. Once commissioned, the vessels' crews became members of the Royal Navy Reserves (RNR) or the Royal Navy Volunteer Reserves (RNVR). The trawlers and drifters, according to Domville-Fife, each numbering well over one thousand, were initially employed in minesweeping and coastal patrols. The ships carried armament in the event they encountered a surfaced U-boat, but were often out-gunned by the submarine. "[Trawler] losses were heavy, both in ships and men, amounting to about 30 per cent," as indicated by Domville-Fife, while drifter "losses amounted to about 20 per cent."[2]

Domville-Fife quoted an article in an American magazine, *Rudder*, written by Henry R. Sutphin, vice president at Electric Boat Company and manager of Electric Launch Company (Elco), one of the businesses purchased by Electric Boat in 1899.

It was February, 1915, that we had our initial negotiations with the British Naval authorities. A well-known English ship builder and ordnance expert [Sir Trevor Dawson] was in this country, presumably on secret business for the Admiralty, and I met him one afternoon at his hotel. . . . I suggested the use of a number of small, speedy gasoline boats for use in attacking and destroying submarines. My idea was to have a mosquito fleet big enough to thoroughly patrol the coastal waters of Great Britain, each of them carrying a 13-lb. rapid-fire gun.[3]

Sutphin was asked how many of the 80-foot vessels could be delivered within a year. "I told him I could guarantee fifty." A short time later, Sutphin was informed that the British Government was interested, and on the 9th of April, a contract for fifty of these "chasers" was signed. A month later, however, the submarine *U-20* torpedoed and sank the Cunard Liner *Lusitania*. According to Domville-Fife, Sutphin's British contact asked him if a larger order could be managed; Sutphin's response: "I told him that I could guarantee to build a boat a day for so long as the Admiralty might care to name." The Admiralty's reply was soon forthcoming, and a contract for an additional five hundred "Chasers" was signed on the 9th of July.[4]

The Admiralty designated these as Motor Launch (ML) class vessels, with a desired speed of nineteen knots. The speed was simple arithmetic. A submerged U-boat may have been capable of as much as ten knots, although most were limited to about six to eight knots. A submarine on the surface, however, could run at nearly seventeen knots, eluding most of the patrol craft available to the Admiralty.[5] Pursuit by a destroyer, however, was a different matter. With speeds over thirty knots, a U-boat risked ramming if spotted on the surface, or if, having fired a torpedo, the destroyer could follow the track of the torpedo back to the submarine.

Right: *The
USS* Aylwin
*(DD-47)
represents
the type of
destroyer used
by American
and British
forces in the
war zone.*
(NHHC *NH
77908)
Before the
development
of effective
listening
devices,
destroyers
would follow
the track of
a torpedo
(below right): in
an attempt
to ram the
U-boat. (Sims,
1919-1920)*

With motor launches carrying hydrophones, it was hoped that a U-boat could be detected before it was in a position to attack a merchant ship. The hunting group, now in pursuit and working in concert with a destroyer, could locate the submarine's position and drop its limited supply of depth charges. The destroyer, in wireless contact with the hunting group, would then steam at full speed to the location and launch a barrage of depth charges. That was the hope. "The tactical methods of anti-submarine attack" expected of the

British motor launch assembly in Canada. (Nutting, 1920)

motor launches, as Domville-Fife had described, "proved impracticable for the more heavily armed but slow-moving trawlers and drifters."[6]

The contract for the 550 motor launches was completed on November 3, 1916. An order for an additional thirty was placed in July, 1917, all of which were launched the following year. Because the United States was considered a neutral country, orders were placed via the Canadian company Vickers, although Electric Boat Company, through Elco at its Bayonne, New Jersey, shipyard was the primary builder of the component parts. The final motor launch assembly was accomplished at shipyards in Quebec.[7] The vessel was an American design, that of naval architect Irwin Chase. The engines for the twin screw, nineteen-knot vessel were produced by the Standard Motor Construction Company. This same engine would be used on the U.S. Navy's submarine chasers, which began production when America entered the war and soon after the British motor launch contract had been filled.

Domville-Fife described the motor launch as "an avenger upon the seas . . . to whom the world appealed to save the lives of their seamen. . . it fought by day and by night, in winter gale and snow, and in summer heat and fog, in torrid zone and regions of perpetual ice to free the seas of the traitorous monster who had, in the twentieth century, hoisted the black flag of piracy and murder." A bit dramatic, but for Domville-Fife, the motor launch, his "avenger upon the seas," and the U-boat were the adversaries in a "guerrilla war at sea."[8]

British motor launch ML-369. (www.naval-history.net)

This may have been an overstatement, though the MLs, as they were referred to, certainly played a major role in British antisubmarine efforts. Until improvements were made in the listening devices, detection and destruction of submarines was a difficult mission; the heroic actions by these small warships would continue to be handicapped. According to Captain C. V. Usborne, RN, in spite of having obtained upgraded devices during the summer of 1917, there were still significant problems. His comments were summarized in *The German Submarine War, 1914-1918* (1931):

> [In] June 1917 I obtained twelve sets of directional hydrophones and thirty to forty sets of 'plate' or 'shark-fin' hydrophones for use in the Mediterranean, the latter pattern then being 'the latest thing' in acoustic detection. Various craft were fitted out with these instruments, but the hydrophones were very crude, and the submarine-detection by sound-listening could only be carried on very slowly.[9]

Until reliable, directional listening devices were developed and deployed, hydrophone flotilla tactics with the early British hydrophones remained inefficient. Domville-Fife described the process when a German submarine was heard:

> It was the call to action. The microphone was hauled to the surface and the chase began, a halt being made every half-mile or so for a further period of listening on the hydrophone. If the sound was louder the commander of the pursuing vessel knew that he was on the right track, and if the sound came up from the sea more indistinct the course was

changed and a run of a mile made in the opposite direction, when the vessel was again stopped and the instrument dropped overboard.[10]

Regardless of any tactical inefficiencies associated with the listening devices carried by British motor launches and American subchasers, hunting with hydrophones was a constant concern of U-boat captains. If a submarine was detected, a destroyer with its supply of depth charges would often be called to the area. When faced with the presence of hydrophone flotillas and other hunting groups, U-boats, also equipped with hydrophones, might quietly head for the bottom and listen to the sounds of the surface vessels. Ernst Hashagen, commanding officer of *U-62*, recalled his experiences while operating just outside the English Channel near the Cornish coast. They had been aware of the distinct sounds of a destroyer's propeller and, in keeping with the game of hide and seek, had settled onto the seabed at a depth of 150 feet. As they prepared to surface after several hours, this from the control room:

> ...the order [is passed] through all voice pipes: "Silence in the boat: listen for propeller noises: surfacing in ten minutes time." The stern compartment repeats "Attention! Report if propeller noises are heard." The coxswain puts on an under-water telephone connected to a diaphragm in the outer hull. But all is quiet.[11]

Listening with what Hashagen called their "bigger ear," which could detect the destroyer's propellers far in the distance, allowed *U-62* to surface and continue on toward the shipping lanes and potential targets while charging their batteries. This tactic, however, could spell disaster for an unwary U-boat captain. Operating in groups of three or more, the hunters might leave one vessel adrift in the area, while the U-boat would hear the rest motoring away. Surfacing could place the submarine in its most vulnerable position, with its hull and conning tower exposed to inevitable shelling by the hunter before the U-boat's gun crew could return fire. In spite of the risks, bottoming the submarine became a common practice when depths allowed. There was nothing for the listeners patrolling on the surface to hear.

Ernst Hashagen served on *U-22* in 1915, took command of *UB-21* in May, 1916, and later *U-62* in December, surviving the war in that submarine. His exploits certainly allow him the credibility to describe the effect listening devices had on U-boat operations, particularly during the last two years of the war. In 1915, listening technology had yet to significantly deter the

Imperial German Navy's undersea raiders, and the U-boat was then very capable of winning that game of hide and seek.

From France, a Supersonic Idea, but Too Late

> Another device capable of detecting a lurking submarine half a mile or more away by the use of a beam of sound waves of very high frequency was perfected too late to be of use . . .[12]

What Robert Millikan described in 1920 became the basis of "active" echo-location for submarine detection. That "beam of sound waves" was based on the piezoelectric properties of quartz crystals, where the crystal expands and contracts when subjected to an alternating electrical current. Throughout the war, the listeners on board submarine hunters relied on "passive" detection by hydrophones of sounds generated by a submarine's machinery and propellers when underway. Now, it appeared that there was a possibility of transmitting sounds from the hunting vessel, those sounds striking a target—the U-boat—and bouncing back in the form of an echo to a receiving hydrophone, which the listener would hear. Knowing the direction of that beam of sound waves and the time it took for the echo to return gave a direct reading of the bearing and distance to the submarine. Had this been available during the war, a U-boat could no longer hide on the bottom.

Soon after the war began, France established a Ministry of Inventions, led by mathematician Paul Painlevé (later serving as prime minister from September 12 to November 13, 1917). Painlevé became interested in one of the many suggestions made to the ministry by French citizens, and in February, 1915, passed one of particular interest to Paul Langevin, physics professor at the *Collége de France* in Paris. Early experimentation with echo detection in the Seine having been promising, Langevin's operation shifted in 1916 to the naval base at Toulon, where the French had established a facility for submarine research, and where he concentrated his efforts on the advantages of using quartz crystals as the transmitting source.[13]

By April 1917, Langevin was able to test a powerful quartz transmitter at his Toulon laboratory, operating at a "supersonic" frequency of 150 kHz (150,000 cycles per second). During this time, he also experimented with the size of the transmitter surface, the width and intensity of the sound beam, and the frequency. It wasn't until February 1918, however, that

Langevin would successfully test his transmitter at sea, receiving an echo from a submerged submarine for the first time.[14]

The work Langevin and other French researchers had completed throughout 1915 and during 1916 aroused the interest of British scientists who, representing the British Admiralty's Board of Invention and Research, established a cooperative relationship with the French Ministry of Inventions. There were indications of a bit of envy by the BIR scientists of the excellent oversight of the research by the ministry, and the importance to the war effort placed on the work of the French scientists.[15] From its inception, the BIR, with its emphasis on science, was often at odds with the pragmatic, make-it-happen-now approach of the military.

When America entered the war on April 6, 1917, an ally with a strong scientific tradition took a leading role in the antisubmarine effort. Exchanges of scientific missions began immediately, and the potential importance of Langevin's transmitter was recognized as a critical topic. The Ames mission from America arrived in France in April, followed by a European mission to America, organized by Painlevé and arriving in Washington at the end of May (chapter 12). The French delegates included two physicists, Charles Fabry and Henri Abraham, who had received commissions as Majors in order that the civilian scientists might better interact with the French military. Several conferences were held in June, where Langevin's work was discussed, although he was not able to participate in the mission. The conferences resulted in a great deal of enthusiasm among the American scientists, followed by the participants taking immediate action. From Admiral Griffin (1922):

> [T]he supersonic work which had been begun in France by professor
> Langevin was presented in full by Majs. Fabry and Abraham. The
> New York group, under the direction of Dr. M. I. Pupin, of Columbia
> University, selected at this time supersonic work at its major activity
> and continued work on this problem at New York, Key West, and New
> London, under the direction of the [Special Board on Antisubmarine
> Devices], during the continuation of the war. The San Pedro group,
> under Mr. Harris J. Ryan, also started work about this time on
> supersonic and kindred lines of research.[16]

Scientists and engineers from universities and industry continued their research on "supersonics" throughout the remaining eighteen months of the war, often bringing their ideas and devices to the Naval Experimental Station in New London. The early experimental work on echolocation is discussed in the epilogue, as this technology would prove to be essential to antisubmarine warfare in the future. The French had planned to install Langevin's latest device on submarine hunting vessels assigned to the Offensive Division of Torpedo-Listeners and on larger vessels beginning in 1919.[17] Armistice intervened.

At the beginning of this section, it was noted that supersonic submarine detection systems using "a beam of sound waves of very high frequency" were not ready for use before Armistice. The British and French antisubmarine efforts had continued throughout the first two-and-a-half years of the war without American help. During those years, U-boats continued their unrelenting pursuit of commercial shipping, which, after their declaration of a war zone around the British Isles in February 1915, resulted in the loss of untold numbers of civilians, including Americans who risked the Atlantic crossing.

NOTICE!

TRAVELLERS intending to embark on the Atlantic voyage are reminded that a state of war exists between Germany and her allies
and Great Britain and her allies; that the zone of war includes the
waters adjacent to the British Isles; that, in accordance with formal
notice given by the Imperial German Government, vessels flying
the flag of Great Britain, or of any of her allies, are liable to destruction in those waters and that travellers [sic] sailing in the war
zone on ships of Great Britain or her allies do so at their own risk.
IMPERIAL GERMAN EMBASSY Washington, D.C., April 22, 1915.

—*New York Times*, May 1, 1915.[1]

This warning was published in many newspapers, along with a
list of the Cunard Line *Lusitania*'s European destinations, prior
to her departure at 10 a.m. on Saturday, May 1, 1915. The German embassy warning was unambiguous—passengers would be traveling
"at their own risk."

On April 30, one day prior to *Lusitania* leaving New York, Captain
Lieutenant Walther Schwieger, in command of *U-20*, left Wilhelmshaven
on Germany's North Sea coast. Bound for the open seas west of Ireland, his
orders were to participate in an aggressive, predatory submarine campaign
against merchant vessels. A week later, nearly two thousand passengers
and crew of the 787 foot long, 44,060 ton passenger ship would sit in the
cross hairs of *U-20*'s periscope. According to the entry in Schwieger's log, at
3:10 p.m. on May 7, 1915, "Torpedo shot at distance of 700 meters, going
3 meters below the surface. Hits steering centre behind bridge. Unusually
great detonation with large cloud of smoke and debris shot above the fun-
nels. In addition to torpedo, a second explosion must have taken place."[2] It
would take only eighteen minutes for *Lusitania* to plunge to the bottom, just
eleven miles from her Liverpool destination, bringing nearly 1200 passengers
and crew with her. There were only 761 survivors.[3]

U-boat flotilla at their base at Keil. U-20, the submarine that sank Lusitania, is in the front row, second from the left. (LOC LC-B2-3292-13)

Headline story about the loss of the Cunard liner Lusitania. (New York Times, May 8, 1915)

When Lowell Thomas, embedded reporter during the war, returned to Europe a decade after Armistice, he searched for German U-boat officers willing to share recollections of their service. The sinking of *Lusitania* would be of particular importance to Thomas's telling of the U-boat campaign through the eyes of the participants. He was meticulous in his selection of U-boat officers, whom he interviewed in order to accurately portray their point of view. His *Raiders of the Deep* was published in 1928, a portrayal of life and death in the German submarine service.

Walther Schwieger could no longer tell his story, having died in September, 1917, while in command of *U-88*, which was lost in the Terschelling Bight mine fields off the Netherlands coast. Schwieger, however, had described the *Lusitania* sinking to his fellow submarine officers immediately after *U-20* returned. One of these officers was U-boat Commander Max Valentiner, and Thomas used the transcripts of their interview to lend Schwieger's voice to that tragic event:

> "I saw the steamer change her course again. She was coming directly at us. She could not have steered a more perfect course if she had deliberately tried to give us a dead shot. A short fast run, and we waited. The steamer was four hundred yards away when I gave an order to fire. The torpedo hit, and there was rather a small detonation and instantly afterward a much heavier one."[4]

When he returned to Wilhelmshaven, Schwieger was congratulated by his peers and throughout his chain of command. Yet the controversy about whether *Lusitania* was carrying war materials began immediately. Having fired a single torpedo, the second "much heavier" explosion was considered evidence of a cargo of munitions, a claim that Lowell Thomas described as "an alleged statement [by the] Collector of the Port of New York, that the *Lusitania* had aboard 4,200 cases of Springfield cartridges, 11 tons of gunpowder, and 5,500 barrels of ammunition."[5] Thomas also interviewed Lieutenant Rudolph Zentner, "a slender, pleasantly smiling chap with fiery red hair. . . [He] tucked a monocle under one bushy brow, and leaned back in his swivel chair."[6] Zentner, who was not aboard *U-20* at the time of the *Lusitania* sinking, had followed his famous (or infamous) commanding officer to his next submarine, *U-88*, after *U-20* ran aground and had to be destroyed by the crew. Zentner, however, was ashore when *U-88* with Walther Schwieger in command left Wilhelmshaven in September 1917, and fell victim to a British minefield; having survived the war, Zentner told Thomas of Schwieger's fate:

Commander Schwieger then assumed command of the *U-88*, a new, big boat of the latest design, and took most of his old crew with him . . . I made two cruises with him and then missed a cruise, just as I had done when the *Lusitania* was sunk. The boat never came back. It was lost with all on board during September, 1917 . . . I have never heard what fate befell my comrades. One rumor is that they hit a mine. . . . Schwieger and his men had gone to join the victims of the *Lusitania* on the floor of the sea.[7]

PRESIDENT WOODROW WILSON'S RESPONSE (*LUSITANIA*)

In view of recent acts of the German authorities in violation of American rights on the high seas which culminated in the torpedoing and sinking of the British steamship *Lusitania* on May 7, 1915, by which over 100 American citizens lost their lives, it is clearly wise and desirable that the government of the United States and the Imperial German government should come to a clear and full understanding as to the grave situation which has resulted.[8]

President Wilson, through Secretary of State William Jennings Bryan, instructed the American Ambassador to Germany, James W. Gerard, to pass this diplomatic protest to the German Secretary of Foreign Affairs, Gottlieb von Jagow, which was accomplished on May 13. Wilson also cited three other cases of attacks on shipping in just over a month prior to *Lusitania*, which resulted in the loss of American lives: the RMS *Falaba* (by *U-28*) on March 28 and the American tanker *Gulflight* (by *U-30*) on May 1, both torpedoed, and the bombing of the American steamer *Cushing* by a German airplane on April 28. Wilson, frustrated by these recent events and the loss of American lives, put Germany on notice that "submarines cannot be used against merchantmen, as the last few weeks have shown, without an inevitable violation of many sacred principles of justice and humanity."[9]

Lusitania fell victim to a U-boat attack, only three months after the proclamation written by Chief of the Admiralty Hugo von Pohl on February 4, 1915, announcing that on February 18, the waters around Britain and Ireland would be considered a war zone. Germany's aggressive submarine warfare against commercial shipping was being justified as "retaliatory measures rendered necessary" because of Britain's policy of "intercepting neutral maritime trade with Germany." Von Pohl expressed Germany's rationale for establishing the war zone: "Since the commencement of the present war

Great Britain's conduct of commercial warfare against Germany has been a mockery of all the principles of the law of nations." Von Pohl's proclamation was quickly and firmly denounced by the United States, expressing that there would be grave consequences "in carrying out the policy foreshadowed in the Admiralty's proclamation to destroy any merchant vessel of the United States or cause the death of American citizens."[10] One hundred twenty-four American citizens died on May 7.

On May 28, in response to Wilson's protest and the worldwide outcry against the sinking of *Lusitania*, Foreign Secretary Gottlieb von Jagow issued Germany's official reply. Von Jagow's contention was that *Lusitania* was armed and carrying war materials, thus, according to Germany, a war vessel. Refusing to accept blame for the loss of *Lusitania*, von Jagow also argued that if "neutral vessels have come to grief through the German submarine war during the past few months by mistake, it is a question of isolated and exceptional cases which are traceable to the misuse of flags by the British Government in connection with careless or suspicious actions on the part of the captains or the vessels." Von Jagow continued his reply:

> The Imperial Government must state for the rest the impression that certain facts most directly connected with the sinking of the *Lusitania* may have escaped the attention of the Government of the United States. It is, moreover, known to the Imperial Government from reliable information furnished by its officials and neutral passengers that for some time practically all the more valuable English merchant vessels have been provided with guns, ammunition and other weapons, and reinforced with a crew specially practiced in manning guns. According to reports at hand here, the *Lusitania* when she left New York undoubtedly had guns on board which were mounted under decks and masked.[11]

In a carefully and diplomatically worded letter to the Imperial German Government, in spite of the loss of 124 Americans, Wilson responded to von Jagow on the 9th of June, insisting that Germany follow "the principles of humanity, the universally recognized understandings of international law, and the ancient friendship of the German Nation." Wilson continued:

> Whatever be the other facts regarding the *Lusitania*, the principal fact is that a great steamer, primarily and chiefly a conveyance for passengers, and carrying more than a thousand souls who had no part or lot in the conduct of the war, was torpedoed and sunk without so much as

a challenge or warning, and that men, women, and children were sent to their death in circumstances unparalleled in modern warfare.

Only her resistance to capture or refusal to stop when ordered to do so for the purpose of visit could have afforded the commander of the submarine any justification for so much as putting the lives of those on board the ship in jeopardy.[12]

Regardless of the possibility that *Lusitania* carried war materials, the press across the world condemned the act, citing the loss of life among so many women and children.[13] It was not long before Germany relented to worldwide condemnation. Schwieger was reprimanded by Kaiser Wilhelm, although this reprimand did not sit well within the German navy, which blamed Britain for necessitating their use of submarines against commerce. Admiral Reinhard Scheer, in his 1920 memoir, was demonstrably angered by the British blockade and their use of armed merchant vessels: "Our enemies acted in an unscrupulous manner, especially when bonuses were offered for merchant vessels which should sink U-boats."[14] By September, 1915, however, the relentless submarine warfare that had begun in February was suspended. U-boats were once again ordered to provide warning before sinking commercial vessels.

Wilson ended his letter to Germany with the following: "The Government of the United States therefore deems it reasonable to expect that the Imperial German Government will adopt the measures necessary to put these principles [of international law] into practice in respect of the safeguarding of American lives and ships, and asks for assurances that this will be done."[15] This would not be the last time the President had to admonish and threaten the Imperial German Government. Because of Wilson's increased antagonism toward Germany, there would be a significant change within his Government. On June 9, his pacifist Secretary of State, William Jennings Bryan, resigned. Bryan felt that there was some merit in Germany's objections to Britain's blockade, and that Wilson, representing a neutral country, should have been more evenhanded. Bryan had preferred expressing some level of protest against restrictions on the free passage of neutral ships bound for German ports imposed by Great Britain. He was succeeded by Robert Lansing who, while also objecting to Britain's blockade, felt that the United States would eventually enter the war as an ally of Britain. Within the German Admiralty, however, there were also objections that went beyond the blockade, pointing out Britain's conduct after the loss of *Lusitania*:

It was particularly striking how the English Press persisted in representing the loss of Lusitania not so much as a British, but as an

American misfortune. One must read the article in The [London] Times which appeared immediately after the sinking of Lusitania (8/5/1915) to realize the degree of hypocrisy of which the English are capable when their commercial interests are at stake. Not a word of sympathy or sorrow for the loss of human life, but only the undisguised desire (with a certain satisfaction) to make capital out of the incident in order to rouse the Americans and make them take sides against Germany.[16]

In his memoir, Admiral Reinhard Scheer, who had replaced Hugo von Pohl as Chief of the Admiralty in January, 1916, expressed his disdain for what he considered the use of this tragedy as a propaganda tool. It was not propaganda, however, that was changing attitudes across America. The reality, which included those 124 American lives, was a realization that remaining neutral in a war that threatened democratic societies was becoming a bitter pill and increasingly untenable as the months went by, as U-boat predation on unarmed merchant vessels continued.

> On the 24th of March, 1916, at about 2.50 o'clock in the after-
> noon, the unarmed steamer *Sussex*, with 325 or more passengers
> on board, among whom were a number of American citizens, was
> torpedoed while crossing from Folkstone to Dieppe.
>
> —President Woodrow Wilson[1]

On April 18, 1916, with these words in his opening paragraph, President Woodrow Wilson delivered his ultimatum to Germany's Secretary of Foreign Affairs Gottlieb von Jagow. *Sussex* was a cross-channel steamer, which had made this passage between England and France many times. The vessel, which did not transit via routes used by troop transports, was well-known, was unarmed, and only carried civilians. Although reports varied, there may have been in excess of eighty passengers lost in the attack. The torpedo destroyed the bow section forward of the bridge, yet *Sussex* remained afloat and was towed into Boulogne Harbor. There was no question that a German U-boat and not a mine was the cause, there being fragments of the torpedo found within the *Sussex* hull.

Wilson's ultimatum continued: "[T]he Imperial Government has failed to appreciate the gravity of the situation which has resulted, not alone from the attack on the *Sussex*, but from the whole method and character of submarine warfare as disclosed by the unrestrained practice of the commanders of German undersea craft . . . in the indiscriminate destruction of merchant vessels of all sorts, nationalities, and destinations."[2]

Less than eleven months had passed since the sinking of *Lusitania*. President Wilson, who had been continuously frustrated by German promises made and broken, ended by putting the German Government on notice: "If it is still the purpose of the Imperial Government to prosecute relentless and indiscriminate warfare against vessels of commerce by the use of submarines . . . the Government of the United States is at last forced to the conclusion that there is but one course it can pursue. Unless the Imperial

The passenger ferry Sussex *torpedoed while crossing the English Channel.* (Wikipedia)

Government should now immediately declare and effect an abandonment of its present methods of submarine warfare against passenger and freight-carrying vessels, the Government of the United States can have no choice but to sever diplomatic relations with the German Empire altogether."[3]

Wilson's ultimatum was delivered to Germany's Secretary of Foreign Affairs on April 18, 1916. The following day, Wilson addressed Congress, with an explanation of his blunt message to Germany: ". . .despite the solemn protest of this Government, the commanders of German undersea vessels have attacked merchant ships with greater and greater activity . . . in a way that has grown more and more ruthless, more and more indiscriminate . . ." Wilson then ended his address to Congress, reiterating his ultimatum to Germany that "if it is still its purpose to prosecute relentless and indiscriminate warfare against vessels of commerce by use of submarines," the next step would be for the United States to sever diplomatic relations, an act that would surely be followed by a declaration of war.[4]

Gottlieb von Jagow, responding from Berlin on the fourth of May to Wilson's ultimatum, continued to complain of Britain's blockade of neutral shipping destined for German ports. "In self-defense against the illegal conduct of British warships, while fighting a bitter struggle for national existence, Germany had to resort to the hard but effective weapon of submarine warfare. . . . Moreover, Great Britain again and again has violated international law, surpassing all bounds in outraging neutral rights. . ."[5] Nonetheless, Germany relented and von Jagow relayed the following decision by the Imperial Government:

In accordance with the general principles of visit and search and the destruction of merchant vessels, recognized by international law, such vessels, both within and without the area declared a naval war zone, shall not be sunk without warning and without saving human lives unless the ship attempts to escape or offer resistance. [original emphasis][6]

The German Admiralty, in particular Reinhard Scheer, understood that once their submarines were required to operate in accordance with prize law, there would be little chance of forcing Britain to capitulate due to a lack of food and fuel. This opinion was shared by his submarine commanders, including Walther Schwieger, who declared that under these conditions there would be "little chance of decisive results." Yet, Scheer relented to the new policy and instructed his submarine fleet to redirect their unrestricted warfare operations to now target naval vessels, including transports and armed merchantmen.[7]

German officials understood, however, that in spite of this latest agreement, the United States would soon enter the war; these diplomatic threats and promises were simply a tactic to stall the inevitable. In fact, Germany was quite willing to cease her policy of unrestricted warfare against commercial shipping. The respite provided an opportunity to intensify the production of long range cruiser submarines: "the monthly rate of commissioning new boats was never so favourable as between April 1916 and January 1917, averaging ten new craft per month. . . . In addition, fifty-two large and eighty-nine small boats were either under construction or about to be delivered."[8]

As U-boat activities subsided, Allied navies also became overconfident in the effectiveness of their antisubmarine capability. This was based on not fully understanding the reasons that Germany had agreed to this slackening of attacks against commercial shipping. "It was both convenient and consoling to presume that counter measures were at last proving effective. For that complacent optimism a bitter price had, a year later, to be paid."[9] The high price of complacency would become evident when Germany unleashed her most destructive U-boat campaign in February, 1917. Meanwhile, throughout 1916, Germany continued her diplomatic fencing with the United States.

DEUTSCHLAND AND U-155

The German submarine *Deutschland*, the first cargo-carrying U-boat, left Bremen on June 14, 1916. Capt. [Paul] Koenig laid his course around the north of Scotland . . .[10]

In 1916, relying on America's neutrality for access to safe ports, the merchant submarine *Deutschland* made two visits to the east coast. Although these were supposed peaceful missions, America's vulnerability to submarines was made clear when the Navy published *German Submarine Activities on the Atlantic Coast of the United States and Canada* in 1920.

It is likely, however, that *Deutschland* was on a dual mission. Germany had purchased raw materials from various sources prior to America's entry into the war and was crossing the Atlantic to collect the merchandise. Her west-bound transit of 3800 miles was accomplished in less than three weeks, including several delays due to potentially dangerous encounters with British submarine hunters early in her transit. This first trip brought *Deutschland* to the port at Baltimore on July 9, where she discharged a 750-ton cargo of a million dollars worth of chemicals and dyestuffs. During her 23-day stay, *Deutschland* loaded 401 tons of crude rubber, 378 tons of nickel, and 90 tons of tin, valued at about $1,000,000 [1916 dollars]. The 22-day return route was 4200 miles, of which only 100 occurred while submerged. *Deutschland* returned to her home at Bremen, Germany on August 23.[11]

Deutschland was in all aspects in 1916, a merchant vessel. She had no torpedo tubes and did not carry the deck guns associated with German U-boats. Her hull, however, was built along the same designs as were the heavily-armed U-boat cruisers that were creating havoc among allied merchant shipping during those first years of the war. These submarines were capable of speeds of fourteen knots on the surface and seven and one-half knots submerged, making them efficient for both commercial and military uses. With a diesel fuel-oil capacity of 240 tons, lengthy cruises of several thousand miles could be expected without refueling.

Was *Deutschland*'s trip to the U.S. purely commercial, or was she also testing the navigation route to America's east coast, in anticipation of our entry on the side of Britain and her allies? Captain Koenig, commenting after his successful Atlantic crossing, was not providing any hints as to his true motives, but did complain about Britain's restrictions on neutral shipping.

> Great Britain cannot hinder boats such as ours to go and come as we please. Our trip passing Dover across the ocean was an uneventful one. When danger approached we went below the surface, and here we are, safely in an American port, ready to return in due course. I am not in a position to give you full details of our trip across the ocean, in view of our enemies. . . . Needless to say that we are quite unarmed and only a peaceful merchantman.[12]

The allied countries would have none of this, and in August, submitted a joint protest to the U.S. urging "neutral Governments to take effective measures [for] preventing belligerent submarine vessels, whatever the purpose to which they are put, from making use of neutral waters, roadsteads, and ports." Their concern was that such vessels can navigate unseen and without any controls, and "that it is impossible to identify them and establish their national character, whether neutral or belligerent, combatant or noncombatant, and to remove the capacity for harm inherent in the nature of such vessels." The allied countries were concerned that neutral ports would effectively become "a base of naval operations" for German submarines operating under the guise of a merchantman.[13]

At a time when this country was still attempting to keep pressure on Germany to restrain from their relentless submarine warfare against merchant ships, the neutral U.S. was reluctant to distinguish a commercial submarine from a warship. The official reply, sent on August 31, a week after *Deutschland* had returned to Germany, notified the "Governments of France, Great Britain, Russia, and Japan that so far as the treatment of either war or merchant submarines in American waters is concerned . . . [the United States] holds it to be the duty of the belligerent powers to distinguish between submarines of neutral and belligerent nationality . . ."[14]

Late in September, another submarine was en route from its base at Wilhelmshaven on Germany's North Sea coast, passing north of the Shetland Islands and down the coast of Newfoundland. It would take seventeen days for this well-armed naval submarine, *U-53*, to reach the coast of southern New England, where she was sighted three miles east of Point Judith, Rhode Island. At 2:00 p.m. on the seventh of October, *U-53*, accompanied by the U.S. submarine *D-3*, entered Narragansett Bay and proceeded to the Naval Station at Newport. When asked about the reason for this unannounced visit, U-boat captain Hans Rose stated that the visit was simply intended "to pay his respects, that he needed no supplies or assistance, and that he proposed to go to sea at 6 o'clock." American naval officers were invited on board for tours of the vessel and given unexpected access to the submarine's capabilities. The German officers spoke excellent, or at least understandable, English, and politely answered the American visitors' questions.[15]

As promised, *U-53* was underway after remaining at the Naval Station less than three hours. The cordial nature of this brief visit ended abruptly the following day when *U-53* sank two British ships less than three miles from the Nantucket Lightship.[16] Later that day a Norwegian, Dutch, and

another British ship fell victim, as this U-bout remained briefly on the east coast before returning to Germany by the first of November.

After *Deutschland*'s very successful commercial venture across the Atlantic in June, she set out again for America on October 10 . . . this time headed for New London, Connecticut, again carrying dyestuffs and chemicals. She arrived on the first of November, the same day U-53 had returned to Germany. Leaving on November 17 with a cargo of copper and 360 tons of nickel purchased from Canada in 1914, *Deutschland* accidentally struck and sank the American Steamship *T. A. Scott, Jr.* near Race Rock Light, causing her to return to New London for repairs. She finally returned to Germany on December 10.[17]

The following spring, *Deutschland* would return to sea as *U-155*, now fully outfitted with torpedoes and heavily armed as a long range cruiser, operating off the west coast of Spain and around the Azores. During her initial cruise, which lasted 103 days, *U-155* sank eleven steamers and eight sailing vessels, including the American schooner *John Twohy*. In January, 1918, *U-155* returned to the waters between the Azores and Spain; during

Right: Germany's mercantile submarine Deutschland *during her visit to New London, Connecticut, November, 1916. (NHHC NH 43610) Below Right: Refitted as* U-155, *she returned to the east coast of America with a much different mission during the summer of 1918. (NHHC NH 111054)*

her 108 days at sea, *U-155* netted ten steamers and seven sailing vessels. In August, this former merchant submarine returned to America . . . now a predator.[18]

By the time *Deutschland* visited the east coast in 1916, the ground war in Europe had raged for two years. German submarines had sunk hundreds of merchant vessels, and it was becoming increasingly obvious to all countries involved that America would soon enter the war effort. This had been a concern for the German hierarchy, and after the sinking of *Sussex*, had resulted in a reduction of submarine predation on commercial shipping. By the end of

1916, however, increased pressure on politicians forced Germany to relent to the wishes of the navy and acknowledge that the only winning strategy was to return to a policy of unrestricted submarine warfare on commerce. If Germany couldn't beat the allies in the trenches, then they would starve Britain into submission. If that brought America in on the side of the allies, the war would be over before she could mobilize and begin transporting troops and materials to Europe. It was a strategic gamble.

Germany knew that sending a fleet of battleships to engage the U.S. Navy was not possible; the only alternative would be her long-range cruiser submarines operating along the east coast. Mine fields would be needed across the primary transit lanes from the strategic port of New York and along the Atlantic seaboard as far south as Chesapeake Bay and Cape Hatteras. Knowing full well that the flow of men and materials could not be stopped, Germany hoped to slow the process, forcing a starving Britain and a war-weary France into capitulating before America could become fully involved.

With two successful Atlantic crossings by *Deutschland* and one by *U-53*, U-boat commanders could expect a transit time of less than twenty days. Much of the voyage from the protection of their Heligoland base to the coast of America was beyond the reach of allied submarine hunters, already stretched to their limit protecting the British Isles, France, and the Mediterranean. In spite of the loss of *Bremen*, sister ship of *Deutschland*, probably after striking a mine, much had been learned. The crossing could be accomplished almost entirely on the surface, with only limited need to submerge if a threat was encountered. These visits in 1916 were not simply commercial or social; they were intended to test the tactical and navigational ability to bring the submarine war to America, and would be the basis for the construction of additional U-boats capable of long-range, extended-duration cruises. Admiral Reinhard Scheer:

> The favorable experiences of the commercial U-Boat U-*Deutschland*
> had led to the construction of U-*cruisers*, of which the first series had
> a displacement of 1,200 tons, which was later raised to 2,000 and
> more. . . . They were fitted with two guns of 15 cm. caliber and two
> torpedo tubes, and could carry about 30 torpedoes in accordance
> with the extended period during which they could be used on cruises,
> cruises which reached as far as the Azores and lasted up to three
> months.[19]

Chapter 8 Preparing for the Inevitable

The press accounts gave daily news of the part that science and invention was playing in the war, of the introduction of new weapons, of the fact that those waging the war were utilizing the best inventive and scientific talent of their respective countries.

—Lloyd N. Scott, *Naval Consulting Board of the United States*, 1920[1]

New and horrendous technologies were being introduced on land and in the sky above the battlefields, and now both on and under the sea, resulting in unprecedented human slaughter. Germany, in particular, had engaged her scientific and engineering talent to the development of these technologies. Throughout 1916, as reports from Europe reached American readers, influential voices from the public and within government were calling for an increase in readiness across America's industries. There would soon be an urgency to respond to an unprecedented need for materials associated with modern warfare. Remaining neutral was becoming less likely as Europe slowly bled to death.

The U-boat represented a technology that naval planners had largely disregarded during the years leading to the war, in spite of those warnings at the turn of the century by the Navy's Engineer in Chief, Rear Admiral George Melville: "As few things are impossible, the submarine may be developed in time to a state of efficiency and reliability that will cause a revolution in the composition of fleets." Melville also warned that: "The naval battles of the future will be won by the nation which has made preparation for a conflict, and has supplied itself with every possible weapon of war."[2]

In the book *Cold Warriors* (2014), this author also noted the relevance of Melville's comments to World War I, as well as modern submarine warfare: "Germany had prepared—America, England, and the rest of Europe had not. The Imperial German Navy would enter the war with a submarine design and construction program capable of winning more than just the battle. [Melville's] observations, as relevant today as they were over a century ago, give insight, through the eyes of the Navy's chief engineer, to the technological potential of submarine warfare."[3]

Many popular and influential figures recognized the lack of preparation for what they saw as America's inevitable entry into the war. Theodore Roosevelt, who lost his bid for the presidency to Woodrow Wilson during the 1912 campaign, was particularly outspoken about Wilson and his government's response to the sinking of *Lusitania*. In the summer of 1915 he wrote an article, "American Preparedness," for the *New York Times*:

> We have been culpably, well-nigh criminally, remiss as a nation in not preparing ourselves, and if, with the lessons taught the world by the dreadful tragedies of the last twelve months, we continue with soft complacency to stand helpless and naked before the world, we shall excite only contempt and derision if and when disaster ultimately overwhelms us.

To emphasize his disdain, Roosevelt cited his concern that where "American men, women, and children drowned on the high seas, as in the case of the Gulfflight and Lusitania . . , [the Government's reaction would be to] appoint a commission and listen to a year's conversation on the subject before taking action."[4]

Losses mounted as a result of Germany's unrelenting U-boat tactics, which concentrated on mercantile shipping; nearly all deaths were associated with civilian crews and passengers, and the public outcry intensified. Those voices were being heard by the Wilson administration. Pacifism and neutrality would stand aside; Wilson's Secretary of State, William Jennings Bryan, a staunch pacifist, resigned on June 9, 1915. "Preparedness" would become a priority within the government, albeit initially behind the scenes. The first sign of this new approach inside Wilson's administration was a letter from Secretary of the Navy Josephus Daniels, sent on July 7, 1915, only two months after the sinking of *Lusitania*. Written to the most well known American inventor, Thomas Edison, the letter may have been designed to stroke the inventor's ego: "Dear Mr. Edison. I have been intending for some time to write you expressing my admiration at the splendid and patriotic attitude you have taken . . ."[5]

Secretary Daniels had proposed to President Wilson an idea of creating a department within the Navy dedicated to warfare technology development. In his letter to Edison, Daniels explained that: "such a department will, of course, eventually have to be supported by Congress, with sufficient appropriations made for its proper development . . . Congress must be made to feel that the idea is supported by the people . . ." Daniels spared no words to persuade the world renowned inventor to join in the effort. "You are recognized by all of us as the one man above all others who can turn dreams into realities and who has at his command, in addition to his own wonderful mind, the finest facilities in the world for such work." Daniels then turned to his most urgent priority. "We are confronted with a new and terrible engine of warfare in the submarine . . . and I feel sure that with the practical knowledge of the officers of the Navy, with a department composed of the keenest and most inventive minds that we can gather together, and with your own wonderful brain to aid us, the United States will be able as in the past to meet this danger with new devices that will assure peace to our country by their effectiveness."

Public acceptance, and thus money from Congress, would not be a problem. Wilson's protest letter to Germany immediately following the sinking of *Lusitania* was widely circulated in the press, and Americans were becoming increasingly concerned. Edison accepted the offer to head the organization Secretary Daniels had envisioned, and on July 13, sent his Chief Engineer, Dr. Miller Reese Hutchinson, to meet with Daniels. Daniels then traveled to Edison's Orange, New Jersey home and laboratory where they discussed the composition and goals of what had been proposed to Wilson.[6]

Drawing representatives from a variety of industries, a formal organizational meeting was held in Washington on October 7, 1915. An initial order of business was naming the organization the Naval Consulting Board of the United States (the NCB).

Preparedness was certainly on Daniels' mind. At a meeting of the NCB on November 4, sixteen committees were formed, encompassing the spectrum of issues that both Daniels and Edison understood would be sure to become urgent if, and, likely, when the United States entered the war: (1) chemistry and physics; (2) aeronautics, including aero motors; (3) internal combustion motors; (4) electricity; (5) mines and torpedoes; (6) submarines; (7) ordnance and explosives; (8) wireless and communications; (9) transportation; (10) production, organization, manufacture, and standardization; (11) ship construction; (12) steam engineering and ship propulsion; (13) life-saving appliances; (14) aids to navigation; (15) food and sanitation; (16) public works, yards and docks. By November, members of these committees had been selected from the NCB membership based on which technology they were best suited for. Additional committees were later created to address fuel and fuel handling, metallurgy, and optical glass. The objectives were far reaching, but each committee was dedicated to the same goal—preparedness.[7]

During the Civil War, as the earlier records of the [National Academy of Sciences] indicate, its committees and its members dealt actively with military and naval problems of precisely the same type as those which have insistently pressed for solution during the present war.[8]

By the fall of 1915, it had become obvious to members of the National Academy of Sciences that the European war was being defined by rapid advances in technology, the direct result of the efforts of scientific minds among the participating countries—Germany in particular.

During the summer following the loss of *Lusitania*, Secretary of the Navy Josephus Daniels had initiated an idea to bring together engineering talent from America's industrial and manufacturing base. Daniels enlisted Thomas Edison to head what would become the National Consulting Board. By October, the NCB had formed committees whose mission was to address the technological needs that were presumed to exist on and over the battlefields of Europe, and on and under the sea. Yet the emphasis would be on improving state-of-the-art technologies through engineering know-how and not through the application of scientific principles.

During the initial NCB meeting in October, when asked why there were only two scientists among the membership, Edison's chief engineer M. R. Hutchison was perfectly blunt in his reply: "... it was [Edison's] desire to have this Board composed of *practical* men who are accustomed to *doing* things, and not *talking* about it."[9]

This attitude would prevail within the NCB; throughout its existence, technological advances would depend on an engineering approach. Daniel J. Kevles, in *The Physicists* (1978), described the relationship between Edison and Daniels: "Edison ... privately advised Daniels that he did not think 'scientific research' would be necessary 'to any great extent'; for the navy could rely on the Bureau of Standards and industrial laboratories. Besides, it would be 'useless to go on piling up more data at great expense and delay ...'"[10] Edison felt that there was already enough data to move technology forward. Members of the National Academy of Sciences, George Ellery Hale in particular, disagreed.

Hale was the director of the Mount Wilson Observatory and had been instrumental in its design and construction. He complained that no one from the National Academy of Sciences had been asked to become an NCB member. Hale, an individual of stature equal to that of Thomas Edison, if primarily among scientists and a scientifically aware public, was miffed by the lack of scientific minds among the membership.[11] Hale fully supported President Wilson's stern warning to Germany after the sinking of *Lusitania* and was delighted when the pacifist Secretary of State William Jennings Bryan resigned. Hale was certain that Wilson would welcome an offer of Academy assistance were the U.S. to enter the war. Yet in 1915, Hale's enthusiasm was not shared by all of the Academy members, and he was urged to hold off from presenting the idea to the President. It would be the torpedoing of *Sussex* by *UB-29* on March 24, 1916, and Wilson's ultimatum and threat of severing diplomatic relations with Germany that brought Hale to the Academy's annual meeting on the 19th of April. He presented a resolution that would offer the Academy's scientific resources to the President, with the expectation that diplomatic relations with Germany would soon be suspended.[12]

Armed with unanimous Academy support, Hale joined a delegation to Washington, headed by Academy president William H. Welch. The delegation successfully obtained President Wilson's endorsement, but because of the sensitive political relationship with Germany, the President asked that any action taken by the Academy be done discretely. The Academy, delighted with Wilson's recognition of the role science could play in the war effort, acted quickly, yet remained behind the scenes as requested.[13]

On June 19, 1916, an organizing committee presented to the Academy a plan "for the formation of a *National Research Council*, the purpose of which shall be to bring into co-operation governmental, educational, industrial, and other research organizations with the object of encouraging the investigation of natural phenomena, the increased use of scientific research in the development of American industries, the employment of scientific methods in strengthening the national defense, and such other applications of science as will promote the national security and welfare." The Academy voted to establish an organizing committee to proceed with the creation of the NRC, which would be far reaching and inclusive of many interests within the worldwide scientific community. In August, President Wilson appointed military representatives from the Army and Navy, as well as scientists at Government bureaus, who would serve on the NRC.[14]

As plans proceeded for establishing an organization responsible for developing military technologies, the Academy decided it would be essential to understand the nature of wartime scientific efforts in Europe. Thus, William Henry Welch, president of the Academy, accompanied by the NRC's organizing committee chairman, George Ellery Hale, crossed the Atlantic . . . a crossing that brought these men through waters patrolled by U-boats. This would not be the only time civilian scientists and engineers would make this same dangerous voyage.[15]

It is likely that Wilson, who continued to hold onto hope for a peaceful resolution, understood the necessity to prepare for war. The obvious technological challenges would have influenced Wilson's decision to support the Academy's proposal for a National Research Council. The complexity as well as lethality of these new technologies led the President and Congress to establish an advisory body within the Government, with the authority to guide the country's civilian war effort.

> [I]t was evident that if the best results were to be obtained not only
> would the existing laws require revision, but there must also be
> created a properly legalized body, under which might be organized the
> scientific and industrial resources of the country.[16]

Congress in 1916, while still engaged in a policy of neutrality, had been willing to fund efforts to respond to a "future war of defense inferentially far distant," and on August 29 of that year acted to establish the Council of National Defense. Created to provide the United States Government, and in particular the President, with recommendations "for coordination of industries and resources for the national security and welfare," council members were from the President's Cabinet, and included the Secretaries of War, Navy, Interior, Agriculture, Commerce, and Labor. Yet during the fall of 1916, the Council remained primarily on paper. Appointments would not occur until November, with the first meeting held on December 11.[17] Eventually, however, the Council of National Defense would serve this administration's efforts to mobilize the country's academic and industrial talents.

According to Lloyd N. Scott (1920), "the aim of the council and its agencies was to serve as a channel through which the best professional and industrial intelligence of the country could make itself most effectively valuable to the Government departments. . . . Although it was not generally recognized, the Council of National Defense was, in fact, the War Cabinet of the administration." With the Secretary of War serving as its chairman, Scott emphasized the importance of the council to the Wilson administration where "a resolution passed by the [council] stood only second to an Executive order of the President of the United States."[18]

As President Wilson turned his attention to the many pressing international affairs, the newly formed National Research Council held its first official meeting, which also served as its organizational meeting, in New

York on September 20.[19] At this same meeting, a fifteen-man Military Committee was formed, chaired by the Secretary of the Smithsonian Institution, Charles D. Wolcott. The Military Committee consisted of the civilian heads of various bureaus, as well as general and flag officers within the Army and Navy.[20] Of these members, the Navy's Engineer-in-Chief, Rear Admiral Robert D. Griffin, and the Army's Chief Signal Officer, Major General George O. Squier, would be primary proponents of the NRC's antisubmarine efforts. As 1916 came to a close and America no longer drifted, but sped toward war, the significance of the decision to establish a Military Committee within the NRC would become apparent in the early months of 1917.

Robert A Millikan was appointed Director of Research and Executive Officer of the National Research Council. NRC chairman, George Ellery Hale, had rented office space at the Munsey Building on E Street in Washington where Millikan had his office, providing ready access to politicians and the civilian staff at the military bureaus. He would be commissioned a Lieutenant Colonel in the Science and Research Division of the Army Signal Corps, thus also providing access to the Army and Navy staff assigned to the bureaus. This was a unique role for this professor and others among his colleagues who also received commissions, as well as their families: "Our wives, no doubt, resented this new assumption of the insignia of *authority*, but took pains to keep us in our proper place, at least at home."[21]

The reality of war, however, was fully understood by every member of the NRC and their families. There was an urgent need to respond to the new technologies brought into twentieth century warfare in the air, on land, and at sea. Robert A. Millikan would be a major influence on the work accomplished by these scientists and engineers: "I was all for a wartime program for it required no prophet to see the impending storm and I knew we had to be in it."[22]

PART II

1917

Does it really make any difference, purely from the humane point of view, whether those thousands of men who drown wear naval uniforms or belong to a merchant ship bringing food and munitions to the enemy, thus prolonging the war and augmenting the number of women and children who suffer during the war?

—Admiral Reinhard Scheer, *Germany's High Sea Fleet*, 1920[1]

Admiral Scheer was expressing the sentiment held by many of his naval colleagues that civilians carrying war materials and items considered contraband according to Prize Law[2] were no different than crews on enemy naval vessels. Many merchant ships, whether flying British flags or those of neutral countries, were transporting war materials, and, according to Prize Law, could be sunk after proper provisions were made for the safety of civilian crews. Scheer's apparent disdain for the civilians on board, which filtered down the chain of command to U-boat crews, resulted in the wanton loss of so many lives.

After the *Sussex* affair in the spring of 1916, and the growing displeasure within America regarding U-boat activities, Germany had assured the U.S. and other neutral maritime countries that submarine commanders would take care to allow shipping to pass after first boarding and checking cargo for contraband. The year 1916, however, still saw well over a thousand ships fall to U-boats and to the minefields that submarines had laid. In tonnage, the last quarter of 1916 saw monthly increases up to about 300,000 tons,[3] in part due to intensified U-boat activity in the Mediterranean. These successes, which continued into January 1917, were nonetheless insufficient to produce the results envisioned by Germany—their goal: starving England into submission.[4]

During this time, particularly in the second half of 1916 when U-boats generally adhered to Prize Law, Germany had escalated her submarine production. At the beginning of that year, there were just over forty U-boats in service, yet by January 1917, after an unmatched number of fifteen were commissioned in December alone, the U-boat fleet had risen to 103.[5]

Throughout 1916, there were differing opinions in Germany over any proposed policy of unrestricted submarine warfare, including hesitancy due to the potential of American intervention. Admiral Scheer described the results of a meeting in September among the principal military and political decision makers where the consensus was to postpone the decision until the course of the ground war was better defined; and "that the final decision would lie with General Field-Marshall Hindenburg." Many in the military, however, including Admiral Scheer and General Ludendorff, were convinced that "[t]here is no possibility of bringing the war to a satisfactory end without ruthless U-boat warfare."[6]

On November 22, Scheer and Ludendorff discussed with Hindenburg their opinion that "the U-boat campaign should be begun as soon as possible. The Navy is ready." German peace proposals made to the belligerents in December were refused, and pressure was mounting on Kaiser Wilhelm II and Chancellor Theobald von Bethmann-Hollweg to return to the aggressive use of the U-boat. That month, Chief of the Naval Staff, Admiral Henning von Holtzendorff, addressed a lengthy memorandum to the Kaiser, which defined the prevailing arguments for a return to an unrestricted submarine campaign against shipping: "If we can break England's back the war will be decided in our favor. . .England's mainstay is her shipping, which brings to the British Isles the necessary supplies of food and materials for war industries . . ."[7]

In this memorandum, Holtzendorff restated his opinion expressed the previous August: "It is absolutely unjustifiable from the military point of view not to make use of the weapon of the U-boat." He also addressed (probably pandering) the concerns of Kaiser Wilhelm and the German Chancellor about bringing the United States into the war. "I am most emphatically of opinion that war with the United States of America is such a serious matter that everything must be done to avoid it. But, in my opinion, fear of a break must not hinder us from using this weapon which promises success." Holtzendorff echoed the opinion of his peers that the effects of the U-boat campaign would bring England to her knees before America could be an effective participant. "Decisive effects need not be anticipated from the co-operation of American troops, who cannot be brought over in considerable numbers owing to the lack of shipping . . . In spite of the danger of a break with America, an unrestricted U-boat campaign, begun soon, is the right means to bring the war to a victorious end for us."

Von Holtzendorff's plea that "to achieve the necessary effect in time the unrestricted U-boat campaign must begin on February 1 at the latest" was accepted at a conference held among the military hierarchy in mid January. Kaiser Wilhelm, who, prior to December when his peace offers were declined, had been reluctant to move forward, relented to the position of his military leaders. With the concurrence of General Ludendorff and Field Marshall Hindenburg, the Imperial German Navy was ready to launch the U-boat campaign.

On January 31, 1917, the same day that the German ambassador to the United States handed the Secretary of State a letter expressing Germany's intent to begin unrestricted submarine warfare on the 1st of February, Chancellor Bethmann-Hollweg addressed the Reichstag about the decision. The following are excerpts:[8]

> On December 12th last year I explained before the Reichstag the reasons which led to our peace offer. The reply of our opponents clearly and precisely said that they decline peace negotiations with us, and that they want to hear only of a peace which they dictate. By this the whole question of the guilt for the continuation of the war is decided. The guilt falls alone on our opponents.
>
> I always proceeded from the standpoint as to whether an unrestricted U-boat war would bring us nearer to a victorious peace or not. . . . When the most ruthless methods are considered as the best calculated to lead us to a victory and to a swift victory, I said at that time, then they must be employed. . . . This moment has now arrived.

The Chancellor also echoed to members of the Reichstag his recent conversation with Field Marshall Hindenburg, who had expressed assurances that "the military situation [on the ground], as a whole permits us to accept all consequences which an unrestricted U-boat war may bring about, and as this U-boat war in all circumstances is the means to injure our enemies most grievously, it must be begun. . . . The Admiralty Staff and the High Seas Fleet entertain the firm conviction—a conviction which has its practical support in the experience gained in the U-boat cruiser warfare—that Great Britain will be brought to peace by arms."[9]

Admiral Scheer was pleased with the decision. "When the starvation of Germany was recognized as the goal the British Government was striving to reach, we had to realize what means we had at our disposal to defend ourselves against this danger." For Scheer, it would be U-boats, which "constitute a danger from which there is no escape. . . ." and that "the submersibility of the boats would also leave the enemy in doubt as to the number of boats with which he had to wrestle; for he had no means of gaining a clear idea of the whereabouts of his opponent."[10] By the beginning of 1917, Scheer was quite confident that the U-boat campaign would force England, followed by their allies, to capitulate within six months. He depended on the inability of the British to know "the whereabouts" of the submarine predators, an expectation fully justified by the inadequate submarine detection technology that Britain had developed.

Bethmann-Hollweg had expressed hope in his address that for England to capitulate, the effects of Germany's planned unrestricted U-boat war would soon become intolerable. But the Chancellor never really favored the use of such a radical mode of submarine warfare, described by others in power as ruthless, but justified. He resigned the following July.

U.S. SEVERS DIPLOMATIC RELATIONS WITH GERMANY

> I have therefore directed the Secretary of State to announce to his Excellency the German Ambassador that all diplomatic relations between the United States and the German Empire are severed . . .[11]

President Wilson addressed Congress on February 3, 1917. He included a portion of a formal note handed to the Secretary of State by the German ambassador on January 31, citing what Germany felt was her legitimate right to respond to the "illegal measures of her enemies by forcibly preventing, after February 1, 1917, in a zone around Great Britain, France, Italy and in the Eastern Mediterranean, all navigation, that of neutrals included, from and to England and from and to France, etc." The note from the ambassador made Germany's intentions perfectly clear: "All ships met within the zone will be sunk."[12]

Prior assurances of restricting submarine warfare against merchant shipping promised on May 4, 1916, after *Sussex* was struck by a torpedo, were now void. President Wilson then informed Congress that "the American Ambassador to Berlin will immediately be withdrawn; and in accordance with this decision, to hand to his Excellency [Count Johann von Bernstorff, German ambassador to the United States] his passports."[13]

Wilson's address to Congress occurred only three days after Ambassador Bernstorff had passed Germany's intent to commence an unrestricted submarine war. Bernstorff continued to claim that after an unsuccessful peace offer, his country was justified in response to Britain's "criminal attempt" to blockade and starve the German people:

> Germany and her allies were ready to enter into a discussion of peace, and had set down as basis the guarantee of existence, honor, and free development of their peoples. Their aims, as has been expressly stated in the note of December 12, 1916, were not directed toward the destruction or annihilation of their enemies and were, according to their conviction, perfectly compatible with the rights of the other nations. . . . The attempt of our four allied powers to bring about peace has failed, owing to the lust of conquest of their enemies, who desired to dictate the conditions of peace. . . . A new situation has thus been created which forces Germany to new decisions. Since two years and a half England is using her naval power for a criminal attempt to force Germany into submission by starvation.[14]

Bernstorff emphasized that "the Imperial Government—in order to serve the welfare of mankind in a higher sense and not to wrong its own people—is now compelled to continue to fight for existence, again forced upon it, with the full employment of all the weapons which are at its disposal." The weapon he was referring to was the submarine. He then became specific in a memorandum accompanying the letter: "From February 1, 1917, sea traffic will be stopped with every available weapon and without further notice . . ." after which he outlined the zones "around Great Britain, France, Italy and in the Eastern Mediterranean," where U-boats would operate.[15]

But there would be another incident, which infuriated an already inflamed American public. On February 28, it was revealed that Germany's Secretary of Foreign Affairs, Alfred Zimmermann, had sent instructions to their Minister in Mexico, Heinrich von Eckhardt, to attempt to create an alliance of Mexico and Japan with Germany. The telegram had been intercepted on January 16 and decoded by British naval cryptographers:

> On the first of February we intend to begin submarine warfare unrestricted. In spite of this it is our intention to keep neutral the United States of America.
>
> If this attempt is unsuccessful, we propose an alliance on the following basis with Mexico:

That we shall make war together and together we shall make peace. We shall give general financial support and it is understood that Mexico is to recover the lost territory in New Mexico, Texas and Arizona. The details are left to you for settlement.

You are instructed to inform the President of Mexico of the above in the greatest confidence as soon as it is certain that there will be an outbreak of war with the United States, and suggest that the President of Mexico, on his own initiative, should communicate with Japan suggesting adherence at once to this plan; at the same time offer to mediate between Germany and Japan.

Please call to the attention of the President of Mexico that the employment of ruthless submarine warfare now promises to compel England to make peace in a few months.[16]

The "ruthless submarine warfare," which Chancellor Bethmann-Hollweg, Admiral Scheer, Zimmermann, and others in Germany had once again endorsed and put into action, would see an immediate increase in the loss of hundreds of commercial vessels and thousands from among their civilian crews.

On April 6, 1917, the day America declared war, the U-boat threat became a national concern, in part due to the Zimmermann telegram. While speculative, what appeared on the front page of New London, Connecticut's newspaper, *The Day*, may have been an attempt to incite fear, anger, and ultimately support for war against Germany. Beneath the headline "PRESIDENT PROCLAIMS WAR," readers found a report from Washington, D. C. of "German submarines waiting in the Gulf of Mexico for the opening of hostilities with the United States." These "persistent but hitherto unconfirmed reports . . ." claimed that "more than a score of submarines were already in Mexican waters." Although that number was questioned, the article contended there was "no doubt that German submarines are somewhere on this side of the Atlantic . . . [and] are being supplied from Mexican shore bases." Their concerns were based on an assumption that "the arrangements proposed by Foreign Minister Zimmermann in his celebrated communication intended for General Cerranza have been achieved . . ."[17]

Although it would be more than a year before U-boat predators appeared along the coast, newspapers had, since the war began, provided readers with genuine reports of the carnage both on land and sea. There was little doubt what would be America's response.

The Day

NEW LONDON, CONN., FRIDAY AFTERNOON, APRIL 6, 1917.—SIXTEEN PAGES.

PRESIDENT PROCLAIMS WAR

WASHINGTON, April 6.—President Wilson at 1.11 today signed the resolution of congress declaring a state of war between the United States and Germany. The president also signed a proclamation formally declaring a state of war between the United States and Germany. In the proclamation he called upon American citizens to give support to all measures of the government.

The navy department immediately wirelessed or telegraphed all its stations, navy yards and ships as follows:

"The president has signed an act of congress which declares that a state of war exists between the United States and Germany."

The war resolution was signed at 12.14 o'clock today by Vice President Marshall. The resolution was signed early this morning by Speaker Clark after its passage by the house by vote of 373 to 50.

Appropriation of $100,000,000 for an emergency war fund to be used at the president's discretion, similar to the $50,000,000 fund given President McKinley for prosecuting the Spanish-American war, was attached today by the senate appropriation committee to the general deficiency bill and passed by the senate, which then adjourned.

Sure U-Boats in Gulf of Mexico

Nearly 100 German Boats Seized by United States

Wilson Urges All to Zealously Aid Country

Headline in the New London, Connecticut, newspaper The Day, April 6, 1917. This town would soon become a center for antisubmarine warfare development.

(New London Public Library Archives)

SIXTY-FIFTH CONGRESS OF THE UNITED STATES OF AMERICA

At the First Session

Begun and held at the City of Washington on Monday,

the second day of April, one thousand nine hundred and seventeen

JOINT Resolution Declaring that a state of war exists between the Imperial German Government and the people of the United States and making provision to prosecute the same.[18]

In his address to Congress on April 2, 1917, urging the passage of this resolution, the President reminded the country that ". . . on and after the first day of February it was [Germany's] purpose to put aside all restraints of law or of humanity and use its submarines to sink every vessel that sought to approach either the ports of Great Britain and Ireland or the western coasts of Europe." Wilson added that "Vessels of every kind, whatever their flag, their character, their cargo, their destination, their errand, have been ruthlessly sent to the bottom without warning and without thought of help or mercy for those on board . . ."[19]

It had been the repeated promises made and broken by Germany regarding the use of unrestricted warfare against mercantile shipping that finally brought the President to Congress and the people. During the weeks that

AMERICA ENTERS THE WAR | 85

followed the commencement of unrestricted submarine warfare, hundreds of lives had been lost, and the situation had become intolerable. Wilson: "The present German submarine warfare against commerce is a warfare against mankind. . . . It is a war against all nations. American ships have been lost, American lives taken, in ways which it has stirred us very deeply . . ."[20]

The predatory nature of U-boats roused Wilson's anger, referring to them as "outlaws when used as the German submarines have been used against merchant shipping . . ." adding: "I advise that the Congress declare that the recent course of the Imperial German Government to be in fact nothing less than war against the Government and people of the United States . . ."[21] President Wilson signed the resolution on April 6, 1917; the United States had changed this from a European war to a world war, known forever as The Great War, and The War to End All Wars.

Germany had, of course, anticipated that America would soon join the conflict, once the policy of unrestricted submarine warfare began. Chancellor Bethmann-Hollweg reacted to President Wilson by placing the blame for the U-boat campaign on the British blockade; the following excerpts from the Chancellor's reply summarize Germany's response to the declaration of war:

> The directors of the American Nation have been convened by President Wilson for an extraordinary session of Congress in order to decide the question of war or peace between the American and German nations. . . . Germany never had the slightest intention of attacking the United States of America. . .[and] never desired war . . . More than once we told the United States that we made unrestricted use of the submarine weapon, expecting that England could be made to observe, in her policy of blockade, the laws of humanity and of international agreements. England not only did not give up her illegal and indefensible policy of blockade, but uninterruptedly intensified it. . . . Then we took unrestricted submarine warfare into our hands . . . If the American Nation considers this a cause for which to declare war against the German Nation with which it has lived in peace for more than 100 years, if this action warrants an increase in bloodshed, we shall not have to bear the responsibility for it.[22]

Woodrow Wilson had won the presidency on the slogan "He kept us out of war!" He would now have to break his promise of neutrality. But the country was ready to put that aside, and most Americans were willing to accept these words from the President: "There are, it may be, many months of fiery trial and sacrifice ahead of us. It is a fearful thing to lead this peaceful people into war, into the most terrible and disastrous of all wars, civilization itself seeming to be in the balance."[23]

No one fully understood the extent of that "fiery trial and sacrifice" into which America would send its citizens . . . there would be sacrifice by young and old on the home front, but Americans would suffer unimagined fiery bloodshed and sacrifice on the battlefields, in the air, and on and beneath the sea.

Chapter 10 Crossing the Atlantic

The Germans, it now appeared, were not losing the war—they were winning it. . . unless the appalling destruction of merchant tonnage which was then taking place could be materially checked, the unconditional surrender of the British Empire would inevitably take place within a few months.

—Admiral William S. Sims, *The Victory at Sea*, 1920[1]

On March 31, 1917, the American passenger steamer *New York* prepared to set sail for Liverpool. A nervous spirit engulfed the passengers, who were very aware that in February, Germany had resumed her policy of unrestricted submarine warfare, once again declaring the waters around Britain a war zone. There was nothing to worry about during the first week at sea, as Germany had not sent its subsea predators to America's coast, and besides, this country remained neutral under a president who had promised to keep the country from joining a European war.

Yet passengers also recalled when, less than two years earlier, during Germany's initial actions in unrestricted submarine warfare, the Cunard Line's *Lusitania* was torpedoed with significant loss of life. *Lusitania* was also in transit from America to Liverpool, and *New York* would travel the same route.

Among the passengers who boarded that cold March morning was S. W. Davidson, a tall, handsome, well-dressed gentleman. He carried himself with the air of one who, at age fifty-nine, had enjoyed a successful career in business. Well groomed with a beard neatly trimmed to fit the contour of his face, he walked on board wearing the stylish suit of someone of his social status.

Another gentleman, V. J. Richardson, who, in his late thirties, appeared the protégé of Davidson, also registered for the Atlantic crossing. To the other passengers and the ship's crew, they both fit the image of America's burgeoning aristocracy and must have been en route to England for yet another international business meeting.

The *New York* had the American flag prominently painted on her hull, as had been stipulated in Ambassador Johann von Bernstorff's diplomatic notice to U.S. Secretary of State Robert Lansing on January 31 regarding the planned commencement of unrestricted submarine attacks on commercial shipping . . . the assurance being that a U-boat commander peering through the periscope would refrain from sending a torpedo into the side of a passenger ship from neutral America. Bernstorff stipulated that "Each mast should show a large flag checkered white and red, and the stern the American national flag."[2] Whether or not this display worked is unknown, but while *New York* steamed across the Atlantic, the large painted American flag would be a liability rather than a guarantee of free passage. On April 6, a message arrived on the ship's wireless that a state of war had been declared against Germany by the United States Congress; the steamship *New York* was now a legitimate target, and it would be another three days before Davidson and Richardson would be safely ashore. On April 9, relieved that they had escaped a U-boat encounter, the passengers relaxed as the ship passed into the port of Liverpool.

A few miles away, passengers on another steamship, the *Tynwald*, watched *New York* enter the harbor. To their horror, the scene was interrupted by a massive explosion when *New York* struck a mine that blew a hole in one of the ship's forward compartments; not fatal to the ship, but a stark reminder of how effective the German U-boat campaign had become. Stunned passengers were brought ashore by *Tynwald*. The two American gentlemen, Davidson and Richardson, who seemed rather undisturbed by these events, were met at the dock and brought to a train which had been sent specifically to carry them to London, where they arrived the following day.[3]

It would be at a luncheon in London on April 13, when United States Ambassador Walter H. Page announced that Admiral Sims and his aide Commander Babcock had arrived in England; Davidson and Richardson had exchanged their civilian clothes for their formal uniforms and joined the ambassador's luncheon—the secrecy associated with their assignment at the British Admiralty no longer necessary.

Less than three weeks had passed since, on March 26, Secretary of the Navy Josephus Daniels telegraphed Sims, then president of the Naval War College in Newport, Rhode Island, requesting him to come to Washington. Daniels had discussed with President Wilson an urgent telegraph from Ambassador Page, sent on the 23rd in which the ambassador expressed the desire within the British government for "closer relations" with the United States, including a suggestion that a submarine base be established on the Irish coast. "I can not too strongly recommend that our government send here an admiral of our own navy," emphasized Page, who must surely have understood the consequences should Germany become aware of such a liaison between a neutral United States and Britain.[4]

Nonetheless, with President Wilson in agreement, Secretary Daniels explained the details of the assignment to Admiral Sims, who arrived from Newport on the 28th. The Secretary described their meeting in his memoir *Our Navy at War* (1922):

> I told him [Sims] the President had decided to send an admiral to England, and he had been selected. Informing him, in confidence, our belief that the time was near at hand when the United States would enter the war, I told him that, in that event, we must prepare for the fullest cooperation with the British navy. But his immediate duty, I pointed out, was to secure all possible information as to what the British were doing, and what plans they had for more effective warfare against the submarine. . . . Impressing upon him the fact that the United States was still neutral, and that until Congress should declare war his mission must be a secret and confidential one, I informed him that it had been decided not to issue written orders detaching him from his duties at Newport, but for him to go quietly as a civilian passenger, and report to Ambassador Page personally before any public announcement was made.[5]

Admiral Sims had been in London only a few days, but quickly assessed the critical situation that Britain faced. After meeting with Admiral Sir John Jellicoe, at that time Britain's First Sea Lord, the effects of Germany's unrestricted submarine warfare became apparent. Sims' first cable from London arrived in Secretary Daniels' hands on April 14, and in his words:

> The submarine issue is very much more serious than the people realize in America. The recent success of [U-boat] operations and the rapidity of construction constitute the real crisis of the war. . . . Supplies and communications of forces on all fronts, including the Russians, are threatened and control of the sea actually imperiled. German submarines are constantly extending their operations into the Atlantic

. . . The amount of British, neutral and Allied shipping lost in February was 536,000 tons, in March 571,000 tons, and in the first ten days of April 205,000 tons. With short nights and better weather these losses are increasing.[6]

Sims was right. As weather improved, losses during April increased to nearly 900,000 tons.[7] However large this number seemed, there was an even greater number of ships that had been damaged but not sunk after striking a mine, or as a direct result of a submarine attack. As with the liner *New York*, which carried Admiral Sims to England, these ships were out of commission while in dry dock. What Sims discovered during his first few weeks in London was that there was little hope of replacing, or repairing, a merchant fleet of sufficient carrying capacity to resupply the allies, and the British Isles in particular.[8]

Sims' warning in April, 1917, that unless the submarine predators were stopped, "the unconditional surrender of the British Empire would inevitably take place within a few months" was not an exaggeration.[9] The U-boat was on the verge of winning the war for Germany. With the United States now engaged, it was no longer an issue of preparedness; it was now essential that immediate action be taken by every nation at war to find these undersea killing machines and destroy them. New technologies had to be developed—and with unprecedented urgency—in a coordinated effort that would see scientists and engineers passing through the gauntlet of U-boats patrolling the Atlantic (*U-117*, for example, shown on the following page).

In March, the Military Committee of the National Research Council organized the first scientific mission to Europe "to ascertain by first-hand contact and to report back to the United States the exact status at that time of scientific development work in Europe in aid of the war."[10] Led by Johns Hopkins University Professor Joseph S. Ames, the group of seven members of the NRC was dispatched to France during the first week of April, the same week Admiral Sims was en route to England.

The French government, headed at that time by M. Painlevé, himself a scientist, not only gave the seven scientists, Messrs. Ames, Burgess, Hulett, Williams, Dakin, Reid and Strong, who constituted the mission, opportunity to come into intimate contact with all scientific developments under way or projected at that time, but he arranged to have a return mission, consisting of some of the most eminent of French, British and Italian scientists . . ."[11]

German long-range mine-laying cruiser U-117. Note the 5.9 inch deck gun. These were formidable vessels. (NHHC NH 92862)

At the same time the NRC sent its scientific mission to Europe, the Council of National Defense was meeting with Pomeroy Burton, an influential British citizen in the U.S. with ties to Lord Northcliffe, a member of Prime Minister Lloyd George's government. In a telegram to Northcliffe, Burton expressed that the Council was "most anxious [to] arrange immediate exchange of commissions of experts on war problems now arising . . . [and] that American experts be sent to France and England and English and French experts be sent here in the quickest possible time, starting this week if possible, cutting red tape, and getting ahead with work . . ."[12] While this may sound redundant with the scientific mission sent by the NRC, it had become obvious that the technology being introduced by Germany during the previous two years would require multiple efforts to enlist the scientific minds among the allied countries. Coordination of these efforts would soon happen.

By April 4, Burton's request had been presented to the Prime Minister's war cabinet. Immediately, Lloyd George forwarded assurances to the National Research Council through Lord Northcliffe that England would be sending a mission to America, led by former First Sea Lord Arthur James Balfour. Nine days later, on April 13, Balfour departed Liverpool, arriving in Halifax, Canada, on the 20th. A two-day train ride brought the British Mission to Union Station in Washington, D. C. Balfour's primary directive from the Prime Minister, however, was not to initiate scientific exchanges, but to encourage American intervention in the war by the transport of troops and materiel as rapidly as possible to the battlefields of Europe.[13]

In a meeting presided over by the Secretary of War, an Advisory Commission of the Council of National Defense met with the Balfour Mission, the members of which were assigned to interact with various departments within the Army.[14] Also in April, Marshall Joseph Joffre, commander of French forces along the Western Front, crossed the Atlantic where he met with Balfour and Secretary of State Robert Lansing to discuss the critical need for American troops in Europe. The United States would soon join the allies on the battlefield; an American Expeditionary Force under General John Pershing left for France in May. While American troops were urgently needed in Europe, the course of the war, and its outcome, would be defined by a singular technology—the submarine.

Ambassador Page, writing to Secretary of State Lansing on April 27, emphasized this. "There is reason for the greatest alarm about the issue of the war caused by the increasing success of the German submarines. I have it from official sources that during the week ending 22nd April, 88 ships of 237,000 tons, allied and neutral, were lost . . ." and then: "Whatever help the United States may render at any time in the future, or in any theatre of the war, our help is now more seriously needed in this submarine area for the sake of all the Allies." Then, on May 4, Page wrote to President Wilson: "The submarines have become a very grave danger . . . It is known in official circles here that the Germans are turning out at least two a week—some say three; and the British are not destroying them as fast as new ones are turned out."[15]

It had become clear that submarine warfare could turn the tide of war in Germany's favor, but neutralizing the threat meant that an effective means to detect, locate, and destroy the U-boats had to be found. Brute force tactics—chasing and ramming a submerging submarine, for example—were insufficient. What Rear Admiral Melville predicted in 1902 had come true: "[The] submarine may not only involve a change in naval construction, but a revolution in naval tactics."[16]

CHAPTER 11 THE FIRST TENTATIVE STEPS

> Our submarine force operating off Pensacola, Fla., during Janu-
> ary, February, and March, 1917, carried out tests and investiga-
> tions of all available listening devices, which were those of the
> Submarine Signal Co.
>
> —Admiral Robert S. Griffin, *History of the Bureau
> of Engineering*, 1922.[1]

The Navy's Bureau of Steam Engineering, renamed Bureau of Engineering in 1920, began investigating the possibility of detecting the sounds from a submarine or surface vessel using Submarine Signal Company's existing underwater communication devices. For more than a decade, ships had depended on the ability to listen to underwater bells suspended from buoys and lightships or mounted on the sea floor as a means of navigating. These devices, in addition to navigation, could be used to send coded signals between vessels outfitted with their own bell and receiving hydrophones, a concept suggested in a 1904 patent:

> The invention is particularly applicable for communication between
> a submerged submarine vessel and a station on shore or on board
> another ship or between two such submerged vessels.[2]

Another underwater signaling device, the Fessenden Oscillator, also designed as an echo-ranging system for detecting icebergs after the loss of *Titanic*, was used on submarines as early as 1915. In tests where Submarine Signal Co. had installed one of their oscillators on the Boston Lightship an-chored near the entrance to the harbor, the range that USS *Colhoun* (DD-85) could detect and understand signals was determined to be in excess of forty miles.[3] The Navy had hoped that the existing Submarine Signal Co. receivers would provide at least some positive results, and the tests at Pensacola (see page 96) were designed to evaluate what was available. The sounds from submarine propellers and machinery were not loud enough to be detected by the Fessenden system at ranges considered necessary for effective antisubmarine operations. At that time, the Navy did not have access to the devices being developed in Britain and France.

> These tests [at Pensacola] were conducted to determine the range of these devices under different service conditions. Submerged submarines listened to surface vessels of different types as well as to other submarines, and tests were carried out from surface craft listening to submerged submarines. It was determined from these tests that the submarine offered a better listening station than the surface craft, and that with the devices then available the probability of successfully detecting submerged submarines was rather remote.[4]

While the results of the Pensacola tests were disappointing, the Navy was certain that advancements in sound detection capability would be made. Throughout the war, U.S. submarines carried Submarine Signal Co. communication equipment as well as improved listening devices as their development proceeded. The vast majority of these devices, however, would be installed on destroyers and a new class of vessel designed specifically as "submarine chasers," described in chapter 16.

Concerns within the Navy's Bureau of Steam Engineering about the importance of solving the submarine problem were well understood. "No work undertaken during the war was attended by greater interest than that conducted under the general direction of the Bureau on the development of devices for the detection of submarines."[5] For the Navy, and in particular for Secretary of the Navy Josephus Daniels, the development of submarine detection technology had been placed in the hands of the Naval Consulting Board.

On February 10, 1917, the NCB called a meeting of its members. A Special Problems Committee was organized to consider "all matters relating to the submarine menace." Various approaches "considered most promising" were assigned to individual members of this new committee, one of which, "detection by sound," was assigned to Dr. W. R. Whitney of General Electric Co. Other topics included: "Mr. Lamme, detection by magnetic, electromagnetic, and electrical means; Mr. Sellers, detection by sight; Mr. Sperry, underwater searchlight; Dr. Hutchinson, bombing from aeroplanes; Mr. Hunt, protection of vessels by nets; and Dr. Webster, miscellaneous special problems."[6] A subsequent review by the committee of files provided by the Navy's Intelligence Department, which included reports from naval attachés in England and France, indicated that there was little of use here and abroad that would solve the submarine problem.

Naval Air Station at Pensacola, Florida, January, 1917. (Courtesy National Naval Aviation Museum)

Dr. Whitney, whose assignment was "detection of sound," invited Submarine Signal Company vice president Harold J. W. Fay to a NCB meeting on February 17. At this meeting, Fay convinced NCB members to attend a demonstration of the company's devices in Boston on the 23rd. While there, Fay discussed the possibility of establishing an experimental station where such devices could be developed and tested.[7]

On March 3, 1917, the Special Problems Committee held a submarine defense conference in New York. The conference was to be classified, so that all aspects of the submarine problem could be discussed. Members of the NCB submitted lists of recommended attendees, which were submitted to the Secretary of the Navy for approval to ensure that the discussions would remain confidential. The topics covered were placed under three headings: detection of submarines, annihilation of the submarine after detection, and the defeat of the torpedo.[8] Conference attendees would become aware of the poor state of affairs regarding existing antisubmarine and anti-torpedo technology. There was an obvious need for keeping the conference discussions classified, considering that it would be another month before America declared war; moreover, many German spies and sympathizers with ties to their homeland were in the country.

Important questions relative to the issues of sound detection using underwater listening devices were asked at this March meeting; they are as relevant today as in 1917, when the U.S. Navy first faced a significant threat of submarine warfare, according to Lloyd Scott (1920):

What is the source of the characteristic noises made by a submarine in motion when submerged, by its commutator, propeller, and bow displacement? Can these noises be suppressed so that sound-detecting devices would become useless? How far can the noise made by existing submarines be heard by microphones or oscillators? How closely can such a system locate a submarine by triangulation from a shore-base line, and is there any hope of reasonable triangulation from the shore-base line available on a ship? Can anyone suggest any sort of a noise filter to exclude sounds due to noise of motion of ships on which listening device is placed? In case submarines become noiseless what are the limitations upon sending out sound waves and listening for the echo? Are there any other types of apparatus available besides the microphone and the oscillator, and can anyone suggest other lines of attack on the problem of detection?[9]

Much progress had occurred within the Naval Consulting Board during February and March: establishing committees, and prioritizing and assigning tasks to members. It was now time to go to work. Harold Fay of Submarine Signal Co. met with the Chief of the Bureau of Steam Engineering on March 20, where they discussed the possibility of establishing an experimental station in the town of Nahant on a peninsula that reached into Boston Harbor. Fay assured the Bureau that property would be made available, and the plan was soon approved, with the suggestion by the Bureau that General Electric Co. and Western Electric Co. work with Submarine Signal Co., which was agreed upon. The laboratory facilities at the Nahant Experimental Station were completed and occupied by the initial staff of scientists and engineers on April 7, with Western Electric joining the others in May.[10] According to Gerald Butler (2012), the experimental station at Nahant was also referred to as the Nahant Antisubmarine Laboratory (NASL).[11]

Nahant Experimental Station. (Courtesy Raytheon Corporation)

THE SPECIAL BOARD ON ANTISUBMARINE DEVICES

> Upon the recommendation of the Chief of Bureau of Steam Engineering
> [Rear Admiral Robert Griffin] the Secretary of the Navy invited the
> General Electric Co., the Western Electric Co., and the Submarine
> Signal Co., to send representatives to Washington on May 8, 1917 . . .
> with a view to securing the active cooperation of the three companies.[12]

The Naval Consulting Board, created by Secretary of the Navy Daniels in the
fall of 1915 and headed by Thomas Edison, was less concerned about pure
science, and would rather use inventive and intuitive thinking to develop improvements in submarine detection systems. Members of the NCB assumed
that enough "physics" was already known. Involvement in their activities
by academic scientists would, they argued, impede the progress that could
be made by the industrial scientists and engineers who were busily experimenting at Nahant. Yet there were no naval personnel involved in the day
to day decision making of the station staff. Unless there was oversight into
the work at Nahant, the Navy's tactical and operational needs could be lost.

Secretary Daniels could see that there would need to be some authority to organize and coordinate the work between the Navy Department
and the three companies that the NCB had assigned sub detection tasks,
namely General Electric, Western Electric, and Submarine Signal Company.
Representatives from the three companies met with the Secretary in his

office on the 9th to discuss the need for a closer relationship between them and the Navy.

This conference resulted in the appointment by the Secretary of a Special Board on Anti-Submarine Devices. On May 11, 1917, Admiral Grant was appointed senior member of this board and Commanders McDowell and Libbey were made members. A representative from each of the three interested companies and one from the National Research Council [Robert Millikan] were appointed as advisory members. Immediately after this, the Nahant station was placed at the disposal of the Special Board on Anti-Submarine Devices and the desired cooperation was in this manner effected.[13]

The May conference also assigned the Special Board the task "of procuring, either through original research, experiment, or manufacture, or through the development of ideas and devices submitted by inventors at large, suitable apparatus for both offensive and defensive operations against submarines."[14] Commander Clyde Stanley McDowell was named secretary of the Special Board and was directly involved with the experimental work that had begun at Nahant, and later at what would become the Naval Experimental Station in New London, Connecticut.

With the creation of an experimental station at Nahant and the early testing of detection devices at Pensacola, the Navy had begun the process of taking those tentative yet serious steps toward understanding the realities and difficulties associated with the goal of early detection and destruction of the U-boat. Yet the devices currently available, including those in use by the British, were insufficient for the task at hand. Submarine detection would require a better understanding of the underlying science behind the way sounds from a submarine propagate through the water, as pointed out by Charles F. Thwing, President of Western Reserve University during the war:

The two chief new forms of attack, the submarine and the airplane, had their origins in the science of physics, and the use of these machines was determined by the laws of physics.[15]

The physics behind submarine detection would need the skills of America's university scientists. Only then could the engineers design the most effective device to listen to and, most importantly, locate and target the source. By early 1917, the President's Council of National Defense had taken more than a tentative step toward developing relationships among America's best minds. To solve the submarine problem, the Council understood that pure science would need to combine with applied science and engineering in order to bring effective submarine detection onto and under the sea.

> [O]n February 28, 1917, the Council of National Defense . . . adopted the National Research Council as its Department of Science and Research. . . .On February 15, 1917, the Naval Consulting Board was adopted as the Board of Inventions for the Council of National Defense.[16]

It was this singular pronouncement that focused the emphasis of the National Research Council and the Naval Consulting Board on antisubmarine warfare.

> By this arrangement there became a differentiation between scientific research and inventions, although inventions are frequently the outgrowth of scientific research, particularly where the arts have reached their highly developed state, as they had at the time of the declaration of war.[17]

Both organizations had originated in the years leading up to America's entry into the war, and each group's membership understood the significance of the submarine threat and were poised to respond to the President's wishes. The development of antisubmarine technology would become international.

Now the problem of submarine detection, as Sir Ernest Rutherford repeatedly pointed out, was a problem of physics pure
and simple. It was not even a problem of engineering at that
time, although every physical problem, in general, sooner or later
becomes one for the engineer.

—Robert Millikan, "A New Opportunity in Science," 1919[1]

After the success of the Ames Mission to England and France,
it would not be long before the combined scientific mission
envisioned by the French Minister of Inventions, mathematician Paul Painlevé, sailed for America on board the trans-Atlantic liner
SS *Espagne*, which served as a troop ship during the war, arriving in New
York on May 28, 1917. Led by University of Marseille physicist Charles
Fabry, the delegation was comprised of civilian and military scientists
from France and England, including Nobel laureate Sir Ernest Rutherford. After arriving in Washington on the 30th, a meeting was held at
the National Research Council building on E Street where they were introduced to Secretary of War Newton Baker and Secretary of the Navy
Josephus Daniels by Robert Millikan, who was at that time the executive
officer of the NRC. Millikan was then asked by members of President
Wilson's cabinet to organize an initial conference between the mission
and a select group of American scientists and Army and Navy officers.
The two-day conference, which began on June 1, resulted in Millikan
being asked to organize a much more inclusive and far-ranging scientific
conference that would deal with, among other topics related to military
technology, that of submarine detection.

Soon after their arrival in Washington, George Ellery Hale, chairman of
the NRC, hosted a formal dinner for the members of the scientific mission.
While the affair was intended as a celebration, the British representative Sir
Ernest Rutherford lent a sober reminder to the gathering of the reason they
had crossed the Atlantic: "Our backs are to the wall. We must have help."[2]

The scientific mission arrived in the United States with an overarching purpose to establish international cooperation in finding a successful solution to the submarine problem.

The members of the mission, however, also brought with them warnings of the grim realities that Europe faced along the Western Front, and the devastation brought on by Germany's unrestricted submarine warfare. Secretary Daniels was anxious to immediately address the practical aspects of developing and deploying antisubmarine devices. The Secretary fully understood that this was beyond the current capabilities of the Navy; the solution would have to come from beyond the military. Daniels turned first to the Naval Consulting Board, which hosted a meeting with the French and British members of the mission on June 9. Speakers included Britain's Sir Ernest Rutherford and Commander Cyprian Bridge, and French Professor Charles Fabry. Also attending was Guglielmo Marconi, then a Commander in the Italian navy. Marconi, who had developed the wireless telegraphy in use by all navies during the war, was a member of an Italian scientific mission and spoke on behalf of his country's efforts. Following the meeting, a luncheon was hosted by the NCB, where the British, French, and Italian representatives were joined by members of the National Research Council executive committee.[3]

Members of the Naval Consulting Board, along with the staff at the recently created Nahant Experimental Station, were focused on the engineering aspects of submarine detection technology and less concerned with the science. The scientific mission, however, had crossed the Atlantic to focus their efforts on the physics of submarine detection. "[A] definite and urgent request on their part has been made for a comprehensive attack upon the scientific side of the problem of submarine detection by American physicists."[4] Facilitating this goal would fall to the National Research Council and Robert Millikan, who, on June 11, set about his task to assemble a more comprehensive conference.

> The National Research Council, which acted as the hosts of this mission in the United States, with authority conferred upon it by the War and Navy Departments, called a conference in Washington of some of the best scientific brains in the United States . . ."[5]

Telegrams were sent to a select group of American scientists with the understanding that the discussions would be classified. The three-day conference, which assembled on the 14th, consisted of forty-five civilians from various universities, many of whom would soon gather in New London,

Connecticut, where a new experimental station would be created. Also included were members of the Naval Consulting Board, the Nahant Experimental Station, and representatives of the Army and Navy.

June was becoming a busy month for the French, British, and Italian scientists, who had brought with them samples of the devices that were being tried by their navies.[6] At the June 14 conference, Sir Ernest Rutherford discussed the listening devices being developed by the British navy, and encouraged the attendees to repeat the experimental work undertaken across the Atlantic to understand the current capabilities. The French delegates, Charles Fabry and Henri Abraham, described their "Walzer apparatus," a system the French navy had been using on its destroyers. Also discussed was the development of a quartz crystal oscillator that was being considered in France for submarine detection using echo-ranging. There was no question in the conference attendees' minds that a cooperative effort between Europe and America would be necessary to confront the twentieth century technologies brought by Germany and its allies onto and above the battlefields and under the sea.

> The visit of the French and English scientists . . . has shown the importance of utilizing the scientific resources and the power of the United States to combat the submarine menace. . . . On account of extensive laboratory facilities, the United States has a capacity for research altogether unapproached in Europe at the present time, and it is most imperative that this capacity be utilized.[7]

In theory, this cooperative effort was the goal; cooperation among America's scientific and technological minds, however, would take time. In February, when the Council of National Defense assigned the National Research Council as its Department of Science and Research and the Naval Consulting Board as its Board of Inventions, these two organizations wasted no time moving forward with their mandates. By April, the NRC had sent the Ames scientific mission to Europe, and the NCB had established their experimental station at Nahant, Massachusetts. Yet there was no authority in place to ensure that there would be cooperation between the scientific approach of the NRC and the inventive focus of the NCB. In May, the Secretary of the Navy had created the Special Board on Antisubmarine Devices, but the Special Board was initially restricted to coordinating the needs of the Navy with the work being carried out at Nahant.

While the international scientific missions were attending conferences in June, Secretary Daniels continued to be concerned that there was still only minimal interaction between the National Research Council and the Naval Consulting Board. Several research and development efforts had been initiated through these two organizations, but without a central authority to guarantee a collaborative effort, there was considerable apprehension about potential inefficiencies and duplication. There were also potential issues associated with the patents that the three companies working at Nahant would be considering, and the presence of university scientists might complicate the proprietary development of antisubmarine devices. Daniels then took the issue firmly in hand in a letter issued on June 23, mandating a cooperative effort between the NRC and NCB, and placing the Special Board on Antisubmarine Devices in charge:

> The department [of the Navy] has approved the plan to coordinate and organize the efforts of various groups now considering submarine and antisubmarine devices and plans . . . It is the department's desire that the special board, of which Rear Admiral Grant, U.S. Navy, is senior member, shall have complete charge of the carrying out of experiments on submarine and antisubmarine devices. . .This plan contemplates the closest possible cooperation between the Navy Department bureaus, Navy Department boards, Naval Consulting Board, and the National Research Council."[8]

The work of the Special Board on Antisubmarine Devices would rapidly grow to encompass experimental work conducted on both coasts. Admiral Grant was certainly anticipating an expanded role for the Special Board; the day before Secretary Daniels' letter was issued, the admiral convened a meeting on board USS *Chicago* at the Philadelphia Navy Yard. Millikan attended and described the various design ideas which the foreign mission had presented at the previous week's conference.[9] It would be an opportunity for naval and civilian interests to be discussed on board a vessel that was about to be assigned to New London as the flagship for the Atlantic Submarine Flotilla.

MORE THAN JUST A PROBLEM OF PHYSICS

> The requirements of a listening apparatus which embodies all that is desired may be stated as follows: It must be able to detect a submarine at considerable distance without interference from noise produced by other shipping, or by wave noise, or by noise produced by the boat upon which it is installed. It should be able to give the distance and

direction of the submarine accurately. It should be sea-worthy, of robust mechanical construction, convenient and rapid of operation. No instrument has been devised that satisfies all of these requirements. In fact no single instrument can give the distance of the submarine.[10]

Harvey Hayes, who would lead much of the effort in New London during the war, listed the design criteria and the issues the scientists and engineers would have to overcome in a 1919 report presented to the American Philosophical Society, published in 1920. The state of the art in underwater listening technology in 1917 held great potential, but needed the combined efforts of the members of the Naval Consulting Board, who had established the experimental station in Nahant, Massachusetts, in early April, and scientists from the National Research Council, who would staff the experimental station forming in New London, Connecticut, that summer.

In his report, Hayes described the variety of underwater sound sensors which the scientists and engineers considered in 1917 (see page 106). At that time, recent developments in telephone and wireless technologies were being employed throughout the military. The evolving microphone systems, which convert sound waves into electrical signals, were being adapted for use underwater and led to the creation of the hydrophone; even faint signals from a vessel operating miles away could be amplified and transmitted to headphones worn by a listener. In 1917, however, amplifiers and the vacuum tubes that were needed were still being developed; reliability issues could not be tolerated when the goal was detecting and destroying submarines. These design concerns would be addressed as the war progressed, and hydrophones, including the early versions being used by the British, eventually provided U-boat hunters with effective and versatile sensors.

But the simplest idea, which was easily adapted to submarine detection and did not require any intricate and unreliable electronics, was the use of binaural listening. The human ear is an example that readers will readily relate to.

In air, a human can distinguish the direction of a sound because the sound arrives at one ear before the other. If you turn your head such that the sound arrives at each ear at the same time, the direction you are facing is the direction from which the sound originated. Underwater, however, the sound speed is much faster than in air—4.3 times faster, in fact—and the person's ears cannot distinguish direction because the sounds arrive at each ear at almost the same time. A person will perceive the sound as coming from all around him.

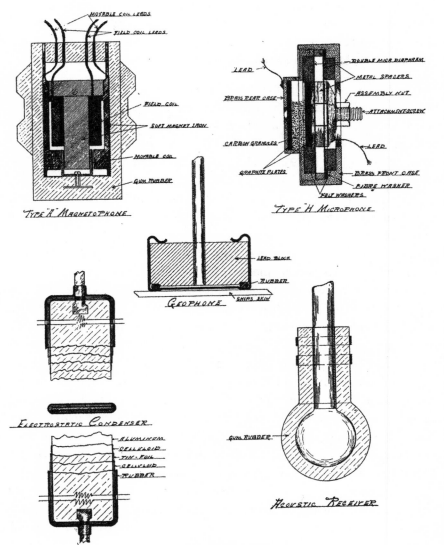

PLATE I. Types of submarine receivers.

A variety of submersible sound receivers available in 1917. Note in particular the spherical acoustic receiver at bottom, right, which was used for the C-tube device. (Hayes, 1920)

Binaural listening underwater, then, requires that the distance between any two sensors be at least 4.3 times the distance between a human's ears—about 25 to 30 inches. If a device could be designed to transmit the sound from each sensor individually to a listener's right and left ears, then the device can be rotated until the intensity of the sound is perceived by the listener as equal, i.e., that the sound source is perpendicular to the underwater listening device, just as is the case for the human listening in air and turning his head.

The physiology of the human head and the acoustic theory associated with sound waves will be left to any twenty-first century scientists who might read this book. What was important to the scientists and engineers in World War I, however, was that sound travels faster underwater than in air. This bit of physics was what had to be incorporated into any underwater listening device, including the rudimentary systems discussed by the scientific mission in June, 1917.

> Sir Ernest Rutherford, the scientific representative from England, described certain experiments conducted abroad with Broca tubes, employing the binaural principal for the determination of direction.[11]

The Broca tube Rutherford referred to was described in 1920 by H. A. Wilson, a scientist assigned to the Naval Experimental Station in New London: "The original Broca tube was simply a stethoscope which could be immersed in water. It consisted of a flat circular metal box one of the circular sides of which was made of a thin metal plate. A tube fixed into the center of the opposite side, led to the ears of the Observer."[12]

Rutherford's underwater Broca tube system included a metallic membrane across the end of a long, air-filled, rigid tube or pipe submerged several feet below the surface. When underwater sound waves struck Rutherford's air-filled tube, the sound waves generated vibrations in the thin metal membrane, similar to the stethoscope sensor. The vibration of the membrane, which reproduced the sound source frequencies, in turn caused the air in the tube to vibrate. With Rutherford's two submerged Broca tubes held in place at the specific distance required for underwater listening, and each length of rigid tubing in turn connected to one of the flexible legs of a stethoscope, the observer above water could hear the sound in each ear. By rotating the device, he could determine the direction of the sound—and a basic binaural underwater listening device was created. The idea only needed refinement, and that would soon happen, leading to a widely-used system installed on submarines and on surface vessels with missions as submarine hunters.

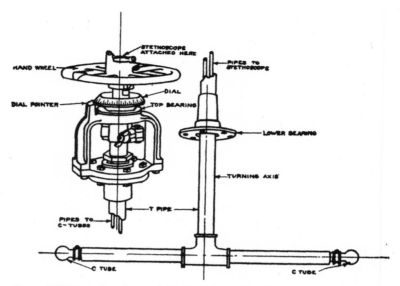

PLATE VIII. *a.* One form of "C-Tube" developed at the Nahant Station.

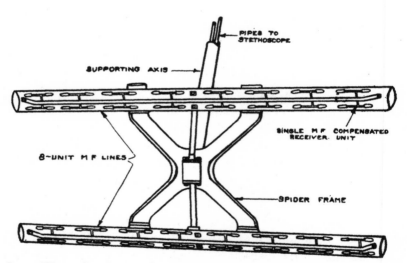

PLATE XI. *a.* One form of Double M-F Tube. Portion of casing removed to show receiver units.

Top: *The C-tube, later referred to as an SC-tube when adapted for subchasers, developed at the Nahant Experimental Station. Bottom: A Double MF-tube from the Naval Experimental Station was also designed to be installed through the hulls of subchasers. Both of these used the "Broca tube" acoustic receivers. (Hayes, 1920)*

Submarine H-5 with installation of a C-tube. The spherical rubber acoustic receivers are visible at each end of the horizontal pipe. (NHHC NH 46757)

Dr. William D. Coolidge, physicist and engineer at General Electric Co. and a member of the Nahant Experimental Station staff, was the first to experiment with binaural listening using Rutherford's Broca tube ideas. After the June conference, Coolidge returned to the General Electric facilities along the Mohawk River in upstate New York where he made his initial experiments. When he returned to Nahant, Coolidge refined his design by replacing the metal Broca membranes with rubber, which was found to be much more efficient in transmitting the sound waves to the tubes.[13]

The Broca tube adaptation to submarine detection became the Coolidge tube or, as far as the Navy was concerned, the C-tube (shown on previous page and above). As devices developed by the staff at Nahant and New London became more complex, eventually including electronic sensors (hydrophones) which no longer depended on a length of tubing to transmit sound, the use of "tube" remained. By the end of the war, listeners were provided with C-tubes, SC-tubes, MB-tubes, MV-tubes, MF-tubes (see previous page, bottom), and electrical versions of these three "M" type devices; also K-tubes, OV-tubes, OS-tubes, OK-tubes, PB-tubes, X-tubes, Y-tubes, Delta-tubes, and AD-tubes. Only the first five of these included a "tube."[14] These listening devices are discussed in more detail in subsequent chapters.

CHAPTER 13 A SOUND DETECTOR OF EXCEEDING DELICACY

> It was developed that the Germans were doing everything possible to reduce the sounds emanating from a submarine, and therefore the problem seemed to be to get a faint sound detector of exceeding delicacy, together with some method of determining the direction from which [the sound] came and the distance it had traveled from the submarine making it.
>
> —Lloyd N. Scott, *Naval Consulting Board of the United States*, 1920.[1]

This was the problem facing the scientists and engineers whose mission it was to devise that "sound detector of exceeding delicacy," which would enable a hunting vessel to locate the position of a U-boat with enough precision to complete the pursue and destroy mission. What had become apparent during the discussions with the scientific mission was that the antisubmarine technologies being developed in Britain and France, while moderately successful, were inadequate to curtail U-boat predation, now accelerated through Germany's policy of unrestricted submarine warfare. Food and fuel reserves in the British Isles were nearly exhausted; starving Britain into submission was a primary objective in Germany's war strategy. On the continent, the inability to replenish the supply of men and materiel needed along the Western Front meant that the war could soon turn in favor of Germany—all due to the effectiveness of the U-boat.

Following the June conference, the scientists, engineers and experimentalists returned to their universities and laboratories with new ideas and enthusiasm. Robert Millikan, however, pursued an idea that would focus the goals of his National Research Council by assembling disparate scientific minds from America's universities at a location where extensive experimentation could be conducted. He understood that success required naval involvement and cooperation in the development of technologies identified by tactical requirements but defined and guided by physics.

[T]he number of men who had any large capacity for handling the problem of anti-submarine experimentation was small. These men existed mostly in university laboratories or in very specialized industrial laboratories, which employed physicists, and we unquestionably had gathered a very representative group of them to gather in the fifty men assembled in the conference in Washington. The success or failure of the war so far as we were concerned depended upon selecting and putting upon this job a few men of suitable training and capacity.[2]

NEW LONDON, CONNECTICUT

Those men of "suitable training and capacity," as Millikan described them, soon found themselves in New London, Connecticut, gazing out onto the Thames River from the Second Naval District base at Fort Trumbull and at the nearby submarine base in Groton. To the north, an equally dedicated team of engineers from General Electric and other companies associated with the experimental station at Nahant, Massachusetts, had left the conference with ideas they hoped needed only a bit of refinement. It would be the Special Board on Antisubmarine Devices that would ensure cooperation between the scientists and engineers from industry who had already begun work at the Nahant station and those from academia gathering in New London. As early as mid-May, the Special Board had established some control over the activities at Nahant.[3] A great deal of work lay ahead.

At the close of that [June] conference a small committee was appointed to select ten men to give up their work and to go to New London to work there night and day in the development of anti-submarine devices. The men chosen were Merritt of Cornell, Mason of Wisconsin, H. A. Wilson of Rice Institute, Pierce and Bridgman of Harvard, Bumstead, Nichols, and Zeleny of Yale, and Michelson of Chicago . . .[4]

The conference had ended in mid-June, and Robert Millikan, who was the tenth person among those listed above, was eager to put the scientists to work. He met with Rear Admiral Robert S. Griffin, Chief of the Bureau of Steam Engineering and member of the National Research Council's Military Committee. Frustrated by the unwillingness of the Naval Consulting Board to include academic scientists on the staff at Nahant, Millikan suggested to Griffin that "You have already a good submarine station at New London.

I should like to see eight or ten of our best university physicists collected there and told to go at these submarine-detection problems in their own way and independently of Nahant."[5]

Admiral Griffin agreed to the idea and promised Millikan that he would receive full cooperation from the submarine base staff. Millikan wasted no time contacting the men he had selected; telegrams were sent and a dinner meeting was scheduled to be held at the Mohican Hotel in New London on Tuesday, July 3rd. The previous day, Millikan had joined the Special Board on Antisubmarine Devices on board the cruiser USS *Chicago*, then at the Philadelphia Navy Yard, where the Board agreed that the group gathering in New London would benefit from an opportunity to thoroughly review the submarine detection devices described by the foreign scientific mission.[6] It was what Millikan wanted to hear. Members of the mission had been "directed by their government to lay before the American scientists every element of the foreign antisubmarine program, whether already accomplished or merely projected."[7] These reports, which Millikan brought with him, provided the basis for discussions held by the men who assembled at the Mohican Hotel. They worked through many ideas until 2 o'clock in the morning, and after some rest, the discussions continued on through the day.

The New London group was particularly interested in binaural listening using Rutherford's Broca tubes, which Dr. Coolidge had just begun experimenting with at General Electric along the Mohawk River. The design had yet to be tried on board a vessel, but it was apparent that the idea had several inherent problems. There were only two sensors, limiting the intensity of the sound reaching the listener. Any vessel using the device would have to stop and shut off its engines, which would otherwise dominate the sounds. Other vessels operating in the area, as well as natural sources of ambient noise, could also mask the faint sounds of a submarine. These were difficult but not insurmountable problems which Millikan was certain his colleagues could address.

Another device, originally proposed by British naval lieutenant G. Walser, but most frequently referred to as the "Walzer" rather than the "Walser" apparatus, had been adopted by France for their submarine hunting vessels. The device consisted of an approximately three to four-foot diameter raised steel "blister" mounted port and starboard near the bow and just above the keel. Each blister had multiple circular diaphragms, each of which vibrated in response to incoming sounds. Because these diaphragms were built into a lens-shaped blister, the sounds from each diaphragm would focus on a

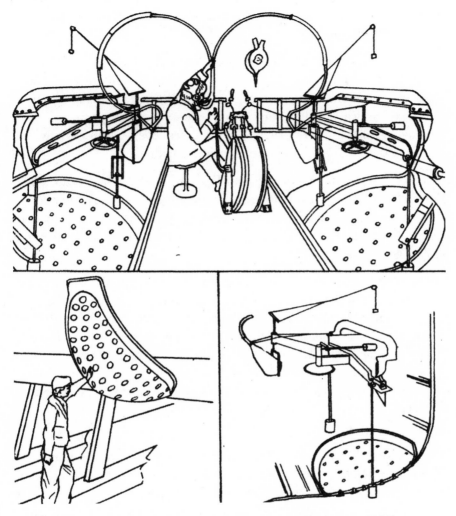

Walzer submarine detection apparatus used by the French. (Hayes, 1920)

trumpet-shaped device inside the ship and connected to the listener's ears. The operator could switch between the port and starboard sound lens and adjust the azimuth position of the trumpet until he heard the loudest response from a group of diaphragms, which were most directly within the path of sounds from a distant U-boat. A major advantage of the Walzer apparatus is that "the device can be operated while moving at considerable speed and good results both as regards range and bearing are claimed."[8]

Millikan was certain that the Walzer apparatus would generate great interest among the scientists gathered together at the Mohican Hotel. He would not be disappointed.

> [F]or two days ten men assembled in a hotel in New London and studied [the Walzer] report, drawing up four or five different variants of this device to develop and try out. The most successful and effective detector which actually got into use in the war was one of these variants . . . Many of our submarines and destroyers which went across during the summer of 1918 were equipped with it.[9]

It was Max Mason (shown on page 144 group photo 3rd from right) of the University of Wisconsin who would take a leading role in the adaptation of the various technologies discussed during those two days in New London. In his autobiography (1950), Millikan related Max Mason's comment about the Walzer apparatus and other ideas conveyed by the scientific mission in June.

> I can see no good reason why one cannot increase greatly both the sensitivity and the sharpness of the direction finding by mounting a whole row of receiver ears on the opposite sides of the hull of a ship and adjusting the lengths of the tubes running to the listener from each pair of such ears so that all the impulses coming from a distant source in front of the bow to the observer's ear by slightly different water-air paths will come together in the same phase when they hit his ear and thus multiply the loudness by the number of pairs of ears and also increase the sharpness of a setting on the direction of the source.[10]

Filled with ideas and enthusiasm, Mason returned to his university laboratory in Madison, Wisconsin, and within a few days was experimenting in Lake Mendota. Mason soon returned to New London with a crude contraption which employed adjustable sliding tubes resembling a trombone. He successfully used this strange apparatus to demonstrate his idea to Millikan and members of the Special Board on Antisubmarine Devices, who had arrived on the waterfront on July 10. For a proper demonstration later that month, Mason needed an appropriate target—a submarine. In his memoir *Take Her Down* (1937), Commander T. B. Thompson described the experimental work he, in the submarine *L-9*, participated in while at New London:

> [A]fter a few days several mysterious gentlemen appeared on our dock. Eventually the secret leaked out and we learned that these men

roosting on the pier were scientists with instruments for tracking down submarines. At last we were doing our bit by impersonating an unwary U-boat. For days we kept up this monotonous performance while the brainy beachcombers twisted knobs and diddled away. . . . The first of our contributions to research was rudely interrupted by telegraphic orders to proceed to Boston where another earnest group of specialists [at Nahant] craved the services of a submersible guinea pig.[11]

Max Mason, one of the "brainy beachcombers" on the pier twisting knobs while *L-9* transited back and forth, was delighted with the success of his demonstration. What had intrigued Mason about the Walzer apparatus, which had inspired his ideas, was its focusing effect. The trumpet-shaped receiver within the hull could be moved by the operator until the sound was loudest. The vibrating Walzer diaphragms focused the sound from a source, a submarine for example, such that the direction the trumpet faced would indicate the bearing to the submarine.

Mason also understood that the intensity of the sound heard by the listener increased due to the accumulation of vibrations from the multiple sensor diaphragms. But it was the effectiveness of the Broca tube as a sound sensor, rather than the Walzer diaphragms, that Mason was convinced could be optimized. If multiple Broca tubes were incorporated into his system, he reasoned, there would likewise be an increase in the intensity reaching the listener's ears.

A brief description of sound waves and the function of a Broca tube might help provide background for the evolving submarine detection devices that would soon come from the university scientists, who became the core of an experimental station in New London, and from the industrial physicists and engineers at the Nahant Experimental Station. I do promise, however, that there will be no additional technical dissertations after the following.[12]

Audible sounds, whether passing through air or water, consist of a cyclic pressure wave of the frequencies we can hear. We might recognize, for example, a violin string vibrating at a musical note known as "A4" or 440 cycles per second (as a scientific term, cycles per second are also referred to as "Hertz" or "Hz"); similarly, a scuba diver might hear a distant vessel's machinery noise of that same frequency underwater. What is "heard" is the cyclic sound pressure reaching our ear drums. Whether from a vibrating ear drum, or a Broca tube, the sensor responds to the maximum and minimum parts of the sound pressure cycle by vibrating at that frequency.

Rather than the hemispherical Walzer apparatus, Mason had conceived of an idea to mount a row of sensors, Broca tubes for example, near the bow of a ship, both port and starboard. If the sound source, a U-boat for example, was perpendicular to Mason's line of sensors, then the sounds from each sensor arriving at the listener's ears would be maximized, providing the tubes over which the multiple sound pulses traveled were equal. Mason referred to the sounds as arriving "in phase," whereby the maximum and minimum levels of each cyclic sound pressure wave from each sensor occur at the same time, thus adding to one another when combined at the listener's ear. If the U-boat were traveling at an angle with respect to the line of sensors, then each sensor will "feel" a different part of the sound pressure wave. For example, when the maximum sound pressure arrived at the first sensor, each subsequent Broca tube would sense a slightly lower pressure, and so on. The individual sensors would be "out of phase," significantly affecting the intensity reaching the listener.

What Mason had recognized was that if the operator could adjust the length of the paths of each tube so that the sound pressure waves were all arriving at the listener "in phase," then he would hear the maximum level. Mason referred to this adjustment as "compensating" for signals arriving "out of phase." As in the example above, if the U-boat were operating perpendicular to the listening vessel, then compensating was unnecessary. When the U-boat was at an angle, then the listener could make these tube-length "compensating" adjustments. The amount of adjustment was then correlated with the angle associated with the sound source, and the listener could then report the "bearing" of the U-boat relative to the direction his ship was traveling.

That was the concept, but several months passed before improvements to the crude mechanism for making this phase compensation, which Mason had initially devised and demonstrated in July, found their way to the war. A description and photos of the compensator are in chapter 20.

Millikan was fully aware that in order to gain credibility for any ideas being presented to the Navy, and in particular to Secretary of the Navy Daniels' Special Board on Antisubmarine Devices, the devices had to be installed and tested on a vessel that closely approximated wartime conditions. Millikan had already been promised access to submarines stationed in Groton, which could be used as "targets," but the listeners would need to operate from a large surface vessel.

Destroyers would have been the ship of choice for the experimenters, but most were being sent overseas, and any new construction was already

The converted steam yacht USS Thetis *(SP-391) assigned to the Naval Experimental Station. (*Merritt Papers, Cornell University*)*

allocated to other priorities. Because of the urgent need for additional surface craft, the Navy had turned to civilian vessels, commissioning many large wood and steel-hulled steam yachts, designated as "Section Patrol" or SP-class ships. The first of these to arrive in New London was *Thetis* (SP-391), commissioned on July 9, 1917. Later that month, *Thetis* was outfitted with an early version of Mason's device.[13] She continued to serve as a test ship throughout the war, patrolling the southern New England waters between Cape Cod and New London.

Another vessel, *Narada*, was in a Staten Island, New York, shipyard being outfitted for naval service. Millikan visited the shipyard at the end of July, viewing *Narada* as a likely candidate for conducting tests of the variety of devices discussed by his colleagues in New London earlier that month. *Narada* was commissioned SP-161 in October and remained assigned to the experimental work in New London throughout the war.[14]

MORE SCIENTISTS ARRIVE IN NEW LONDON

Of the ten scientists who met at the Mohican Hotel early in July, many returned to their universities to begin work on the devices they had expressed interest in. Millikan had already visited New London, anticipating that the

Navy would agree to an idea he had for the National Research Council to establish an experimental station in the area. On June 25th, he wrote to his friend Ernest Merritt (see photo page 144 3rd from right) at Cornell University describing his intentions. In the letter, Millikan expressed his optimism in the future, particularly with the administrative oversight that Secretary Daniels had assigned to the Special Board on Antisubmarine Devices:

> This arrangement appears to have removed all the difficulty between the Research Council and the Naval [Consulting] Board so that there is now nothing to prevent the most intensive work upon the problem of submarine detection by all the brains and resources which we can command.[15]

Most of these scientists would return to New London from time to time where they could test their ideas. Max Mason, as already mentioned, had been busily experimenting with a device at the University of Wisconsin. After returning with a few university engineers, they would remain in New London. Cornell physics professor Ernest Merritt and Harvard physics professor George W. Pierce also remained in New London that summer. During July and August, 1917, the scientists were provided a temporary home in a portable building at the submarine base in Groton. Two months later, the Naval Experimental Station was established on and around the grounds of Fort Trumbull in New London.

By the fall of 1917, with activities at the experimental station in full swing, another professor joined the ranks. Details of his early work are limited, but Professor Harvey C. Hayes had already been working on a device for several months while chairman of the Swarthmore College physics department. Many of the other scientists, who were associated with devices being developed in New London, began their work at their respective universities, including Harvard, Yale, Cornell, University of Wisconsin, and Wesleyan, later moving or commuting to New London where they could concentrate their efforts. Professor Hayes' interest in designing an antisubmarine device was apparent in an article that appeared in his hometown newspaper, the *Oneonta* [New York] *Daily Star,* on December 27, 1917. Few details were given, due to secrecy issues as the reporter indicated:

> [S]hortly after the outbreak of war between America and Germany [Hayes] set about designing an implement that would be useful in combating the submarine. He submitted his designs to the government and about two weeks ago he was summoned to appear before a board

having power in the matter to explain the construction and operation of the device. . . Further descriptions of the device [are] barred by the regulations of the sensor.[16]

The following day, another article about Professor Hayes appeared in the *Oneonta Daily Star*, mentioning he was departing Swarthmore and heading for an undisclosed location:

He refused yesterday to disclose particulars of his new venture, adding that he has been forbidden to disclose the location of the laboratory where he is to continue his research work. Professor Hayes will be joined by five other physicists from the best universities and laboratories in the country in the government research work. They will commence on January 1.[17]

Hayes was undoubtedly summoned to New London where the "board" referred to above was the Special Board on Antisubmarine Devices. All of the scientists were required to present periodic status reports to the Special Board, and it appears that Hayes was finally asked to move himself and his family to the Naval Experimental Station. Secrecy associated with their work would have been paramount, and it was simply not necessary to provide details to a hometown newspaper. One headline on another clipping from an unidentified paper might have appealed to a German spy or sympathizer, anxious to relay any information about Hayes, his "Device to Defeat Submarine," and this "Secret Laboratory":

SWARTHMORE INVENTOR CALLED BY U.S. TO FINISH U-BOAT DEVICE . . . Prof. H. C. Hayes, College Physicist, Perfecting Device to Defeat Submarine—To Work in Secret Laboratory."[18]

Harvey C. Hayes (shown on the next page and on the group photo, front row, far right, page 144) remained in New London throughout the war, continuing after Armistice and into the following year where he experimented with the application of listening devices for peacetime use. After the experimental station closed in August, 1919, Hayes, who had resigned from Swarthmore, continued his government work at the Annapolis Experimental Station and soon at the newly created Naval Research Laboratory, where he became Superintendant of the Sound Division in 1923, remaining in that position until 1947.

(L-R) Professors Harvey C. Hayes (Swarthmore) and G. W. Pierce (Harvard) at the Naval Experimental Station. (Hayes Family Archive)

A highly qualified, but most importantly, motivated staff was assembling at both Nahant and New London, unified in their focus by the coordinating authority of Secretary of the Navy Josephus Daniels' Special Board on Antisubmarine Devices. These individuals provided the brains behind the antisubmarine technologies which President Wilson promised the country when he addressed Congress days before the United States declared war on Germany:

> It will involve the immediate full equipment of the navy in all respects but particularly in supplying it with the best means of dealing with the enemy's submarines.[19]

CHAPTER 14 FROM THE LABORATORY TO SEA

9 July, 1917. Submarine Base, New London, Conn. Memo. For Professor Merritt

I have directed the Executive officer of the Base to give necessary carpenter and electrical facilities for installing your apparatus. Capt. Johnson of the THETIS will use his crew and help with all apparatus but it is requested that a representative of your board be present when apparatus is being moved in order to safeguard same.

—Commander Yates Stirling Jr., 1917.[1]

Thetis (SP-391) had arrived in the Thames River, and the commanding officer of the submarine base, Commander Yates Stirling Jr., instructed the captain of *Thetis* to provide assistance to Professor Merritt. His research team was anxious to put their vessel to work. The Special Board on Antisubmarine Devices had been given authority over all experimental activities as specified in a letter from Secretary of the Navy Josephus Daniels, with day to day decision making placed in the hands of the Board's secretary, Commander C .S. McDowell (group photo page 192, center). This meant that McDowell was to receive periodic reports from the various test facilities, including the scientists in New London.

On July 23, one month after the Special Board was given this oversight and only two weeks after *Thetis* had been assigned to the researchers, Ernest Merritt provided McDowell with his first "Report on Work of the New London Group." The Special Board, which Merritt referred to as the Submarine Board, at that time operated from the cruiser USS *Chicago*, flagship for the Atlantic Submarine Flotilla. The "New London Group" was working from the submarine base in Groton, though often referred to as being in New London; the Naval Experimental Station would not be officially established until October. However, with *Thetis* available, Merritt was able to report several accomplishments. The following are excerpts from Merritt's July 23rd report.

At New London. Test of the Rutherford hydrophone. Observations were made from the Thetis, lying off Race Rock Lt with all machinery stopped. Submarine G 3, running on surface at different distances from 400 yds to 1200 yds. Test greatly disturbed by presence of numerous vessels in neighborhood. Steamer at 3 to 4 miles louder than submarine at 1200 yds. At occasional intervals when vessels were not near instrument was very quiet and responded so strongly to sub at 1200 yds that range could undoubtedly have been greatly increased.

Madison, Wis[consin]. First test of "trombone" modification of Walzer method highly satisfactory. . . Apparatus is to be brought to New London for test as soon as possible.[2]

The "trombone" modification, which Merritt referred to, was the device that Max Mason had built and tested at the University of Wisconsin on Lake Mendota, returning to New London in July for a demonstration to members of the Special Board at the end of the month (see chapter 13).[3] Mason's first concept of adjusting and equalizing the sound path from each Broca tube in his device was incorporating sliding tubes similar to what is used to adjust the length of a trombone tube. Regardless of the number of Broca tubes that Mason experimented with—there were ten in one of his designs—equalizing the path length of the sound from each sensor maximized the total sound that would reach the listener's ears.

A week later, on July 30, Merritt expanded the next status report in a seven-page letter to McDowell, which included tests of the Mark I hydrophone brought by the British delegation in June. The tests had the Mark I mounted in a streamlined wooden housing six feet long and 18 inches at its center, towed aft of the test vessel, Thetis. Installing a hydrophone in a rigid or flexible housing that could be towed far aft of the vessel was done in order to isolate the ship's own noise from the device so that the sounds received by the hydrophone would be from another vessel, hopefully a submerged U-boat. In Britain during October, 1917, after a successful demonstration in July, the Admiralty conducted operational trials of the "Nash Fish," which was one of their versions of a towed listening device (see chapter 3). The tests in New London provided for remotely rotating the Mark I to achieve directionality, which was also used in the British Nash Fish.[4]

Merritt also described in his weekly report additional tests of Mason's "trombone" device, which had been completed during the last week of July, his device suspended from a barge in the Thames River. By August, Mason's device was ready to be tested on board a ship. Thetis would soon be put into a dry dock in preparation for multiple tests, including Mason's trombone apparatus, in cooperation with submarines stationed at their base in Groton.[5]

Meanwhile *Narada* (SP-161), which Robert Millikan had visited at the end of July, was about to be outfitted with a variety of designs which the scientists in New London were anxious to try. All work anticipated for *Narada* and *Thetis* would be coordinated with the Special Board, specifically Commander McDowell. In a letter dated August 1 to one of the researchers, Dr. H. A. Bumstead, Millikan outlined the types of devices that would be installed on *Narada*. Because the Walzer apparatus was of particular interest, and had inspired Max Mason's ideas, Millikan proposed its installation on *Narada*: "On the port side, the original Walzer, as nearly as possible like that used by the French." Because the hemispherical blister of the French design created turbulence as the ship moved through the water, a modified apparatus was to be installed on the starboard side. Another modified Walzer device was being designed to be installed within the hull "for testing whether the Walzer apparatus could be made to work inside the boat."[6]

Also discussed in Millikan's letter was for Max Mason and Ernest Merritt to install two ten-foot rows of Broca tubes on either side of the ship, as near the bow as possible. In addition, there were provisions made to include hydrophones being tested by Submarine Signal Company and Western Electric Company, two of the industries staffing the Nahant Experimental Station. Also being considered were British listening devices which had been brought with the European scientific mission in June. Millikan ended his letter to Bumstead by recognizing the complexity of the *Narada* installations: "It looks as though we were making a pretty formidable job out of this installation, but . . . a little time and expense put in now is preferable to wrong installation and necessity of changes." Millikan had confidence in the effort, as the installation of each device would be in the hands of knowledgeable individuals.

The tests Millikan had described in his letter were proposals, but the component parts were being built by various organizations, including university laboratories and industries. The Special Board, and Commander McDowell in particular, had final decision-making authority. The Navy had purchased the twenty-eight-year-old wooden-hulled steam yacht from a Maryland owner at the end of June, but *Narada* soon became a permanent resident at the experimental station in New London.

That summer, the staff at Nahant was likewise busy with their testing.[7] The C-tube design, which Dr. William Coolidge had experimented with at General Electric in July, was looking promising. The thin, metal diaphragms used on the British Broca tubes brought by the scientific mission in June were being replaced with a rubber sphere, which transmitted the underwater sound more efficiently.[8] By August, the Nahant team was ready to run a simulation of a U-boat pursuit. As with the New London group, the Navy had provided them with a submarine.

> On the 21st of August, 1917, a very interesting practical demonstration of the use of the C-tube was given in Boston Harbor. The test was arranged to duplicate as nearly as possible an actual offensive attack against an enemy submarine; with three chasers equipped with C-tubes and various signaling apparatus to intercommunicate the bearings obtained on the submarine. . . . Miniature depth bombs, consisting of electric light bulbs designed to explode 50 feet below the surface, were dropped near the submarine to indicate that it had been located and could actually have been destroyed.[9]

The three "chasers" mentioned in the above article must have been small craft assigned to Nahant, as the Navy's SC-class Submarine Chasers would not begin to be commissioned and available until October. What was significant, however, was the need for three vessels, each carrying a listening device (the Coolidge C-tube in this case). An individual C-tube would provide a fairly accurate direction, or bearing to the target, but not distance. A second vessel with a C-tube provided a second bearing. Each vessel then transmitted their bearings to a third vessel, which would also be listening on its C-tube. After plotting the three bearings, the target was located where the three lines crossed. These tests by the Nahant group in the nearby waters of Boston Harbor had demonstrated that, while this early version was somewhat crude, the C-tube was reasonably accurate during a chase at close range.

The initial C-tube apparatus developed at Nahant was designed to be portable, lowered from the gunwale of the hunting vessel and secured during the listening period. As this binaural device evolved, it was configured for the Navy's new class of 110-foot vessels designated "submarine chasers," construction beginning in the spring with deliveries starting in the early fall of 1917. The improved device, referred to as the S.C.C-tube (see page 249) and then simply the SC-tube, was attached to a vertical pipe passing through a stuffing-tube in the hull. The sensors, normally secured up against the hull when the vessel was underway, were then lowered below keel depth during the listening process. The SC-tube was then raised into a protective housing against the hull when the vessel obtained the bearing and resumed the pursuit. A similar SC-tube device was also designed for submarine use (see page 109).

The Navy had assigned a Section Patrol (SP-class) vessel to the Nahant station, and at the end of August, USS *Margaret* (SP-524) became involved with additional testing. Excerpts from the test plan, written on August 23rd, show the optimistic detection ranges anticipated for the listening devices. It should be noted that secrecy was required, and in many cases, documents described the general test operations, but did not include any details as to the devices. These tests, as implied in the test plan (excerpts below), were intended to determine range and bearing accuracy for a submarine operating in a stealthy mode.

> Location: 6 ½ miles 60° from Boston Light Ship . . . The Margaret will remain at anchor or drift depending on weather conditions from 9:30 AM until 2:30 PM
>
> The submarine will leave the Navy Yard about 8 AM and proceed towards Margaret. Before reaching a point 6000 yards from the Margaret the submarine will submerge 12-14 feet (i.e. keep periscope visible for range finders on Margaret). . . . The submarine will then proceed on any course to a point 2000 yards of the Margaret at a speed not greater than the speed at starting after submerging. . . .The submarine will then go away from Margaret on a course other than the one she approached on at full speed until she is AT LEAST 6000 yards distant. The approaching maneuver given above is to be accomplished 2, 3, or 4 times within the time prescribed . . . The main objective of the test is for the submarine to approach within 2000 yards of the Margaret without being detected by overboard devices & therefore it would be desirable to approach at a low speed. On the approaching maneuver motors should be shut off for short periods at irregular intervals.[10]

The submarine *G-2* had been sent to Nahant from its base in New London to support antisubmarine testing. It is possible, however, that the submarine mentioned in the August, 1917, test plan involving the steam yacht *Margaret* was *L-9*, which had just arrived at the Boston Navy Yard, having recently been involved with submarine detection tests in New London (see chapter 13). *L-9* executive officer T. B. Thompson recalled his time supporting the Nahant scientists:

Converted yacht USS Margaret *(SP-524) assigned to the Nahant Experimental Station. In the center is the torpedo boat* Blakely *(TB-27). (NHHC NH 100560)*

Without any fussy preliminaries, experiments began off Nahant. Early every morning, fair weather or foul, the L-9 would stand out and be met by a flotilla of assorted small craft, each armed with some sort of U-boat detector. . . . A small steam yacht joined our flotilla [possibly *Margaret*] fitted with a listening device of such beautiful simplicity that any plumber's helper could have duplicated it in a few hours.[11]

Likely referring to the simplicity of the C-tube, other "overboard devices" mentioned in the August 23 test plan were also carried. Thompson expressed amazement at the vessel's ability to track *L-9*, despite many evasive maneuvers. "To our surprise the yacht was astern of us. . . Again and again we zigzagged beneath the surface, but in vain. We couldn't shake her."[12]

By the end of October Nahant saw the arrival from New London of three newly commissioned subchasers, *SC-6*, *SC-19*, and *SC-21*.[13] These three vessels eventually returned to Long Island Sound where they were heavily involved with offshore operations at the Naval Experimental Station throughout 1918.

Testing that summer at Nahant was being accomplished with a clear idea that U-boat predators attempted to approach their prey undetected to within a range of 2000 yards before firing a torpedo. Specifying a low speed would ensure a quiet approach, while the shutdown "at irregular intervals" was designed to deceive the listeners. The mention of overboard devices may have included, in addition to the C-tube, hydrophones that were being developed at Nahant, possibly based on a microphone design by Thomas

Edison. As head of the Naval Consulting Board, Edison was directly involved with the activities at Nahant.

The physicists and engineers at Nahant and New London were anxious to adapt microphone-based hydrophones to a listening device which could provide directionality. As early as July 12, Millikan had suggested in a letter to his colleague in New London, Ernest Merritt, that a representative from Nahant meet "with the New London group and show you in detail the whole situation as far as he can. The construction of their microphones and the principles underlying them will be helpful. They have more hope from one of their microphones than from any other device yet available."[14]

A week later, Millikan informed Merritt that he "asked Mr Fay of the Sub. Sig. Co. to send you the best microphone detector which the Nahant group has yet found for comparison with other devices. You should receive it in a day or so . . ."[15] There was no mention of the particular device being sent from Nahant, but the intent was to run comparison tests of the several detection designs which the Special Board on Antisubmarine Devices was interested in considering.

There had been plenty of tests of single sensors, whether a hydrophone or a Broca tube, which gave the scientists a measure of the relative sensitivities of the sensors to underwater sound, but at least two sensors were required to provide an indication of direction. The C-tube, based on the binaural principal, was able to provide the listener with a fairly accurate bearing, but its range was limited. Tests of hydrophones, used in conjunction with an amplifier, provided a significantly higher range, which had been a focus of the experimental work at Nahant.

The first multi-hydrophone device developed at Nahant was the K-tube, which was comprised of a triangular frame with a hydrophone at each corner. The device was designed to be lowered from a listening vessel, with flotation and weights to suspend the K-tube device well below the surface. The vessel would drift with the wind and current, or simply from the headway of the vessel's momentum after the engines were shut down, until there was sufficient distance between it and the device. Additional floats were added to keep the cable on the surface. The hydrophone signal ran through the electrical tow cable and to an amplifier and switching box where the listener (shown on page 130) could select between any pair of the three hydrophones. Based on which pair of hydrophones provided the loudest signal, the listener then determined a general bearing to the U-boat. Later improvements to the electronics enabled the listener to obtain a more precise bearing.

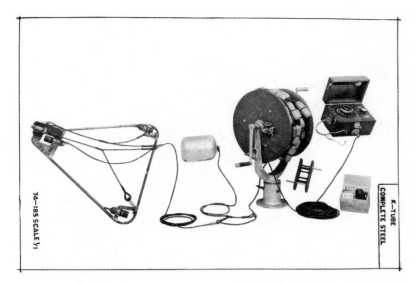

Left:
*Components
of the K-tube
listening
device. (Hayes
Family
Archive).*
Bottom Left:
*The K-tube
deployed aft of
a subchaser.
(Courtesy
Raytheon
Corporation)*

The rapid increase in offshore tests of these rudimentary detection systems, in spite of their unrefined nature as prototypes, was showing promise of success. Secrecy, therefore, became of particular concern. Knowledge of the capabilities of an effective submarine detection technology would be critical to Germany. If such devices were to be made available to allied naval forces, U-boat predation on merchant shipping, and the intended goal of starving Britain into submission, would be severely constrained. "The navy cloaked listening devices with top-secret status, [and] warned the scientists at Nahant and New London against breaches of security. . ."[16]

Right: Subchaser listener operating his K-tube compensator to obtain a bearing to the target, which he would provide to the bridge via the speaking tube to the right of the compensator. (Stockbridge, 1920) Below Right: K-tube components mounted port side of a subchaser at New London. (detail from image of SC-19, NHHC, NH 2458)

Secrecy—a Paramount Concern

[To] Prof. Ernest Merritt, Submarine Base, New London, Conn.

Sir: You are hereby notified that much of the experimental work you are doing or witnessing must be kept absolutely secret. This can be assured if no one discusses the work with others outside of it. You are therefore requested to hold no communication whatever regarding the work with persons not engaged in it . . .[17]

This August 15, 1917, directive from Commander McDowell and the Special Board on Antisubmarine Devices was intended for the civilian staff in New London. McDowell undoubtedly sent the same instructions to Nahant and other facilities where antisubmarine technologies were being developed. The need for secrecy also extended to suppliers of raw materials and to companies with unique capabilities, as was noted after the war by Admiral Robert S. Griffin in his *History of the Bureau of Engineering* (1922). "In order to preserve secrecy, it was necessary in some cases to distribute the manufacture of parts among several manufacturers. . . . The manufacturing firms equipped to do the work of the novel character and nicety required were few at best . . ."[18]

The experimental work underway in the waters off New London would certainly have attracted German spies, or at least sympathizers who might be enlisted as agents for Germany. In a letter to Robert Millikan, Ernest Merritt, at that time working from the temporary building at the submarine base, expressed some uneasiness about the sympathies of an individual who was being considered for the research team in New London. His name, coincidentally, was Mr. F. E. German, an instructor and colleague of Merritt at Cornell.

> I feel confident that German would not be guilty of any act of intentional disloyalty. However, his sympathies are undoubtedly with Germany. . . . Under these circumstances it would not be advisable for him to be given any position where he would be in touch with information of value to the enemy.[19]

Any new technology, certainly the listening devices and the wireless telephones that were just finding their way into the fleet, were of great interest to Germany—spies and German sympathizers abounded, and New London had its share.

> [U]nder a shroud of rubber-heeled secrecy, a wireless telephone system was being installed in the radio shack. . . And, as the maintenance of the wireless equipment was one of my responsibilities, I helped the civilian technicians with the work of the installation. The wireless telephone was little more than a legend in those days. . . . Furthermore, it was firmly impressed upon every man that under no circumstances was he to breathe a word about wireless telephones ashore. It was certain that

Poster warning of the ever-present spies. (LOC 3b30552)

German spies were lurking in New London and would attempt to get information about the Navy's new communicating system."[20]

The above concerns about secrecy were related by Ray Millholland, chief engineer of a subchaser assigned to New London, in his book *The Splinter Fleet* (1920). After the installation of the wireless telephones in his subchaser, *SC-124*, Millholland claimed that he "came face to face with a German secret agent." The following are excerpts from his encounter:

I had just gone ashore for a last good dinner at one of New London's leading hotels. . . . I had just ordered my dinner when the head waiter ushered a dignified guest to my table [who] seemed inclined to be sociable while we waited to be served.

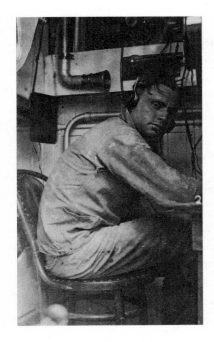

Left: *Subchaser radio operator. (Courtesy Todd Woffenden)* Below: *Western Electric Model CW-924 radio used on submarine hunting vessels during WWI. (Courtesy Timothy Straw, New England Wireless and Steam Museum)*

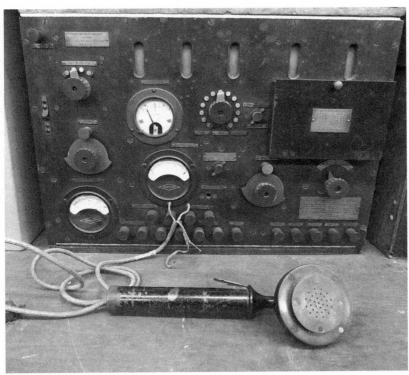

'Well,' said he, 'I suppose you won't have many more dinners here, eh?'

At another table close by sat a man, taciturnly eating and apparently paying no attention . . . The warning not to discuss naval matters with strangers was still fresh in my mind.

'I can't say,' I replied to my chance companion's question. 'Here to-day and gone tomorrow—that has been the Navy since its beginning.'

My companion nodded. Only a banal remark or two passed between us during the rest of the meal. When I had finished my dessert, I leaned back and fumbled in my coat pocket for my pipe, [but] decided to wait until I went into the lobby.

'Have a cigar?' suggested my companion, offering his case. I accepted one with thanks, and fired it up. . . .When the waiter brought our dinner checks, my companion reached for both. 'Thanks. No,' I said, picking mine up. He nodded amiably and pushed back his chair. 'Suppose we go out into the lobby and finish our cigars,' he suggested.

In order to reach the door, I had to pass around the table where sat the taciturn civilian . . . He also was rising to leave, but stood back to let me pass. I acknowledged the courtesy . . . [and] for one fleeting instant, I looked him in the eyes. I can remember them yet—they were dark brown. I passed out of the dining room and found my dinner companion waiting for me in the lobby.

Setting ourselves in two chairs, my companion remarked, 'I understand they're not allowed to serve drinks to men in uniform. That right?'

'Yes, that's orders,' I agreed. He glanced at his watch and rose. 'Well, I must get back to my office and finish a little work there.' He nodded toward a window in an office building across the street. 'I'm up there in room 323. Drop in when you've finished your cigar and we'll have a little drink together, eh?' He gave me a friendly smile . . . bought an evening paper, and went across the street. A moment later, the man with the brown eyes dropped into the vacant chair.

'Your friend isn't coming back, is he?' he asked. I shook my head and went on smoking. 'Know Mr. Brown very well?' he asked. 'Not any better than I know you,' I replied impersonally.

He smiled at the end of the cigar he was lighting; then suddenly got up and walked over to the key desk and spoke to an officer in naval uniform.

The whole train of incidents was common experience to any man in uniform during wartime. Civilians frequently spoke to us when we were ashore, and seemed to get a lot of pleasure out of taking men in uniform in tow and acting as host for a show or a drink. I had about finished my cigar when a Sergeant of Marines, pistol belted over his greatcoat, came into the lobby and walked directly to my chair.

'Hello, Chief,' he said as if we had known each other all our lives, 'grab your coat and let's go.'

Right then I realized something was wrong. . . . I got up, slipped on my greatcoat, and followed him out on the street. . . . We went down an alley, then turned to enter the hotel by a rear entrance. We took the service elevator up, and the Marine Sergeant knocked on the door. . . . The door swung open. 'Come in, Chief. That's all Sergeant.' Then the door closed behind me. I saluted the naval officer and glanced over at the civilian with the brown eyes.

'Just tell us all you know about the man you took dinner with, Chief,' suggested the civilian . . . 'He interests us, officially.' I related the extent of our conversation and included his invitation to drop over for a drink. 'Room 323, you said that was?' questioned the civilian. I nodded.

'Thanks, Chief. That's all,' said the naval officer, nodding toward the door. 'Keep your mouth shut and forget about that drink.'[21]

The phrase from World War II, "Loose Lips Sink Ships," was just as appropriate in 1917. What Chief Millholland had related was a brief encounter with a suspected German spy, who had attempted to befriend a sailor and loosen his lips with alcohol. Always watchful of these encounters, naval and civilian intelligence officers were suspicious of "Mr. Brown" and questioned Millholland about their conversations. There was no mention of what happened to the man in room 323, but it is likely that the intelligence officers continued to keep an eye on his activities.

CHAPTER 15 MATTERS OF LIFE AND DEATH

Whenever I think of the naval situation as it stood in April, 1917, I always have before my mind two contrasting pictures, that of the British public, as represented in their press . . . and the other, that of British officialdom, as represented in my confidential meetings with British statesmen and British naval officers.

—Admiral William S. Sims, "The Victory at Sea," 1919-1920[1]

Admiral Sims, recalling his first few days in London as the newly-appointed commander of U.S. naval forces in Europe, described the "atmosphere of cheerful ignorance" among the British public. The press had purposely understated the shipping losses by Germany's unrestricted submarine warfare, in part to retain the morale among the population. What Sims learned after being briefed by senior officers in the British Admiralty, however, showed losses "three and four times as those indicated" by the press, the same news reports the Admiral and his colleagues had been reading and mislead by at home.[2] According to Sims, the reality he discovered in London was this:

> The best authorities calculated that the limit of endurance would be reached about November 1, 1917; in other words that, unless some method of successfully fighting submarines could be discovered immediately, Great Britain would have to lay down her arms before a victorious Germany.[3]

Was the development of antisubmarine devices truly a matter of life and death? For Britain, and likely the rest of allied Europe, it certainly was. And for the scientists at New London, Nahant, and other facilities under the wing of the Special Board on Antisubmarine Devices, the urgency was kept in the forefront of their minds, as more reports of U-boat depredations continued to flow across the Atlantic. Between February, at the beginning of Germany's unrestricted submarine warfare, and August, when submarine detection development was well underway in the U.S., more than four million tons of shipping had been sunk by U-boats in the Atlantic and Mediterranean. That number represents over two thousand ships with their crews lost at sea.[4] For anyone who ventured out to sea, whether on an allied vessel or neutral, every minute was a matter of life and death. Such was the situation in 1917, which the staff at Nahant and New London faced.

> Dr. Pierce and Prof. Bridgeman of Harvard University started experimenting on anti-submarine devices in the summer of 1917 at the Submarine Base near New London, Conn. It soon became evident that in order to make the desired progress, a machine shop and laboratory with capable assistants were necessary. It was also desirable to have a station independent of the Submarine Base in order to cut out unnecessary red-tape.[5]

Ensign James Bean, who had known Professors Pierce and Bridgman (both shown in the photo, page 144), wrote about the establishment of the Naval Experimental Station in a paper written after the war while a student at Stanford University. As a naval officer, Ensign Bean was familiar with that "red-tape" and understood the necessity of providing a working environment where the New London scientists could efficiently move ahead with their antisubmarine devices. Bean recognized how inadequate the detection technology was prior to the U.S. entering the war: "[N]o device then in use could get the actual position or location of a submerged submarine, [which] was absolutely necessary in order to follow up and destroy them."[6]

Prior to February, much of the destruction of shipping had occurred when a U-boat had surfaced and used its deck gun, saving the limited number of torpedoes until necessary. Britain's Admiral Jellicoe described the change in U-boat operations: "When the enemy commenced unrestricted submarine warfare, attack by gunfire was gradually replaced by attack by torpedo, and the problem at once became infinitely more complicated."[7] Detecting a submarine had been largely visual, but once submerged, that was no longer an effective option. Even by 1917, listening devices and hydrophones, according to Jellicoe, "had been in the experimental stage and under trial for a considerable period, but it had not so far developed into an effective instrument for locating submarines ..."[8] That was the message the European scientific mission brought to the American scientists, along with the warning that, for Britain in particular, the submarine problem had in fact become a matter of life and death.

By September, it was apparent to the Special Board that the work among the scientists and other groups under their oversight was rapidly expanding,

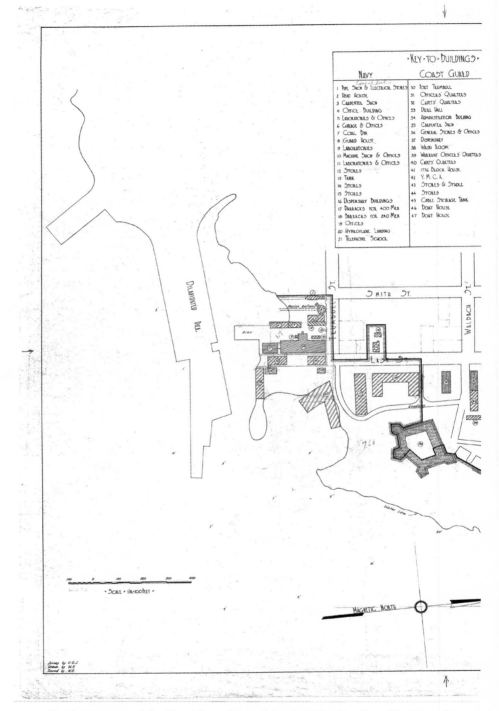

Southern sector of the Naval Experimental Station, New London, CT., November 12, 1918. (Courtesy Fort Trumbull State Park)

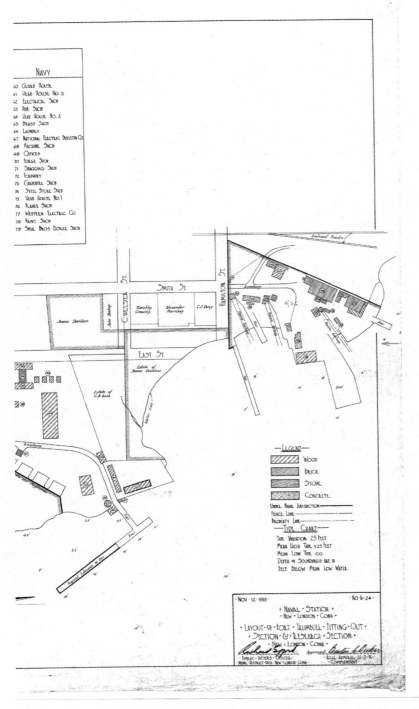

Northern sector of the Naval Experimental Station, New London, CT., November 12, 1918. (Courtesy Fort Trumbull State Park)

Aerial view of the New London coastline along the Thames River taken in 1934 (North facing right). The area which encompassed the site of the Naval Experimental Station is above; the town of New London is on the facing page. Several changes had been made since the station was there 1917-1919. (Courtesy Connecticut State Library)

and a dedicated location where the majority of the development and testing could be centered was going to be essential. That location would be on and adjacent to the grounds of the Fort Trumbull Military Reservation, along Connecticut's Thames River. With convenient access to the submarine base for support, and Long Island Sound for at sea testing, this area was ideally suited. The cruiser USS *Chicago*, which hosted members of the Special Board, would be assigned to New London as flagship for the Atlantic Submarine Flotilla.

THE NAVAL EXPERIMENTAL STATION IS ESTABLISHED

Initially, an abandoned machine shop was leased and renovated to accommodate the experimental work. The Coast Guard was located on the Fort Trumbull grounds, but there was plenty of room for the future experimental station, which officially began operations in October, now fully funded by the Navy.[9] See pages 138-141 above for schematic and aerial views of the Naval Experimental Station. According to John Merrill (2000):

> In October 1917, [Assistant Secretary of the Navy Franklin D. Roosevelt] was involved with expediting the transfer of funds for this Navy research. The Navy released $300,000 in support of the work. On October 12, the Navy took over the research effort; and the location was designated the Navy Experimental Station at New London.[10]

Additional buildings were constructed, including barracks to house the increasing number of naval personnel; marine railways were put back into service to facilitate the installation of the submarine detection devices being tested. A view of the southern end of the station is shown on the opposite page; the large brick building, which housed most of the scientific staff and the listening device assembly area in the back, was previously the LaPointe Broaching Machine Company.

Naval personnel were assigned to the station as machinists and electricians, as well as serving on the various test vessels. As an indicator of the rapid growth in operations, personnel increased from ten enlisted men in October, 1917, to two hundred in January, 1918, with over seven hundred stationed there by Armistice, on November 11.[11] The civilian staff remaining in November posed for a photograph soon after Armistice (see page 144).

As the amount of experimental work increased, the Special Board recognized that the New London staff just could not keep up with the demand for prototype construction and enlisted help from many manufacturing companies. The diversity of these companies reflected the range of expertise

The main building housing the scientific staff, located at the southern end of the station, adjacent to one of the marine railways used for installation of the various listening devices on subchasers. (Hayes Family Archive)

needed to support the operations at New London and Nahant: Ford Motor Co., Locomobile Co. of America, Willys Overland Co., Victor Talking Machine Co., Westinghouse Electric and Manufacturing Co., Bryant Electric Co., United Wire & Supply Co., Pittsfield Machine and Tool Co., and others.[12]

In the meantime, scientific attachés had been assigned to offices in London, Paris, and Rome, where nearly daily reports were being sent on the research being accomplished in the U.S. The London office would, in turn, send reports back to Washington on developments among the allied anti-submarine activities. According to Charles F. Thwing (1920): "The French, English, and Italian scientists were in constant cooperation, both in person, by post, and by cable . . ."[13] Robert Millikan described carrying these reports to the scientists working in New London:

> [The National Research Council] reviewed all the reports from abroad each week and put the workers on this side into the closest touch with the developments on the other side. In the submarine field, for example, all anti-submarine work in England, France, and Italy which was reported by cable and by uncensored mail immediately to the Research Council in Washington, was taken each Saturday night to New London and presented in digested form to the group of scientists which was working there continuously on submarine problems.[14]

Scientific staff remaining at the station after Armistice (photo dated November 21, 1918). Front Row (L-R): H. B. Smith, E. M Hewlett, E. Merritt, Captain J. R. Defrees, M. Mason, G. W. Pierce, H. C. Hayes. Back row: W. T Coyle, R. R Ireland, H. M. Trueblood, G. E. Stebbins, P. W Bridgman, J. R Roebuck, O. D. Kellogg, C. C. Bidwell, R. Haskell, F Gray. (Hayes Family Archive)

The Special Board, whose mission it was to ensure that all the research on antisubmarine devices would progress in as efficient a manner as possible, held weekly meetings attended by the principal researchers. Robert Millikan, who by that time had returned to his duties with the National Research Council at his office in Washington, would take the overnight train, arriving in New London at five o'clock Sunday morning. Millikan then returned on the eleven o'clock night train to Washington, a travel schedule he followed throughout the war.[15] An important aspect of the Special Board, and one of the reasons Secretary of the Navy Daniels created it, was to also ensure that the devices being considered would lead to a practical method of detecting a U-boat. The Navy's Engineer in Chief, Rear Admiral Robert S. Griffin, expressed the concern that the scientists, unfamiliar with the demands of wartime conditions at sea, would place insufficient emphasis on the operational use of their devices, which would eventually be in the hands of the sailors:

It was in this connection that the organization of the special board, composed of naval officers working in close relation with physicists of the highest attainments, proved of the greatest value. The question of practicability from a naval standpoint was kept always in the foreground . . . to prevent development along impracticable lines, however promising the outlook from the point of abstract theory.[16]

For effective oversight of the development of devices, which were promising "from the point of abstract theory," naval personnel became involved with all the experimental work, ensuring that the "practicability from a naval standpoint" was always being considered. A close relationship had to be established between naval members of the Special Board and the scientists, who might be inspired by that abstract theory, but less concerned about conditions on board a naval vessel outfitted with their devices. This task was effectively carried out by Commander Clyde S. McDowell, who was recognized for his efforts by Admiral Griffin: "To Commander McDowell, who acted in the capacity of secretary to the [Special Board], the Bureau is indebted for nearly all the material related to its work."[17]

LISTENING DEVICES NEEDED LISTENERS

As the development of the antisubmarine apparatus progressed it was realized that the Navy personnel who were to operate the devices on the ships should have a special training, and a listeners' school was therefore authorized by the Bureau of Navigation in August, 1917. The first class was started in September at the submarine base, but in July, 1918, the school was moved to State Pier, New London.[18]

These words by Admiral Griffin recognized the need to train the listeners who would serve on vessels with a critical objective—seek and destroy the U-boat. Griffin estimated that by Armistice, over 1,500 enlisted men had qualified as listeners.

Submarine hunting, using these new listening devices, became a critical mission for destroyers, U.S. submarines operating in the war zone, shore-based listening stations, and soon, the newly-commissioned SC-class submarine chasers. It was not enough, however, just to test and develop this new technology; it was essential that naval enlisted personnel be trained not only in the use of the detection technology as listeners, but in the care and maintenance of the systems. The operators who manned the listening positions required specialized training, and New London became the focal point for the U.S. Navy. The students would find themselves tracking submerged submarines in Long Island Sound.

By the summer of 1918, the Navy also recognized the need for training "hydrophone officers," who were responsible for the installation and operational readiness of the detection systems. After an initial class of fifty officers completed a trial course in July, an official hydrophone school was established in New London in September, continuing until the end of the war. "The school was equipped very completely with models of the latest antisubmarine devices, and several boats were assigned to its use for practical training at sea."[19] Ensign James Bean, who attended the hydrophone officer school,[20] described the listener's school for enlisted men:

> To qualify as a listener it was necessary to locate the direction of a submarine within five degrees. Practice tests were made daily to familiarize the students with various noises encountered. Each type of vessel can be distinguished by the peculiar beat or rythm [sic] of its engines or propeller. . . . Students who graduated from this school were given active service on subchasers in the English Channel and the Mediterranean Sea.[21]

It was not sufficient that a listener simply be able to remain alert and focused on his task for long periods. The expectation was that a listener would also understand the operation and maintenance of the submarine detection devices, which became more complex as time went on. According to Ensign Bean, enlisted men who graduated from the Navy's radio school in Cambridge, Massachusetts, known as the Harvard Radio School as classes were held in buildings owned by the university, "were given assignments with the fleet, on merchant vessels, shore stations, or to the Radio Telephone School in New London, Connecticut."[22] Some of these radio operators would then attend listeners' school.

The telephone school was on the grounds of the Naval Experimental Station. The wireless radio telephone, at that time a new technology, became a critical addition to the vessels used for submarine hunting, and in particular the new submarine chasers, which began arriving at the station late in the fall of 1917. According to Ensign Bean: "All submarine chasers and most of the larger naval vessels carry radio telephone sets so it was essential that operators assigned to these boats be thoroughly familiar with maintenance and repair as well as with the operation of telephone (radio) sets and spark sets. Three to six operators were assigned to each of the larger vessels."[23] What Bean didn't include was that radio operators and listeners who attended the schools in New London were also assigned to submarines.

Raymond Whannel, who had served in the submarine service during World War I, was interviewed in 1955 for an article appearing in the U.S. Navy Underwater Sound Laboratory weekly newsletter, ECHO. At that time, he was head of the laboratory's General Engineering Division.

> After attending the Brooklyn Navy Yard Electrical School and the Harvard Radio School, [Whannel] was transferred to the Submarine School at the Submarine Base, Groton. The 3-month training period included attendance at the Listeners' School, sea duty aboard the converted yacht THETIS, and service at the listening post operated by the Navy at Ocean Beach.[24]

As an Electrician Second Class (Radio), Ray Whannel was assigned to the submarine USS *E-1* in December, 1917. In addition to his duties in the radio room, he served as a listener during antisubmarine operations overseas, returning in September, 1918. His submarine, assigned to duty in the Azores, had joined a group of L-class boats preparing for the Atlantic crossing. *L-9*, *L-10*, and *L-11* (among the submarines shown on the photo, page 1) continued on to Bantry Bay along the southwest tip of Ireland, accompanied by the submarine tender, *Bushnell* (AS-2). It was a tough crossing, but "the gallant little E-1, with those fine engines, eventually made it to Ponta Delgada . . ."[25]

L-9 had participated in the early experiments with submarine detection devices, first in New London and then sent to Nahant. After spending time around Boston working with the Nahant scientists, the crew received word that *L-9* would be heading overseas later that fall: "One September afternoon the Skipper came rolling down the dock, stepping along at a high speed as usual," as T. B. Thompson, *L-9*'s executive officer, recalled. "'People,' he exclaimed, 'hot dang it, we're going to Europe! Let's get ready.'" Thompson's memoir summed up the mix of anxiety and excitement:

> [N]ews of the very heavy losses of Allied submarines had filtered through to us. We had heard that casualties were greater than any other arm of the land or sea forces; that at times out of every three Allied submarines that ventured into the North Sea, one disappeared, usually without a trace. . .
>
> Fortunately there was not much time to dwell on this disquieting information amidst the hurried preparations for service overseas. . . The Navy yard installed new listening devices that we had helped develop, also one new periscope which was somewhat an improvement over the old one but still subject to fogging in damp weather. Finally the nerve-shattering rattle of riveting hammers ceased and orders came to join the expedition assembling at New London.[26]

Submarine E-1 *Underway. The inset shows the submarine bell used for underwater communication enlarged. (*NHHC *NH 41946)*

L-9 and her sister vessels had been outfitted with a listening device similar to the triangular K-tube design, intended for subchasers but adapted for use by submarines (see photo, page 1. The three sensors are visible on the deck of *L-10*). These devices, as effective as the experimental work had demonstrated, were worthless unless the operators had been sufficiently trained. That training was available in New London; it can only be surmised that *L-9*'s listener, as was the case for Ray Whannel on *E-1*, had attended that same school.

The British had recognized the necessity for adequate listener training soon after the Admiralty had established their Hawkcraig Experimental Station in the Firth of Forth, under the leadership of Commander C. P. Ryan. Shore-based listener schools had been established in the Forth and naval bases in the Mediterranean. Ryan had also created mobile training opportunities with his vessel, HMS *Tarlair*. (See chapters 2 and 3.)

In the United States, it was understood that for any critical military operation to be successful, training was essential; for that, the Navy turned to New London. The urgency was obvious. Every month, hundreds of ships carrying food and fuel, bullets and bombs were being torpedoed and sent to the bottom by the relentless predators that lurked unseen beneath the sea. For thousands of sailors in the merchant marine, and for the tens of thousands of soldiers waiting for critical war-fighting supplies that were being shipped to the Western Front, the mission for the listeners, whether assigned to subchasers, destroyers, or submarines, was a matter of life and death.

By the end of 1917 the submarine detector had been so perfected that its manufacture had begun, and Capt. R. H. Leigh, U.S.N., was detailed to head a special party of American officers and enlisted men and civilian engineers to take a quantity of the apparatus to England and test it out under actual service conditions. The American submarine-detector proved its value at once.

—Frank P. Stockbridge, *Yankee Ingenuity in the War*, 1920[1]

harles P. Scott, an engineer with General Electric Co., crossed the Atlantic with Captain Richard H. Leigh in what was always a dangerous voyage, passing through waters constantly patrolled by U-boats. There were several other civilian engineers who accompanied them, but Scott was there to supervise the installation of the listening devices. He later reported his adventures in the war zone, which were quoted in *Yankee Ingenuity in the War* (1920) by Frank Stockbridge.

The special party under Captain Leigh took over about ten tons of antisubmarine detection devices and had also worked out the tactics necessary for the detection, pursuit, attack, and destruction of the enemy submarine. A request was made of the British Admiralty for the use of three boats capable of making eighteen knots, on which this apparatus could be installed and a demonstration made. No vessels of this speed were available, so we were forced to accept three fishing trawlers of nine to ten knots speed.

The three trawlers were the *Andrew King, Kunishi*, and *James Bentole*. These trawlers were fully equipped with all the American submarine-detecting devices, radio telephones, etc., at H. M. dockyard at Portsmouth, England, and on December 30, 1917, we steamed out of the harbor for our first real patrol in English waters. The English Channel lived up to its reputation of being the roughest body of water for its size in the world.

A 'P' boat, a small type of destroyer with high speed, developed for the war, had accompanied us, as the Admiralty feared we might be attacked by the submarine coming to the surface, and detailed one of these vessels as an escort.

The day after New Year's we received a wireless from an airship that a submarine had been sighted. We steamed over, got our devices out, but couldn't hear a thing. Another message from the airship changed the sub's position, so we altered our course and obtained a clear indication from the listening device. The Hun was slowly moving up the Channel, submerged.

We gave the P-boat a 'fix' [cross bearing] on the spot where our indication showed the submarine to be. She ran over the place, dropping a 'pattern' of depth charges, and soon we began to see tremendous amounts of oil rising to the surface. Evidently our first experience was to be successful. How successful we did not learn until afterward.

A trawling device had been developed which indicated whether contact with a submarine had been made. After the oil came up we got out our trawling device and ran over the area for about an hour and finally got an indication. We threw over a buoy to indicate the spot and anchored for the night, as it was getting dark. Next morning we trawled again and got another contact within a hundred yards of the buoy. We had destroyed a submarine in our first test and the 'sub' was given out by the Admiralty as a 'probable.'[2]

There is no current evidence that a U-boat was lost anywhere within the English Channel during those first few days of January, 1918, when Scott described the chase and the oil slick resulting from the depth charges. U-boat commanders often released a quantity of oil to fake its destruction and then remained motionless on the bottom, waiting for the hunters to leave the area. A 1918 publication by the Office of Naval Intelligence (ONI) specifically addressed the question: "Is oil, seen on the surface, any proof of a submarine having been destroyed?" Their answer, in part: "German submarines are fitted with an arrangement for ejecting oil fuel and use this to mislead or delay their pursuers."[3] This could be a lethal tactic, however, if the vessels on the surface continued to drop depth charges in order to be certain the sub was lost. According to Scott, they used a trawling device to locate the U-boat, but did not continue the attack. This may very well have been a case of a successful ploy on the part of the U-boat.

Before the Admiralty would confirm that a U-boat had been sunk, irrefutable proof was required. From the following report, it appears that Scott remained in the war zone or returned later to accompany other vessels equipped with these devices. He related an incident, which occurred during the summer in the Mediterranean, where listeners had engaged in another chase. Depth charges were dropped, and the hunters stopped in order to listen for additional sounds.

> A propeller was heard to start up and run for about thirty seconds, and then a crunching noise. It was quite evident that the 'sub,' having been put out of control, sank to the bottom and had collapsed, due to the tremendous pressure at these depths. We went back to the spot the next morning and found an oil slick 2 miles long by 800 yards wide on the surface of the water.[4]

The incident was reported to the area naval commander, Commodore Kelly, who expressed interest, but once again, it was that irrefutable proof needed in order to record a definite kill. An oil slick wasn't enough. "[W]hat we want," Kelly said, "is a few arms and legs with it."

An incredulous Scott: "We replied that we wished we could do it, but under the circumstances the water was too deep. . . . We were rather amused at reports that after a submarine was sunk how chairs and everything else came to the surface. For my part, I never saw anything the size of your hand on a submarine that would float."[5]

Admiral Sims, as commander of U.S. naval forces in Europe, recognized the difficult problem posed by U-boats. Implementation of the convoy system was effective, but the stealthy submarine remained an elusive enemy. "[D]espite the wonderful work which had been accomplished by the convoy, the Allied warfare upon the submarine was still largely a game of blind man's buff." But Sims was confident in the ability of scientific minds to win the game.[6]

> Our men could not detect the submarine with their eyes; could they not do so with their ears? The enemy could make himself unseen at will, but he could not make himself unheard, except by stopping his engines. In fact, when the submarine was under water, the vibrations due to the peculiar shape of its propellers and hull, and to its electric motors, produced sound waves that resembled nothing else in art or nature. It now clearly became the business of naval science to take advantage of this phenomenon to track the submarine after it had submerged.
>
> A listening device placed on board ship, which would reveal to practised ears the noise of a submarine at a reasonable distance, and which would at the same time give its direction, would come near to solving the most serious problem presented by the German tactics.[7]

Referring to the staff scientists and engineers at Nahant and New London, Sims praised their efforts to produce "several devices . . . which seemed to promise satisfactory results." It was this confidence in the work of the American scientists which led to Captain Leigh being sent to Europe "to test, in actual operations against submarines, the detection devices which had been developed in New London." The devices, in particular the C-tube and K-tube, which had originated in Nahant and been tested in New London, were found to be "superior to anything in the possession of the Allies. . . . They were by no means perfect," as Sims observed, "but the ease with which they picked up all kinds of noises, particularly those made by submarines, astonished everybody who was let in on the subject."[8] That success, of course, was due to a great extent to the trained ears of the listeners. There was no mention, however, if those were American sailors' ears or British, though probably included both, as detection systems from both countries were being compared.

The astonishment of the Admiralty, however, is what the Americans had hoped to see. Perfection was not expected at this stage, just an improvement over what the allies had in hand. "[T]he greatest advantage which these new devices had over those of other navies was that they could more efficiently determine not only the sound, but the direction from which it came. . . . The net result [of Leigh's] trip," according to Sims, "was a general reversal of opinion on the value of this mode of hunting. The British Admiralty ordered from the United States large quantities of the American mechanisms, and also began manufacturing them in England."[9]

The results of Leigh's demonstration certainly pleased Admiral Sims, yet he recognized the inherent difficulties that any sub hunting group would encounter. The speed of the pursuing vessels had to exceed that of the submerged U-boat. The trawlers that Leigh used were much too slow to depend on as a tactical unit. Most importantly, however, was the ability of the listening devices to detect the submarine and plot the location with accuracy. U-boats, also equipped with hydrophones, knew when they were being pursued and would take evasive action, causing them to abandon their patrols along transit routes used by vulnerable merchant ships. Creating and outfitting the most effective hunters involved mechanical design issues. The solution? Depend on the scientists and engineers to design the most efficient detection devices and create a fast, seaworthy vessel specifically equipped with these devices for the pursuit.

Commander Babcock had a Corona typewriter, which he was able to work with two fingers, and on this he laboriously pounded out the reports which first informed the Navy Department of the seriousness of the submarine.[10]

When Admiral Sims and his aide, Commander J. V. Babcock, arrived in London just days after America declared war on Germany, they immediately became aware of the dire situation in Britain brought on by Germany's unrestricted submarine warfare. It was essential to enlighten the U.S. Navy, at that time unprepared for the far-ranging operational capabilities of the U-boat.

Early in the war, according to Admiral Sims, "Hardly any one, except a few experienced submarine officers, had regarded it possible that these small boats would successfully attack vessels upon the high seas." Sims related an opinion held by many that "certain very prominent naval men of great experience declared that the submarine 'could operate only by day and in fair weather; that it was practically useless in misty weather,' [and] that it had to come to the surface to fire its torpedo . . ."[11] As far as U.S. naval strategists were concerned in 1917, there was little threat from U-boats prowling along the American coast, yet as early as March, a small, fast antisubmarine vessel had been authorized. The assumption had always been that, eventually, the U.S. would enter the war, and ramping up ship construction would have to begin. Admiral Griffin:

> Immediately upon entry of the United States into the war it was determined to concentrate construction upon such types as were most necessary . . . reports from our representative at the seat of war emphasized in the strongest terms possible the urgent need of destroyers . . . [and] of small craft that might be utilized in combating the submarine.[12]

Antisubmarine warfare would set America's naval priorities. The "representative at the seat of war" was Admiral Sims, whose reports emphasized that destroyers should top the list; submarine chasers would be next. Early communication from America's ambassador to England, Walter Page, also stressed the need for destroyers as well as fast, maneuverable, and armed U-boat hunters. In a letter to President Wilson sent May 4, 1917, Page wrote: "The greatest help, I hope, can come from us—our destroyers and similar armed craft—provided we can send enough of them quickly. The area to be watched is so big that many submarine hunters are needed." Two months later, in a letter to his son Arthur, Page expressed his certainty that

"Five hundred such little boats might end the war in a few months; for the Germans are keeping the spirit of their people and of their army up by their submarine success."[13]

When merchant ships had arrived in the waters around Britain, the coast of France, and the Mediterranean, the vessels left the protection of destroyer escorts and headed for their destination ports. Unprotected, they were easy prey for U-boats watching for lone targets. After the war, Sims described the problem and his assessment of the subchaser:

> Thus we had to deal with an entirely new phase of the submarine campaign; the new conditions demanded a light vessel, which could be built in large numbers, and which could hunt out the submarines even though they were sailing submerged. The subchaser, when fitted with its listening devices, met these new requirements . . .[14]
>
> About the time [Capt. Leigh had] shown that these listening devices would probably have great practical value, the first 'subchasers' were delivered at New London, Conn."[15]

The concept of creating a fast, maneuverable vessel for coastal patrol had already been proposed, but with America's entry into the war, and with Sims' first hand reports from London, subchasers would take on a priority at numerous shipyards. Admiral Griffin, as the Navy's Engineer in Chief, agreed with Sims' assessment.

> By the time the earliest subchasers were approaching completion the development of submarine detection devices and antisubmarine weapons had reached such a stage that the long-sought means for direct and practicable offensive action against submarines appeared to be in sight. The first subchasers were accordingly assigned to experimental work along this line . . .[16]

The subchasers, with hoped for speeds approaching nineteen knots, were driven by three propellers, hence three independent engines. In addition, a small two-cylinder auxiliary engine was included for a fire and bilge pump, air compressor, electric generator, and other systems requiring power. These four engines constituted one set per vessel. The Bureau of Steam Engineering selected Standard Motor Construction Company to produce the engines. Their 220-horsepower engine had already proven itself under wartime conditions.

> The engines had been well tried over several years of service and had given satisfactory performance in the British 80-foot patrol boats, of which 550

had been built [see chapter 5]. The manufacturers were just completing the last British and a small Italian order; their shops and those of others upon whom they relied for important parts were equipped for quantity production; and they could proceed immediately with our work. . . ."[17]

With the recent experience building the 80-ft motor launches for the British, American manufacturers were prepared to mount an aggressive construction program. Across the country, contracts were provided to thirty-eight shipyards, large and small. While the majority of subchasers were produced at the Brooklyn Navy Yard (facing page), with a total of sixty-two, other manufactures were allotted a number commensurate with their capabilities. Burger Boat Co. of Manitowoc, Wisconsin, and American Car and Foundry Co. of Wilmington, Delaware, each built one chaser, while the Puget Sound Shipyard of Bremerton, Washington, and Hiltebrant Dry Dock were contracted for twenty-five. Electric Launch Co. (Elco) of Bayonne, New Jersey, the primary supplier of British motor launches, produced twenty chasers. Elco had become a subsidiary of Electric Boat, previously the Holland Torpedo Boat Company, in 1899.[18]

Chaser hulls were being completed before the engines were ready; between May and August, only seventeen sets of engines had been built, tested, and accepted for installation. By the end of the year, engine sets for another one hundred vessels were ready.[19] That, of course, limited the availability of operational vessels during 1917, though the rate of launching and commissioning rapidly increased throughout 1918 as engine manufacture likewise increased to meet the demand. Wartime subchaser production totaled 403, of which one hundred were supplied to France. An additional thirty-eight were completed after the war.[20]

One of the first chasers was *SC-6*, built at the Brooklyn Navy Yard and commissioned on August 19. The New London scientists, at that time working from the small, portable building at the submarine base, had been experimenting with several listening devices using the converted steam yacht *Thetis*. When *SC-6* and other subchasers arrived in the Thames River, the experimental station staff now had access to vessels designed specifically for antisubmarine operations; they were anxious to put the subchasers to work. These newly commissioned vessels were soon on one of the marine railways (see page 158) being outfitted with SC-tube and K-tube listening devices, then sent out into Long Island Sound to conduct tests with submarines from their base in Groton. In one case, the submarine *G-4* had been instructed to employ evasive maneuvers, yet *SC-6* successfully tracked *G-4* for two hours, much to the delight of the listening device designers.[21]

Subchasers under construction at the Brooklyn Navy Yard, August, 1917. Soon the completed vessels would arrive in New London. (NHHC NH 83620)

These small but seaworthy vessels carried a complement of two officers and a crew of twenty-two enlisted men—a chief petty officer with a team of five in the engine room, three radio operators, a boatswain's mate, quartermaster, coxswain, three listeners, a cook, mess attendant, and five seamen.[22] Many subchaser crews and their vessels began their wartime duties with as little as three or four months of tactical training and outfitting in New London. During the war, 103 chasers successfully made the Atlantic crossing via Bermuda and the Azores (chapter 23), the first contingent leaving U.S. waters in February, 1918. Another thirty arrived just as Armistice came into effect.[23] In addition to those built for the U.S. Navy, orders for one hundred chasers were manufactured and delivered to France.

The subchaser as an effective antisubmarine vessel was at first looked at with disdain by all levels among naval personnel used to their battleships and dreadnaughts. As the war progressed, it became apparent that the massive capital ships were ineffective against the U-boat. Soon, these small, fast, maneuverable, wooden-hulled, 110-foot naval vessels earned the respect of all navies, friend and foe. Ensign John L. Leighton, intelligence officer on Admiral Sims' staff in London, described them:

Subchaser SC-21 on the marine railway adjacent to the main experimental station building; photo taken in November, 1917. (Merritt Papers, Cornell University)

The submarine chaser was a very vicious-looking little war vessel for its size. Forward, there was mounted a three-inch gun [facing page], and aft, the necessary and elaborate paraphernalia [Y-gun] for launching depth charges . . . With the help of three high-powered gasoline engines, the chaser had more speed at its disposal than it could often use. It was manned by two officers and twenty-two men.[24]

It would take more than being vicious-looking; these vessels had to withstand the rigors of heavy seas and a bitterly cold winter, which would test not only the chasers but also the officers and crews, some with little previous naval experience.

Eight of the boats built at Kingston [Hiltebrant Dry Dock Co.], a hundred miles or so up the Hudson River from New York, were caught by the early freeze-up of 1917 that locked the river tighter than it had been locked within the memory of the oldest inhabitant. Twelve-inch ice paralyzed navigation—but the boats were needed. . . . Five of the boats were placed on a floating drydock with the remaining three made fast astern, protected from the ice by a barge on either side, and a fleet of ten tugs commandeered to tow the outfit down the river.[25]

The transport down the Hudson River began with the temperature 24 degrees below zero, but, as Lieutenant Junior Grade (LTJG) William Nutting stressed, "the boats were needed." There would be no delays due to weather and no relief from the cold throughout the winter of 1917-1918.

While primarily outfitted to detect, locate, and drop lethal depth charges, the "vicious-looking" subchasers also carried a 3"/23-caliber deck gun if they encountered a surfaced U-boat. (Courtesy Marist College; Lowell Thomas Archive)

The tests of American-designed listening devices conducted in the English Channel by Captain Richard H. Leigh and described at the beginning of this chapter were critical to establishing America's submarine hunting strategy throughout 1918. Official communications from Captain Leigh and Admiral Sims are available on line at the Naval History and Heritage Command.[26] Among these, a January 9, 1918, cable to the Chief of Naval Operations labeled "Very Secret" included the following urgent request from Admiral Sims:

> The maximum possible number of submarine chasers equipped with listening devices and manned by personnel trained for this work should be placed in service in war zone without delay. This is a matter of the highest importance warranting extraordinary effort.

PART III

1918

CHAPTER 17 THE COLDEST WINTER ON RECORD

It is a cold day, 14 below. All the exposed metalwork, bolts, steel plates, port fittings etc. in the quarters, is covered with ¼ inch of frost. The pilot house windows coat with frost faster than it can be removed, so they have to be kept open when under way.

—Ensign George S. Dole, 1917[1]

Commissioned on December 4, 1917, *SC-93* received her commanding officer, Ensign George S. Dole, while the 110-foot vessel waited at the Brooklyn Navy Yard. The new submarine chaser and her crew soon departed for New London, Connecticut, where Ensign Dole wrote to his family about the brutally cold conditions they faced. *SC-93* joined other chasers in New London where the first order of business was the installation of the latest listening technology and other antisubmarine devices, which might take only three days in one of the experimental station's marine railways. Once completed, the work of the chasers began. Training would proceed regardless of the bitter cold and accumulating ice, and would involve submarines from their base in Groton, a few miles above the station. Ensign Dole:

Had motors warmed up and ready to start at 6:00 a.m. Came up from the experiment station to sub wharf alongside the subs. The weather was thick owing to the water giving off a dense vapor. Could just see the masts of the vessels lying in the harbor when close aboard. Had to just crawl along with steerageway. The subs are waiting for the sun to clear the fog when we will proceed. There is considerable wind loose, and expect we will be busy cutting ice from decks as soon as we get outside.[2]

Only two weeks after Ensign Dole took command of *SC-93*, he was in Long Island Sound with his crew, undoubtedly "cutting ice from the decks" while listening for one of these submarines. Winter winds made offshore duty difficult aboard the 110-foot vessel. In a letter dated December 15, Dole described how *SC-93* behaved: "When we stop to use the detectors, the boat rolls to the gunwales on either side, and you have to hang on tight to stay with the ship."[3]

Ensign George Wallace, commanding officer of *SC-253*, described similar experiences in New London that winter, ". . . going morning, noon and three to four nights a week, and if you recall the winter of 1917-18, this meant operating in ice anywhere from six to twelve inches thick."[4]

Even Admiral Sims, in London during that winter as commander of U.S. naval forces in Europe, was keenly aware of the conditions that the newly commissioned subchasers faced as more and more of them were sent to New London. It wasn't just that the vessels were in need of repairs; Sims was concerned that the crews were largely inexperienced and in dire need of instruction in basic seamanship prior to the long and challenging Atlantic crossing:

Day after day the poor subchasers, coated with ice almost a foot thick, many with their engines wrecked, their planking torn and their propellers crumpled, were towed into the harbor and left at the first convenient mooring, where the ice immediately began to freeze them in. As was inevitable under such conditions, the crews, for the most part, suffered acutely in this terrible weather; they had had absolutely no training in ordinary seamanship, to say nothing of the detailed tactics demanded by the difficult work in which they were to engage.[5]

SUBCHASER TRAINING IN NEW LONDON

Admiral Sims had long recognized the importance of the antisubmarine work being carried out in New London, both at the experimental station and further up the river at the submarine base—he was anxious for the subchasers to cross the Atlantic. For Sims, however, their training was essential before his expectations could be realized.

It now became known that a subchaser training base had been established at New London. The news was apparently a godsend to the builders, who began to hustle their chasers into the water and send them to the Connecticut harbor in all stages of unreadiness for sea.[6]

As Sims anticipated, however, the chaser units would be under the command of enthusiastic naval reserve officers. Ensign Wallace, one of these reservists, was very specific about his time in New London:

It was my good fortune to be assigned to sub-chaser experimental work before many had been launched. There was a fleet of twelve of us at New London, Conn. whose job it was to test out all listening apparatus and to make practical use if possible of these inventions which were laboratory successes but had not as yet bridged the gap between that and the grueling work of the open sea.[7]

Only six months had passed since the first devices had been designed and tested at both Nahant and New London. As the brutal winter weather began to break in March, more opportunities became available for *SC-253* and the other chaser crews to participate in the experimental work and to train for what lay ahead. What Wallace saw as his and his fellow subchaser crews' mission was first to ensure that the "laboratory successes," which had been subjected to countless experimental trials throughout the summer and fall, could be applied to the latest submarine hunters as practicable antisubmarine devices:

After finding what was best we then had to evolve chaser tactics, which included maneuvers, special signals, hunting, patrol and attack formations, and at the same time take men who had never been to sea before, and not only cram practical seamanship into their heads and bodies, but the specialized knowledge so necessary to efficient, lightning-fast sub-chaser operation, and all this in the short space of three or four months.[8]

The SC-tube and K-tube listening devices were becoming standard gear for the chasers assigned for overseas duty, and Long Island Sound was an ideal location for training. A brief stay in one of the Station's marine railways (see page 158) was all that was needed to install an SC-tube or one of the other experimental listening devices. These devices were dependable, and the listeners adapted well to their operation, which was essential in order to expect the chaser crews to prepare for operations in the war zone after only a few months at New London. The anticipation of success for the listening devices was later reported on by the Office of Naval Intelligence:

> A demonstration of the use of the "C" tube has been given by a listener named Ross on the *151*. This man picked out and definitely stated that a convoy was approaching on a certain bearing. There was nothing in sight at the time in the direction given. One-half hour later smoke was sighted and two steamers escorted by two destroyers came into view. The convoy must have been picked up at a distance of at least 25 miles.[9]

While that report described a convoy over the horizon, detecting the sounds of vessels operating at a distance of twenty-five miles is a credit to these early listening devices. A U-boat, however, would be significantly quieter. Hunting tactics were the name of the game, and for *SC-253* and Ensign Wallace's fellow chasers, Long Island Sound became a busy place. "When March came blustering along, we hunted subs—American ones to be sure, but we had all the local color of the English Channel, produced by the fog and winds of Block Island and old Montauk."[10] While the conditions were difficult, everyone knew that it was only a prelude to what could be expected.

The chasers needed to practice their U-boat hunting techniques with as much of that realism as possible. Not having a U-boat at their disposal, there was an ample supply of U.S. submarines at their base in Groton eager to act as surrogates. Although the newer L-class boats in the Atlantic Submarine Flotilla would be sent to the war zone, older D-class and G-class subs remained as coastal patrol assets and for experimental work and training. With unflinching support from the submarine base and an increasing presence of newly commissioned subchasers, there were opportunities to develop rudimentary chaser tactics for those heading across the Atlantic, where the realities of U-boat hunting would provide the final test.

The listening devices carried on the chasers gave a reliable indication of the direction of the sound source—a submerged U-boat running away from its pursuers at speeds from six to ten knots. In reality, however, U-boat captains had practiced evasive tactics and maneuvers, which might include running very slowly or quietly settling onto the bottom when depths allowed. Admiral Sims recognized that the tactics employed by hunting units would evolve and improve as their experiences in the war zone progressed. He was, however, pleased with the performance of the chasers which arrived at Plymouth, England, at the end of June.

In company with a number of British hunting units, Captain Cotton's detachment kept steady at work from June 30 until the middle of August, . . .[and] not a single merchant ship was sunk between Lizard Head and Start Point [the English Channel] as long as these subchasers were assisting in the operations.[11]

Captain Lyman A. Cotton commanded the flotilla of thirty-six subchasers—twelve hunting groups of three chasers—at Plymouth. Their tactics, which originated in Long Island Sound, quickly adapted to the conditions experienced in the English Channel as described by Admiral Sims:

By the time Captain Cotton's squadron began work, the hunting tactics that had been developed during their training in New London had been considerably improved. Their procedure represented something entirely new in naval warfare. . . The fight against the submarine, under this new system, was divided into three parts—the search, the pursuit, and the attack.

[The search] included those weary hours which the little group spent drifting on the ocean, the lookout in the crow's nest scanning the surface for the possible glimpse of a periscope, while the trained listeners on deck, with strange little instruments, which somewhat resembled telephone receivers, glued to their ears, kept constantly at tension for any noise which might manifest itself under water. It was impossible to use the listening devices while the boats were underway, for the sounds of their own propellers and machinery would drown out other disturbances. The three little vessels therefore drifted abreast . . . [and] formed a new kind of fishing expedition, the officers and crews constantly held taut by the expectation of a "bite."

A hunting group of three subchasers heading to their assigned operating area. (Sims, 1919-1920)

[S]uddenly, one of the listeners would hear something which his experienced ear had learned to identify as the propellers and motors of a submarine. The great advantage of the American tubes, as already said, was that they gave not only the sound, but its direction. The listener would inform his commanding officer that he had picked up a submarine. "Very faint," he would perhaps report, "direction 97"—the latter being the angle which it made with the north and south line.

The middle chaser was the flagship and her most interesting feature was the so-called plotting room. Here one officer received constant telephone reports from all three boats, giving the nature of the sound and, more important still, their directions. He transferred these records to a chart, as soon as they came in, rapidly made calculations and, in a few seconds, he was able to give the location of the submarine. The process was known as obtaining a "fix.". . . the "fix" being the point on the ocean where the three lines, each giving the direction of the detected sound, cross one another.[12]

Maximizing the efficiency of obtaining the "fix" on a submarine was essential in the pursuit phase of hunting. As Sims had mentioned, the three vessels had to stop and lower their SC-tubes before obtaining a bearing to the target. Each vessel's bearing was then transmitted to the center or "flagship" chaser. At New London, a mechanical "position plotter" had been developed

Position plotter used by the lead (center) subchaser to obtain the bearing or "fix" (inset) to the target obtained from each vessel in the hunting group. (Hayes Family Archive; Inset from Sims, 1919-1920)

for use by the officer plotting the track of the submarine. Ensign Hilary R. Chambers, commanding officer of *SC-128*, had trained in chaser tactics while in New London and described the plotting process:

> [The position plotter] consisted of movable dials with three movable arms. Reports of the submarine bearing came from each of the three ships to the officer who was handling the plotting instrument. He adjusted the arms in accordance with the reports, and knowing the

distance between ships he got what is called a "fix" of the submarine where the arms met. These movable arms were proportioned relative to the distance between ships, and he could read the distance and bearing of the submarine on the instrument.[13]

An Uncooperative Target

A U-boat captain, who likely knew his sub was being pursued, may have been running on a zigzag course. The chasers would need to continue to adjust their course accordingly, using the position plotter after having to stop and obtain another set of three bearings. It was expected that the speed of the hunting group, which exceeded that of the U-boat, would eventually enable them to cross over the submarine and launch their attack. Admiral Sims:

> Putting on full speed, all three chasers rush up to the latest "fix," drop depth charges with a lavish hand, fire the "Y" howitzers, each one of which carries two depth charges . . . In many of these hunts a destroyer accompanies the subchasers, always keeping at a considerable distance, so that the noise of its propellers will not interfere with the game; once the chasers determine the accurate "fix," they wire the position to the larger ship, which puts on a full head of steam and dashes with the speed of an express train to the indicated spot, and adds ten or a dozen of its twenty to thirty depth charges to those deposited by the chasers . . .[14]

The training received in New London could not anticipate all of the evasive maneuvers that German submarine captains engaged in. Aware that these U-boat tactics were not included in the training, officers at the submarine base expressed their concerns through Lieutenant Ford who attended an experimental station department meeting in May. Ford suggested that "the exercises in connection with the chasers for training of listeners was unsatisfactory . . ." adding:

> Commanding Officers of the submarines claim that if they are allowed to run at less than 6 knots they can always get away from the chasers. Felt that the chaser people are making these problems easy for the chasers and making it a sure thing. [The submarine commanders] seemed to feel that the development of listening apparatus would be helped if they were to work under conditions most likely to occur in the war zone."[15]

Thus it was, that the chaser units left New London and crossed the Atlantic in 1918, at least having trained in what Ensign Wallace had described as the basic "chaser tactics, which included maneuvers, special signals, hunting, patrol and attack formations." Admiral Sims recognized that for the new chaser units sent to the war zone, "it was only after much experience that the procedure began to work with clock-like regularity."[16]

As the winter months of 1918 continued to restrict the amount of testing and training that could occur, the naval and civilian staff at New London's experimental station, and the submarine and subchaser crews who were stationed at the submarine base, were anxious for spring. Elements of the Naval Reserve Flying Corps were also involved with the experimental work and had been flying from their air stations on Long Island during the summer and fall of 1917. They had been trying various listening devices, which they deployed after landing on the sea surface, but these early devices were cumbersome and required improvements before a practicable system could be used. One of the pilots, Wells Brown, noted: "After being [in New London] about a week, we saw that there was no use in spending more time on the experimental work because the apparatus was so bulky that it needed to be redesigned." The winter, however, soon put an end to the flights.[17]

> Several flights were made in connection with submarine operations. . . . At various times [the pilots] joined in this sport of hunting the shy submarine. . . . They continued into December, until freezing weather came and ice formed on New London harbor and river.[18]

The winter months provided time for the experimental station scientists and engineers to redesign the initial listening devices and create new ones that could be more readily adapted to these aircraft. Spring would provide many opportunities for these aerial submarine hunters to test a variety of these devices. Soon, lighter-than-air airships, which the Navy had recently contracted to be built, would also arrive over Long Island Sound. In the meantime, the various seaplanes and flying boats sat idle while their pilots waited for spring.

CHAPTER 18 THE NAVAL RESERVE FLYING CORPS

> Allied victory was so gravely imperiled that every resource of
> naval and scientific ingenuity was focused upon the problem of
> combating the ravages of submarines, of hunting and extermi-
> nating them like noxious vermin.
>
> —Ralph D. Paine, *The First Yale Unit*, 1925[1]

In his 1925 book *The First Yale Unit: A Story of Naval Aviation 1916-1919*, Ralph D. Paine (journalist who worked for the Navy Department during the war) emphasized the importance that aviation would have on anti-submarine warfare during the Great War, and that it would take significant scientific ingenuity to combat the submarine. "Aeroplanes seemed likely to supersede destroyers as the eyes of the Fleet," adding that the "submarine was the mobile weapon of offense which Germany employed with a skill and audacity that dismayed her enemies. The barbarity of her methods horrified civilization and stained the ancient chivalry of the sea with abominable cruelties."[2]

Aircraft, as effective military assets, were beginning to be felt over the battlefields of Europe. These same aircraft, with wheels replaced with pontoons, could now operate on and above the sea in spite of objections by "Crusty old admirals with ossified prejudices, who had cursed aviation as a nuisance in time of peace," but were now "compelled to change their minds," as Paine described:

> It was soon perceived that the air service could be made tremendously useful as one factor of the anti-submarine patrol. Even a swift destroyer could detect a U-boat only by the telltale periscope or when the hull was awash. An aviator, however, sweeping over hundreds of miles of sea in the day's work, could discern the dim shape if not too deeply submersed, or spy the distant patch of foam when the boat broke water. Aircraft could also assist in convoying troop transports and supply ships.[3]

In America, as the war raged in Europe, patriotic men urged the creation of flying units, including those that arose from the student body at Yale University—the basis for Ralph Paine's book. The efforts at Yale were initiated in 1916 by F. Trubee Davison, class of 1918. Davison made several trips to Washington, hoping to convince Secretary of the Navy Josephus Daniels to give official recognition to Davison's proposed creation of Aerial Coast Patrol units. Daniels, who at that time remained unconvinced, but interested, wrote to Davison on July 14, 1916. The following is from Secretary Daniels' letter:

> You will understand, of course, that the Department cannot give official recognition to persons or organizations over which it had no official control. It is certainly most pleasing to hear of the patriotic desire of independent citizens of the country to organize themselves to assist in time of danger in the protection of their country, and in wishing you all success in your enterprise I am trusting that some provision can be given whereby Government recognition will be extended to these organizations.[4]

Daniels was not, however, shutting the door to Davison. In the summer of 1916, America was still a neutral country, although everyone in President Wilson's government anticipated that war with Germany was highly likely. Davison was finally rewarded for his efforts, when, during the early months of 1917, the Yale unit received official recognition. In March, these enthusiastic students enlisted in the recently created Naval Reserve Flying Corps. Now able to receive formal flight training in aircraft designed for operations over and on the water, these would-be Navy pilots earned their "wings."[5] During the winter of 1917-1918, crews trained in Florida at the Palm Beach (following page) and Pensacola Naval Air Stations (shown on page 96); at other times, pilots trained at the several air stations on Long Island, New York.

The pilots were introduced to several varieties of aircraft referred to as seaplanes, also known as floatplanes. Many of this type were equipped with both wheels and pontoons, which allowed them to safely fly over the water on submarine scouting missions, yet return to a land-based airfield. Early in the second decade of the twentieth century, aircraft were also being tested with a fuselage specifically designed to support the plane on the water. After two years of experimentation, Glenn Curtiss, in 1913, had produced his Model-F aircraft, which he referred to as a "Flying-Boat."

Right: *Naval Reserve Flying Corps training at Palm Beach, Florida. Pilot F. Trubee Davison is at center.* Below: *Huntington [New York] Naval Air Station on Long Island where some of the Yale pilots continued their training.* (Paine, 1925)

Left: *Curtiss aircraft at the southern end of the Naval Experimental Station.* (Courtesy Submarine Force Library and Museum, *Ensign J. Bean, 1917*) Below: *Curtiss R-6 seaplane being outfitted for an experimental run over Long Island Sound.* (Courtesy Victor Marolda)

Ralph Paine, referring in his book to the aircraft being used by the Naval Reserve Flying Corps, described the differences between these types of aircraft: "Equipping an aeroplane with pontoons in place of wheels enabled it to take off and land on the water," but "stouter construction was needed to withstand the battering of the waves. This necessitated larger machines. The logical development was the flying-boat with a hull instead of pontoons."[6] While naval reserve units had several types of aircraft available at their air stations, contemporary photos of the Naval Experimental Station indicate that both the Curtiss R-6 seaplane and the HS-2 flying boat saw service over Long Island Sound supporting antisubmarine tests.

THE NAVAL RESERVE FLYING CORPS ARRIVES AT NEW LONDON

Throughout 1917, multiple naval air stations were being established along America's Atlantic coast. The experimental stations at Nahant, Massachusetts, and New London, Connecticut, made frequent use of the air stations on Cape Cod and Long Island. Albert Ditman, one of the pilots from Yale and now enlisted in the naval reserves, found much to interest him in the technical part of his assignment at the Bay Shore, Long Island, air station: "I made regular trips to the submarine base at New London, flying from Bay Shore in an R-6 . . . and while at New London I would either experiment with the Davis gun or listening devices."[7] Ditman's Curtiss R-6 Seaplane may be the one seen among the aircraft depicted in the Naval Experimental Station waterfront photographs on the previous page.

One of Ditman's duties at Bay Shore was as an instructor for new personnel assigned to the air station. He recalled concerns regarding German sympathizers, who had been suspected of tampering with aircraft at his and other air stations.

> It was found that acid had been used on the turn-buckles so that they broke under a strain. I made it my business to keep in touch with the different stations on these matters, and I suppose that for this reason whenever a suspect was rounded up he was put on my crew.
>
> Several of the men whom I was instructing had to be closely watched, and I always had the feeling that some trick might have been played on every plane I took up. The only safeguard was to make the suspects fly as much as the rest of us. They never knew at what time I might call on them to go up. For the sake of saving their own necks, I think, no accidents occurred at the station from this cause.[8]

HS-2 flying boat flight crew at the Naval Experimental Station. (Hayes Family Archive)

Commander Yates Stirling Jr., commanding officer for the submarine base in Groton until the end of July, 1917, immediately recognized the significance of aircraft when Yale's naval reserve pilots (note the HS-2 Flying Boat in the background) arrived in New London, landing their aircraft at the submarine base on the Thames River.

[Stirling] had great confidence in the value of aircraft for spotting submarines and showed more foresight than many of the departmental officials in Washington. He wished to assemble all the data possible. How far beneath the surface could a submarine be detected? What were the varying effects of light and wind and rough or smooth water? Would the aeroplane compel the submarine to change its tactics? What about bombing from the air?[9]

Stirling understood that to answer his questions, teamwork between the submarine crews and the flight crews was essential. He encouraged his submarine officers to participate on flights and "observe how their submarines behaved," also inviting "the aviators to go down in a submarine to learn for themselves how it dived and steered." Wells Brown, one of the pilots, related his experiences:

[W]e did get some experience in flying over submarines and in determining at what depths they could be seen, and at what depths they disappeared from sight. Commander Stapler [commanding officer of the submarine *D-1*] and I made several flights of this character and watched closely the maneuvers of submarines from the base. I think we came to the conclusion that submarines could be found and followed quite easily at about thirty feet underneath the surface, but below that depth they were pretty hard to see. We also decided that this depended a great deal upon the type of bottom, which was very muddy at New London.[10]

It appears that submarine officers were just fine with their flights, yet for pilot William Rockefeller, submarine life was rather unappealing:

Submarine officers also took flights with us to observe the visibility of subs while submerged under different conditions. I had my one and only trip in a submarine at this time, as the officers very kindly let us go out with them when we were not otherwise occupied. I don't want another ride. All I remember is a good deal of noise, being told I was under the Sound, seeing the water go by through the little glass portholes in the conning tower, or whatever it is called, and coming up again.[11]

Gradually, Commander Stirling's questions were being answered, in spite of the poor water conditions in Long Island Sound, where pilots attempted to observe submarines operating below a depth of thirty feet.

Dirty water made the conditions unfavorable. The submarines were usually invisible after submersion, but it was discovered that they left a white wake after diving and this was conspicuous from the air. When the water was fairly clear, as happened once or twice, the hull could be seen perhaps twenty feet down. It was learned that the submarine could be easily bombed, for the planes circled as low as fifty feet without being seen through a periscope. Attempts to drop bags of flour on them failed to score hits for lack of a bombing sight.[12]

SUBMARINE LISTENING DEVICES FOR DETECTION OF AIRCRAFT

Periscopes were not capable of looking up into the sky, making submarines vulnerable to attack, particularly if prior to surfacing, the area was determined to be free of hunting vessels. In his September 17, 1917, weekly report to Commander McDowell, Ernest Merritt described the test of a device intended to enable a submerged submarine to detect the presence of enemy aircraft.

It has been suggested that it would be advisable to provide our submarines with listening devices mounted on top of the periscope so that as soon as the periscope comes out of the water it would be possible to determine whether an enemy air plane was near. To test the practicability of such a device, a small funnel, 5" in diameter and 4 ½ in deep was connected to ¾" pipe which led from the periscope through the conning tower hatch to the interior. With ear pieces at the end of this tube, a seaplane could be heard at a distance of 1,000 yards.[13]

Merritt also noted that the detection range by a listener when the submarine was operating at periscope depth "was practically the same as that of the unaided ear when the observer was on deck." He then suggested that including a microphone and amplifier inside the sub, "a considerable increase of range would probably be practicable." As Ralph Paine noted, naval reserve aircraft from Long Island were used to conduct these tests, which would continue into 1918:

For practice in hunting submarines, [William] Rockefeller, [Kenneth] MacLeish, and [David] Ingalls were ordered from Huntington [the air station shown on page 174] to New London for temporary duty. They stayed there a week or ten days. 'During this time,' says Rockefeller, 'we made several flights over submarines operating in the Sound while they tested out various devices by means of which they hoped to be able to detect the presence of aircraft.'[14]

Always mindful of their vulnerability, submarines typically waited until after dark to surface and charge their batteries. Among the documents reviewed for this book, a very brief reference was found where the Special Board on Antisubmarine Devices, Commander McDowell, sent a memo to Ernest Merritt. "[I]t is desirable that tests be made of Professor Stewart's Airplane Listening Device for listening to a submarine on the surface charging her batteries. Professor Smith will be informed of this and the problem assigned to you." No details were found regarding Professor Stewart's device and no further discussion about the proposed tests. It is important to realize, however, that all U-boats would eventually have to surface at night. This would certainly have been another task for the naval reserve pilots.[15]

After gaining experience in New London and above Long Island Sound and in the air on coastal patrols off New York, many of the Yale pilots were sent to Europe. Lieutenant David Ingalls became the first American pilot to become an ace, flying for the Royal Air Force in a Sopwith Camel. Ingalls was later appointed Assistant Secretary of the Navy for Aviation by President Herbert Hoover.[16] His fellow pilot, Lieutenant Kenneth MacLeish, was shot down over Belgium on October 14, 1918. His body wasn't found until December 27.[17]

Aircraft, both seaplanes and dirigibles, possess certain advantages for detection of submarines over surface craft. On account of the height of the observer from the surface, a very large area may be observed; in addition, the wake of a periscope appears as a white ribbon against the dark background of the sea, and the superior speed of the aircraft permits them to reach any supposed location of a submarine.

—Admiral Robert S. Griffin,
History of the Bureau of Engineering, 1922[1]

Admiral Robert S. Griffin, Chief of the Bureau of Steam Engineering, writing in 1922, understood that an aircraft's primary advantage over surface craft was as an aerial observer. He did, however, recognize that a seaplane could also be used for submarine hunting when a U-boat was suspected of running beneath the surface in an area away from subchasers. "To be able to detect a submarine totally submerged, aircraft must be able to drop some form of listening device under water, because a submarine, save in exceptionally clear water with sandy bottom, becomes invisible from the air as soon as the periscope is entirely under water."[2] The Naval Experimental Station was working to provide exactly that for the Navy's airmen.

A test was carried out by Ensign Case with the cooperation of the test department, of two forms of overboard devices for use on flying boats. . . Device shows reasonable sharpness of focus and good range . . ."[3]

In his daily log for May 15, Ernest Merritt was encouraged by the tests conducted by Ensign Case using a subchaser, and eagerly recommended "to try this apparatus on a seaplane or flying boat even though it is not yet in its final form. Such a trial will suggest important points to be considered in the final design." There was no indication of which "overboard devices" Merritt was referring to, a likely consequence of the details being considered classified.

By spring, it had become evident that any device intended for use by aircraft required mechanical and operational design considerations which differed from those devices used on surface craft. For aircraft, weight of the device was a major consideration, as was ease of deployment and retrieval by the listener. Aircraft engines would have to remain on when the device was deployed to ensure the aircraft could readily take off from the sea surface; the listener, therefore, would have to wear headphones designed to muffle the engine noise.

The results of aircraft listening device testing during the fall of 1917 had been largely unsatisfactory, which led to their primary use as observers in operational trials while in New London. By spring, however, improvements had been made with various designs that could be adapted to the strict requirements of seaplanes. Once again, the Naval Reserve Flying Corps found themselves descending out of the sky and onto the surface of Long Island Sound.

The aircraft were hauled out of the water at a protected cove adjacent to the experimental station buildings (page 175 shows this area with three of the aircraft facing south toward Long Island Sound), and set in cradles where they were outfitted with their experimental devices.

Curtiss HS-2 in its cradle at the Naval Experimental Station. (Courtesy Victor Marolda)

In April, one of the first devices to be tested was described by Professor Merritt at an experimental station department meeting, as "a simple listening device for a seaplane alighting on the water and having a light microphone device drop from it." Merritt continued, describing it as light and compact, and "nothing but a microphone with a screen which gives it a reasonable sharp, directional quality." Merritt noted that he had been reading reports related to sound screens, and would be ready for more testing "in a day or two."[4]

During the first week of June, Merritt provided updates to the Special Board on Antisubmarine Devices (Commander McDowell) on the status of listening devices, including the screened microphones, being considered for seaplanes and flying boats.[5]

June 1

A number of devices have been designed and several have been constructed and tested. Some of these devices use screened microphones. Others are electrified C-tubes. The support is to be either flexible cable with sufficient resistance to twist, or some telescoping rod or similar scheme. The essential thing is to get something compact and easy to handle. As a result of tests on a sea-plane designs have been made for installing [these devices]. . . . Continuation of work [includes] installation on sea-plane or flying boat. Further development [is recommended] for cases where this type of apparatus is more suitable than a C-tube or MB-tube . . .

June 3

The Screened Microphone for overboard use has now reached a point where the device can be produced in quantity. . . It seems to me that this device should be manufactured in sufficient quantity so that it can be supplied promptly to such vessels as wish to use it.

June 4

Ensign Case has completed designs for installing a listening device upon a seaplane and the necessary parts have been built so as to fit the plane upon which he made a test about ten days ago. The pilot operating the machine when Mr. Case made his previous tests was of the opinion that the installation could be made without in any way interfering with the operation or balance of the plane.

In the June 3rd memo, Merritt noted to McDowell that, in addition to aircraft, the screened microphone could be made readily available "to such vessels as wish to use it." This simple device, which only required a battery and amplifier with the stethoscope-type earphones, would be appropriate for small craft used as patrol boats which would not carry the more complicated devices produced for subchasers.

The screened microphone tested in New London, however, was intended for aircraft which could rapidly fly to any offshore location, lower the device, listen for a submarine, and if one were detected, radio the location to a subchaser hunting unit in the area. When the success of the New London

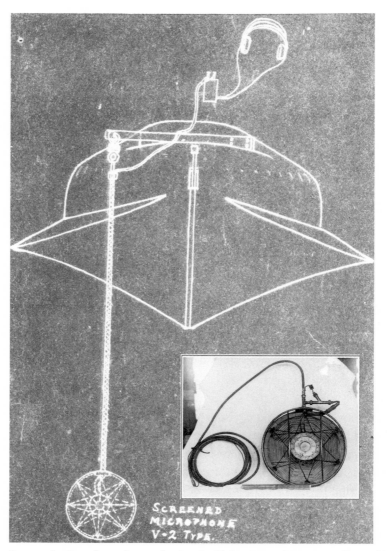

Screened microphone for use by Curtiss Flying Boat. (Hayes Family Archive)

testing reached Admiral Sims in England in June, Sims immediately cabled the Bureau of Steam Engineering, asking when "two sets of Merritt's screened microphones for use on flying boat can be obtained for testing at sea plane station abroad . . . ." His request was passed to the submarine base at New London and then to the experimental station, where delivery to the American Consul in Liverpool was promised by July 9.[6]

Comparison tests of the four screened devices—the lantern, saucer, balloon, and basket shown (in that order) on the following page—continued throughout July, with all four suspended from the USS *Thetis* (SP-391). As the experimental work in New London continued, so did shipments of the devices. The basket design did not perform as hoped and was not among the designs shipped. The British had experimented with screened microphones for their various hunting vessels to obtain directionality, but the application for aircraft piqued their interest. The British liaison officer, Lieutenant Commander Houghton (shown in the group photo, page 192), joined Merritt on board *Thetis* for the tests, the purpose of which was "to determine which ones to send to England this week for further experimental work over there."[7]

While the screened microphone was by far the simplest device carried by the seaplanes, Merritt had also recommended, in his June 1 memo to McDowell (above), the development of an apparatus "more suitable than a C-tube or MB-tube." The C-tube (more accurately called an SC-tube) and MB-tube mechanisms for subchasers were much too heavy for aircraft use. The installation of both of these devices required that the vertical pipe portion be mounted through a watertight seal in the heavy wooden chaser hull, impossible for the thin aluminum-hulled flying boats. An attempt to mount one of these devices had been tried the previous year, as related by pilot Albert Ditman:

> On November 30th I received orders to make an investigation of the new listening device that had been invented by the Western Electric Company at Lynn, Mass. I proceeded to Buffalo where plans were made to install this device on an H-12. This comprised cutting a hole in the bottom of the boat, and after the boat had landed on the water the device was lowered about twenty feet under the surface. This installation was later given up because it was found impossible to make the hole water-tight.[8]

This would not happen again. The acoustic sensors of the MB-tube subchaser device being considered by Merritt in 1918 were readily adapted for overboard use, rather than installed through the aircraft's hull. For the aircraft MB-tube, twelve hydrophones were mounted in a horizontal line on a metal bar. Once the aircraft had landed on the sea surface, the listener in the bow compartment

Four types of screened microphones tested at New London. Examples of these (except the far right) were shipped overseas for use by the British. (Hayes Family Archive)

unfolded and lowered the horizontal portion of the T-shaped mechanism beneath the water, such that six of the twelve hydrophone signals were directed to the listener's left ear, the other six to his right ear (opposite page).

The listener then rotated the mechanism (see inset). When the sound source was perpendicular to the line of hydrophones, all twelve received the sound wave at the same time (i.e., the sound at each microphone was "in phase"; see chapter 13 for a description of sound waves and phase). In this position, the sound heard in both of the listener's ears was equal, thus giving a general indication of the direction of the submarine. The ability to determine the direction of the sound was a desirable feature of the MB-tube, but the listener would have found it nearly impossible to operate the apparatus as the aircraft pitched and rolled on the sea surface. Other solutions were needed.

One of the initial electronic listening devices developed at the Nahant station for subchasers was the K-tube, a triangular device with a hydrophone mounted at each corner (see chapter 14). The listener selected any pair of hydrophones, and by making adjustments on an instrument that compensated

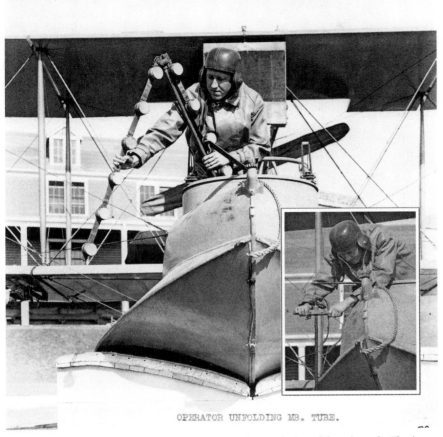

OPERATOR UNFOLDING MB. TUBE.

*HS-2 listener deploying the MB-tube listening device designed for aircraft. The inset shows the listener rotating the device. (*Hayes Family Archive*)*

for the time delay between the two hydrophones, he obtained a bearing to the sound source (compensators are described in chapter 20). Rather than towing a triangular frame while the aircraft drifted or slowly taxied, the engineers in New London set individual hydrophones in a small lead sphere, each lowered from the forward cockpit through three rings that formed a triangular arrangement referred to as a PB-tube (following page). The lead spheres kept the hydrophones suspended vertically as the aircraft conducted its search. The listener, comfortably sitting in that forward compartment, could make adjustments on the compensator and determine the direction of the submarine.[9]

Right:
PB-tube arrangement on an HS-2 Flying Boat. Below Right: The PB-tube components including the electrical compensator. The inset shows the hydrophone removed from the lead sphere. (Hayes Family Archive)

Left: *HS-2 Flying Boat on Long Island Sound with experimental listening device.* (Merritt Papers, Cornell University)
Below: *Search pattern for submarine hunting using aircraft.* (Hayes Family Archive)

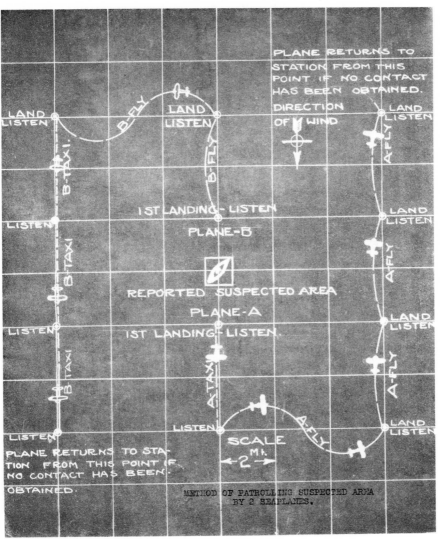

As mentioned at the beginning of this chapter, the tactical use of aircraft required the plane to land on the surface and lower its listening device, report any contact, then move to another location. Encouraged by positive test results, a plan for this operation shown on the previous page was produced at the experimental station.

The primary mission of the experimental station was to outfit subchasers, destroyers, and submarines with every means possible to detect, locate, and destroy the enemy's submersible predators. The expectation for aircraft was that they provide additional coverage over areas that surface craft were unable to patrol at any particular time, their numbers being far too few. Aircraft could cover hundreds of square mile of open ocean and had the ability to land on the sea surface if conditions allowed. If outfitted with even a basic listening device such as the screened microphone, an aircraft could listen for a submarine lurking in an area far from the hunting units. Thus, throughout 1918, engineers at New London continued to design and improve submarine detection technology for both surface craft and aircraft.

LIGHTER THAN AIR

The scope of the work was greatly enlarged as the station grew, and apparatus was designed for use on Destroyers as well as on seaplanes and air ships. . . . Five sea-planes were used at the Experimental Station for observation tests and balloons were obtained from the Montauk Point air station for tests.[10]

Ensign James Bean, who had attended the Navy's hydrophone school in New London, wrote about the experimental station while a postwar student at Stanford University. Although Bean did not provide any details about the various aircraft that had been employed in antisubmarine development in New London, he did mention that the station designed listening apparatus for airships. These lighter-than-air aircraft were either constructed of a rubberized fabric envelope over an airframe, referred to as a rigid airship, or the envelope had no supporting airframe and took its shape when inflated. These non-rigid airships have been referred to interchangeably as blimps or dirigibles—the term dirigible used by the experimental station staff.

From the start of the war, both sides included airships and observation balloons in their tactical planning for use at sea and over the battlefields. For Germany, their massive Zeppelins conducted bombing raids over London

B-class dirigible aloft. (Hayes Family Archive)

and other locations along the coast, thus making aerial bombardment of England of strategic importance. With the appearance of the U-boat in 1914 and the inability of the allied navies to combat its predatory efficiency, England, France, and Italy all increased their use of airships to patrol the skies over vast expanses of ocean, searching for Germany's illusive submarines. Several foreign military officers joined Commander C. S. McDowell, secretary of the Special Board on Antisubmarine Devices, at the experimental station, standing for a group photograph (following page). At the far right is an army lieutenant who was a member of the Italian airship service within the *Battaglione Specialisti del Genio*.

Throughout the war, allied navies sent airships aloft as convoy escorts and to continue their submarine hunting mission over the western Atlantic and Mediterranean. The British created their Submarine Scout, or SS-class, airships specifically for this mission, even carrying bombs in the event a U-boat was encountered on the surface.

Richard G. Van Treuren (2009) described the amazing history of these aircraft in *Airships vs. Submarines*, covering in great detail each year, from 1914 through 1918, in his chapter five, "The Great War." Van Treuren quoted Ladislas D'Orcy, from his *Airship Manual* (1919): "Airships have played an extremely important role in the Great War, particularly in connection with naval operations, although, owing to the secrecy which surrounds such work in wartime, their achievements have received little publicity."[11]

In the United States, when it was becoming apparent that war was inevitable, naval authorities decided to create an airship suitable for coastal patrol. In 1915, a single airship, the DN-1, was contracted for construction by Connecticut Aircraft Company of New Haven, Connecticut, but construction delays resulted in this airship not being delivered until November 1916, more than a year late. In the meantime, the Navy Department decided to develop a separate class of dirigible, and on February 4,

Foreign visitors on the experimental station waterfront. (LR) unnamed French naval lieutenant; Lieutenant G. Abetti (Italian naval pilot); at center is Commander C. S. McDowell, secretary of the Special Board on Antisubmarine Devices; Lieutenant Commander S. C. Houghton, Royal Navy Volunteer Reserves; Italian army lieutenant and dirigible pilot. (Hayes Family Archive)

1917, Secretary Josephus Daniels ordered that construction of sixteen commence immediately. Goodyear had produced observation balloons for the Army in 1916 and was ready to accept a contract from the Navy, as described by Hugh Allen in *The House of Goodyear: Fifty Years of Men and Industry* (1949):

> [A]s early as 1915, Comdr. J. C. Hunsaker, chief aircraft constructor, and Donald Douglass, his assistant, were instructed to develop a design for a dirigible. Lieut. (later Admiral) J. H. Towers, Naval attaché in Europe, brought in considerable information in 1916, and a design was completed for an airship similar to the British type B. . . The early blimps were not too complicated a job. It was merely a matter of suspending a car and engine under the gas bag, well under it to keep sparks away from the lifting gas, hydrogen, which was highly flammable. An airplane fuselage would do, so Curtiss built the early ones, open cockpit

cars with a windshield in front. There were no landing wheels, just a pneumatic bumper bag underneath to take the shock of landing. . . The important job was the gas bag, and only Goodyear and a company in Connecticut had any experience with this.[12]

On March 19, 1917, just three weeks before America entered the war, contracts for those sixteen dirigibles were awarded to several companies. The first of these B-class airships was flown on May 24, an incredible accomplishment in only two months. B-1 was finally delivered to the Navy in July, arriving at the naval air station at Pensacola, Florida, on August 7. Within a year, all sixteen had been delivered to the Navy, having received their airship numbers, A-235 to A-250.[13] Naval airship stations were established at Chatham, Massachusetts; Montauk Point and Rockaway Beach [on Long Island], New York; Cape May, New Jersey; Hampton Roads, Virginia; and Pensacola and Key West, Florida.[14]

Ensign Bean had mentioned the experimental station having obtained balloons from the Montauk Point naval air station at the eastern tip of Long Island. These may have been kite balloons used for observation while tethered to destroyers during submarine hunting patrols. But it was the dirigible as a submarine hunter that was of most interest to the staff at both Nahant and New London. Dirigibles were available at the Chatham Naval Air Station (on Cape Cod) to support the offshore tests at Nahant, and from the Montauk Naval Air Station for the New London staff. Admiral Griffin (1922):

> On account of its ability to stay practically stationary in the air, the dirigible can utilize a form of listening device which can be lowered from the craft and towed underwater. Several towed listening devices were developed to accomplish this, the most satisfactory being the "electric eel" and the OK-tube, compensators being used by the listener in each case.[15]

The two listening devices mentioned above by Admiral Griffin were initially designed to be towed behind a destroyer or other large vessel; sufficient cable length minimized the amount of sound the hydrophone sensors would pick up from the ship's own propellers and machinery, the advantage being that the vessel could continue the chase, listening while underway. Although the tactics had evolved to make the small 110-foot subchasers effective hunters, their SC-tube and K-tube devices required the hunting groups to stop and drift with the current in order to listen for a submarine.

The K-tube, which consisted of a metal frame with a hydrophone mounted at each corner, was designed to be set overboard and follow well behind as the chaser drifted with the current (see page 129). The listener, as described in chapter 14, selected any pair of hydrophones; with his electrical compensator he could determine the approximate bearing of the sound source. In order to tow such a device, it was necessary to streamline the triangular framework using metal piping, creating what was referred to as the OK-tube, intended to be towed by vessels as well as airships. In the spring, a lightweight OK-tube was tested from an airship traveling between four and five knots, tracking a submerged submarine at a range of 1000 yards.[16]

Its success led to the development of the OV-tube, where the frame was made of wood and much lighter than the metal OK-tube. These devices were developed at the Nahant station for use by surface ships and airships, examples having been provided to the New London experimental station where the photos on the following two pages were taken. For all of these towed devices being tested in Long Island Sound, the delicate hydrophones were protected within streamlined housings. The housings also minimized unwanted sound, known as "flow noise," produced as the device was towed through the water.

Submarines were also outfitted with a variation of the OV-tube design. These streamlined Y-tube devices were rigidly secured to the hull, both far forward on the deck for operation while submerged, as well as on the keel when surfaced (shown on page 197).

Another device based on the three-hydrophone K-tube was referred to as the OS-tube. Unlike the OK-tube, where the hydrophones were mounted on a metal tubular frame, the OS-tube consisted of a metal "spreader" from which three separate cables ran to each hydrophone encased in their individual, hydrodynamically-shaped housings. When the vessel was underway, the three hydrophones would tow in the required triangular arrangement. Although there is no indication as to where the 210 OS-tube units that were built were eventually shipped, each one was tested at Nahant "before shipment."[17]

The second device Admiral Griffin referred to was the "electric eel" (shown on page 199). Recalling the MB-tube with twelve sensors, the engineers used similar hydrophones housed in a long, flexible rubber hose (an elongated wooden version was also tried), where, again, the signals from six of them were sent to the listener's right ear and the other six to his left ear. The difference, however, was that the MB-tube listener rotated the line of hydrophones until the sounds were equal in each ear. In contrast,

Left: *An OK-tube with its streamlined metal tube framework. Below Left: A 4-point towed device with a hydrophone at all four corners, allowing for one to fail and still operational with the three remaining sensors. (Hayes Family Archive)*

276

Right: *A streamlined wooden-framed OV-tube. These were designed to be towed by airships as well as destroyers.*
Below Right: *Another OV-tube shown with a dirigible airframe and the electric compensator. (Hayes Family Archive) The inset photo shows the streamlined pod opened with the hydrophone. This is from the one remaining OV device, which is located at the Naval Undersea Warfare Center (NUWC), Newport, Rhode Island. (Courtesy NUWC)*

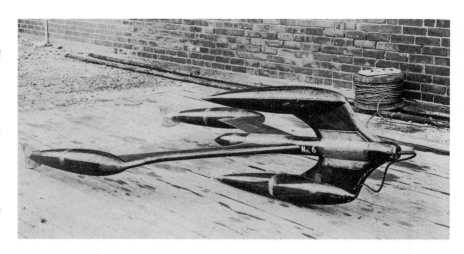

Left: *The Y-tube listening device mounted at the submarine bow. Note the streamlined housings designed to reduce flow noise across the hydrophones.* (Stockbridge 1920) Below: *Submarines were also provided with a keel-mounted Y-tube for use when surfaced; this one installed on USS G-1 for testing in Long Island Sound. Note the opened hatch at left used to enable a diver to exit the submarine.* (Hayes Family Archive)

the line of hydrophones in the electric eel always moved in the direction of the vessel or aircraft. A compensator (chapter 20), similar to those used for the PB-tube, as well as those for the K-tube and towable variants, was designed that would adjust for the time that the sound signal would take to reach each of the electric eel's twelve hydrophones. The amount of adjustment, or "compensation," necessary to put the signal in phase for the line of hydrophones, was an indication of the direction (or bearing angle) of the submarine.

Harvey Hayes had worked with George W. Pierce on the eel concept. Hayes saw the potential use of the towable eel for destroyers, where a pair of them would be towed astern. With only a single eel, there was the ever present problem of determining if the sound source was on the port or starboard side, referred to as the left/right ambiguity. Compensators used with eel systems were able to tell the listener if the sound source was forward or aft of the device, but not from which side the submarine was traveling. By towing a pair of eels, the operator was able to determine which eel received the sound waves first, thus whether port or starboard. The pair of eels, which Hayes referred to as the U3-tube, was towed at depths up to one hundred feet, depending on the amount of tow cable used.[18] Single eels, however, continued to be tested on aircraft. The goal was to detect the presence of a submarine, the information then radioed to a nearby subchaser or destroyer, which would conduct the pursuit and attack.

Several variations of the electric eel were carried out onto Long Island Sound by an HS-2 flying boat (facing page) as well as on a dirigible (see page 200), much of that work occurring in the summer of 1918. In June, Ernest Merritt reported the following to the Special Board, indicating the difficulties his colleague, Professor G. W. Pierce, was having: "[T]he plans are made for the dirigible device. [Professor Pierce] said that the weight was about 100 lbs; that it would require 500 feet of cable and that this would weigh about half of that . . . He also stated that microphones are holding him back; that the best delivery he can get will be the 22nd of June." The problem seems to have been corrected a week later, when Merritt reported that Pierce "had two 12 unit eels but that he has microphones for making more."[19]

Whether on a ship or in the cockpit of a flying boat or dirigible, the listener, unencumbered by the device now deployed and streaming aft, could readily adjust the compensator until the sound heard in both ears was maximized. The flying boat could taxi on the surface, while the dirigible was able to hover above the surface, lower the OV-tube or electric eel, and then slowly move forward under power.

The capabilities of the listeners, whether operating from ships or aircraft, rapidly improved in the spring, as did the devices available to them. Patent 1,482,980 for the OV-tube, referred to as a "Direction Detector for Submarine Sounds," was filed by Richard D. Fay of Nahant, Massachusetts, in June, 1919, and issued on February 5, 1924: "My invention relates to the reception of compressional or sound waves and an apparatus embodying it . . . especially designed to receive submarine signals or the noises originating in submarine or other vessels, seen or unseen." There remains a single example of this device, now at the Naval Undersea Warfare Center in Newport, Rhode Island.

Left: *One of several Eel towed devices tested on aircraft and ships. Note the tow cable is 425 feet long.* Below Left: *Another Eel ready for testing by an HS-2 Flying Boat.* (Hayes Family Archive)

Although there was a great deal of experimental work on Long Island Sound with aircraft and listeners, as well as some airship tests performed around Britain, there were those ever present difficulties associated with landing on rough water and the equal uncertainties that the plane could take off. Being stranded on the ocean surface would not have been an option. In practice, seaplanes, flying boats, and airships in the war zone served primarily and most effectively as spotters, often as aerial convoy escorts. Listeners remained aboard hunting vessels or listened from shore.

Fuselage on Dirigible No. 237.

An Electric Eel installed along the fuselage adjacent to the aft cockpit of the B-class "No.237" dirigible. (Hayes Family Archive)

CHAPTER 20 THE CRAZY AMERICAN–U-BOATS BEWARE

Mason and other scientists at the Naval Experiment Station at New London, Connecticut, worked feverishly to perfect the device, then called the M-V tube. Once it was adapted for seagoing conditions, the decision was made to equip vessels in the war zone with it. Mason went to France to supervise its installation and to instruct crews in its use. In France he found a golf course, and became known as the 'crazy American who played golf and solved submarine problems between holes.'

—Caryn Hannon, *Wisconsin Biographical Dictionary*, 2008[1]

Although Max Mason began his MV-tube installations in England, the lure of golf courses along the French coast would have been an enticement for Mason as he moved his efforts across the Channel, which could be readily accomplished; many vessels regularly brought passengers to and from French ports. There were several options, as golf seemed to be a common diversion from the rigors of the war, the following (from a 1920 golfing magazine) being surprisingly close to the Western Front:

It is not generally known that his lordship [General Sir Douglas Haig] during the critical and black periods from 1915 to 1918 used to steal away from the headquarters to the links at Le Touquet to seek fresh inspiration and renewed confidence. No one will ever know what part those fateful rounds on the French links played in the destinies of the British Empire. But it may be assumed that the Commander-in-Chief came away with a clearer vision and the clouds of doubt rolled away.[2]

It appears that Mason was easily distracted, particularly in his younger years as a university student. According to Daniel Kevles (1978): "[Mason's] seemingly effortless talents had gone more into chess, golf, bridge, the violin, and billiards than into research." Yet, as Kevles continued, Mason, "with swift insight [had] suggested replacing the blisterlike Walzer apparatus with a horizontal row of short capped pipes, or Broca tubes, connected by more piping to an earphone." Mason's "swift insight" was the basis of the listening devices he was installing on destroyers in England and France.[3]

After nearly a year, Max Mason, working with several other members of the experimental station staff in New London, had finally proven the ability of his device to detect a submerged submarine while the ship was underway. It would no longer be necessary to stop a vessel, deploy a device, listen, and then head off to another position and repeat the process. For larger vessels, as with destroyers, hunting while underway was a necessary improvement.

Two horizontal arrays of sensors had been mounted port and starboard near the bow of vessels assigned to the station, including *Narada* (SP-161), the destroyers *Jouett* (DD-41) and *Aylwin* (DD-47), as well as the torpedo boat *Blakely* (TB-27), which can be seen alongside USS *Margaret*, page 127. To protect the device and minimize flow noise over the surface of the sensors, the entire length of the device was enclosed in what Mason referred to as a "blister." *Jouett*, running at seven knots, was able to detect a submarine at a range of 2400 yards. By the spring of 1918, "tests of a blister MV resulted in its adoption for our destroyers abroad. . ."[4] The upper image on the facing page shows a section of an MV-tube installation in progress on an unidentified vessel; also shown is another MV-tube installation along the keel of the submarine *G-2*.

> The installation of an MV-tube on a destroyer [in Navy shipyards] was done normally in a week's time. . . . After the device was made standard equipment for destroyers outfitting in the United States, the writer [Max Mason] was sent to England.[5]
>
> During the summer of 1918 the writer was engaged with the destroyers and chasers of the United States Navy in European waters, installations being made in English dockyards. . . . The work was done under direct control of Captain R. H. Leigh, head of the anti-submarine division of the Navy in European waters, whose cordial and complete co-operation stimulated all to maximum effort.[6]

After the war, Captain Leigh praised Mason's MV-tube "as the best listening device, with which I have had experience, for destroyers."[7] American destroyers began arriving at the naval base in Queenstown [now Cobh], Ireland, in the spring of 1917. There were, however, no listening devices associated with these vessels, as the work at Nahant and New London had only recently begun. It would be the following year before Mason and others began the installation of hull-mounted listening devices on U.S. destroyers, and those of the Allies. The destroyer *Jouett* had been

Left:
Installation of MV-tube near the keel of a steel hulled ship (possibly Jouett (DD-41)). Below Left: *Another MV installation along the keel of the submarine G-2. The acoustic sensors of these devices were of the "Broca tube" design with flexible rubber caps at the ends of the rigid tubing. The MV-tube devices would be enclosed in a protective housing or "blister."* (Hayes Family Archive)

assigned to support experimental work in New London, later being involved with submarine patrols along the east coast when U-boats began arriving in the summer (chapter 22). The *Aylwin* (shown on page 48), for example, had been conducting experimental work with submarine detection devices at both Nahant and New London, and sailed for the American destroyer base at Queenstown in January, 1918, possibly carrying Mason's device. In the meantime, the naval base along the French coast at Brest was expanding, and as fuel storage tanks and repair ships were brought from the U.S., this became the strategic base for destroyers tasked to escort American troopships.[8]

The acoustic MV-tube Mason had designed, and Captain Leigh praised as "the best listening device" for destroyers, was a complicated piece of hardware. Daniel Kevles provided a concise description of the operation of this device: "Transmitted through the pipes, a sound from the water would lose very little energy, and simply by varying the pipe lengths until the sound was loudest, a listener could determine with considerable accuracy the direction from which the noise was coming."[9]

In practice, however, "simply varying the pipe lengths" was not so simple. Mason and his colleagues spent months creating a device that allowed the listener to adjust the pipe lengths, such that the sounds from each "Broca tube" sensor would arrive at the listener's ears "in phase," thus at maximum intensity. This was not an issue for the rotatable SC-and MB-tubes, as the listener turned the device by hand; when the sound was loudest, the sound source was perpendicular to the horizontal arm of the apparatus. Acoustic listening devices rigidly mounted on a ship's hull could not be rotated, and the targeted submarine was almost never perpendicular to the line of sensors. The instrument that maximized the signal strength reaching the listener's ears was referred to as an "acoustic compensator," which had its origins in New London with Max Mason (Chapter 13).[10]

Listening devices, where the sound path was through multiple air-filled tubes to an acoustic compensator, included Mason's hull-mounted MV-tubes. His acoustic MB-and MF-tubes, being rotatable devices, did not require a compensator.[11] Care was also taken by the experimental station engineers to minimize extraneous audible distractions that might affect the quality of the sound reaching the listener's ears. "The compensator . . . was placed in the listening booth, a small compartment with sound proof walls, directly above the keelson and at the middle of the lines. The connecting tubes were held on sound-insulated mountings, and the compensator was supported on a sound-insulating spring suspension of a type devised by Professor Bridgman. Communication with the bridge was furnished by a voice tube."[12] Before Mason was able to optimize his design, a monumental effort was underway at the station:

> Thousands of tests were made on hundreds of types of sound receivers. The spacing of receivers, their position on the ship and the method of mounting, the size of conducting tubes, methods of sound insulation, all received detailed study. Compensators of widely different design were tested, before a combination of acoustic excellence with mechanical simplicity was reached.[13]

Binaural acoustic compensator assembled (at top) with its upper grooved component (left) and the mating surface (right). (Hayes, 1920)

What Max Mason designed was referred to as progressive compensation.[14] The goal was to ensure that the time it would take for the sound from each acoustic sensor to reach the listener's ears would be in phase, thus of equal (and maximum) intensity. The length of the sound paths had to be easily adjusted by the operator. Mason demonstrated the concept using a binaural device, consisting of two acoustic sensors. His assembled compensator is shown at the top of the above figure. Its upper plate (image, bottom left), which could be rotated by the hand-wheel, contained two concentric grooves; when assembled, the raised blocks on the fixed lower plate (bottom right) fit snugly into the grooves of the upper plate. As the operator rotated the upper plate, the length of the grooved path on one side of the blocks shortened the acoustic path from one sensor, at the same time lengthening the acoustic path along the groove on the other side of the blocks. Visible at the perimeter of the lower plate are two short tubes that run from either side of the longer block; these connected to the tubes coming from the binaural sensors. The two horizontal tubes running from either side of the shorter block directed the compensated sound to flexible hoses (not shown) of stethoscope headgear worn by the listener.

Using Mason's binaural device as an example, sound waves produced by a submarine transiting in the distance crossed the two sensors at slightly different times, depending on the position of the submarine relative to the path of the listening ship. Only when the submarine was perpendicular to the ship did the sound waves cross the sensors at the same time, and only under this condition would an acoustic compensator be unnecessary. A listener would hear the sound in both ears at a maximum level because the sound waves arrived in phase. As the angle, or bearing, of the submarine increased, there would be an increasing time delay as the sound waves passed the two sensors in succession. The sound, now increasingly "out of phase," resulted in lesser net intensity at the listener, reaching a minimum when the submarine was dead ahead.

As mentioned above, turning the hand-wheel increased the groove length—thus the total path—from one sensor and decreased the groove length for the other sensor. The net difference in the groove lengths compensated for the time delay between the two sensors, ensuring that the sound arrived at each ear in phase. The difference in the groove lengths was a measure of the direction, or bearing, to the sound source—the target, a U-boat. The bearing was then read from marks on the top surface of the upper plate. The more sensors Mason used, a commensurate number of grooves were required—two sensors, two grooves; four sensors, four grooves, and so on; the complexity of the compensator followed suit. A Type "H" multi-layered acoustic compensator[15] (facing page) was typical of those used with Mason's MV-tubes designed for installation on destroyers heading to the war.

When listening devices incorporated microphone-based hydrophones rather than the acoustic sensors used with Mason's MV-tubes, an "electrical compensator" was needed. Examples included the sea-bottom-mounted tripod (chapter 22, page 236), the K-tube (page 129) and its towable variants (pages 195 and 196), the aircraft PB-tube (page 188), and the electric eel (pages 199 and 200). Mason also incorporated hydrophones in his multi-element "M"-type devices.

Above: *The four layers of a Type "H" multi-sensor acoustic compensator.* Left: *The assembled Type "H" used by listeners on destroyers. The two outlet tubes that connect to the listener's stethoscope are visible at the left of the center component.* (Hayes Family Archive)

The development of an electric M-V tube on principles corresponding to the straight acoustic M-V was undertaken at New London by Professors G. W. Pierce and H. C. Hayes. Special microphones served as individual receivers. Their electrical outputs were compensated on the plan of progressive compensation of the acoustic M-V, the required time lags being introduced to proper amounts by the aid of a switch which passed the current from each receiver through an artificial line giving the required retardation. Compensation was not continuous but in small steps.[16]

One method of stepped compensation developed at the Naval Experimental Station was accomplished with multiple time delay circuits and a dial that allowed the operator to switch from one circuit to another. Adjusting the time delay until the hydrophone signals were in phase provided the listener with the bearing to the target. The complexity of the circuitry increased with the number of hydrophones, as with the electric eel, for example, with a total of twelve.[17]

Simple yet very effective listening systems were those with hydrophones in a triangular arrangement, also known as "three-point" detectors (for example, the K-tube for subchasers and the PB-tube for aircraft). The operator switched from one pair of hydrophones to another in order to listen within 120-degree sectors, thus only requiring compensation between two hydrophones to obtain a precise bearing.

Harvey Hayes tested an electric MV device during an Atlantic crossing on USS *Von Steuben* (ID-3017), a transport ship bringing troops home after Armistice. He discovered that the line of hydrophones mounted on the ship's hull also detected the ship's own machinery noise reflected off the bottom, resulting in the concept of using the MV design as a fathometer.[18] Admiral Sims, in a post-war letter to the Secretary of the Navy regarding the Naval Experimental Station, praised the MV apparatus, "which has proven in service that listening could be carried out in exceptional cases with the listening ship making twenty knots. . . This apparatus has proven its utility as a navigation instrument as well as a means of detecting submarines."[19]

Spring of 1918 was a busy time in New London and on nearby Long Island Sound, where the experimental station staff and naval personnel were constantly at work developing the next best U-boat detector, and where listeners practiced their craft.

> Several different types of devices were perfected for use on Destroyers and Sub-chasers. Stationary [hull mounted] devices were found to be best for Destroyers while the smaller vessels carried both stationary and portable devices.[20]

Ensign James Bean, who had completed the hydrophone school for officers in 1918, was familiar with the "stationary and portable devices" being tested for use on destroyers, subchasers, submarines, and aircraft. As more and more subchasers arrived in the Thames River, some were assigned directly for support of the experimental station, while others were there specifically for operational training prior to their Atlantic crossing. By the summer of 1918, both the listeners' school, previously at the submarine base, and the new hydrophone school were located on New London's State Pier, where most of the subchasers were berthed.[21]

Ensign Hilary R. Chambers, who served as commanding officer of *SC-128* and later executive officer on *SC-215*, wrote about his time in New London in a memoir, published in 1920.

> At New London the State Pier was the base for these little motor boats. As soon as they had been equipped, the training of the men began. Each week day morning the officers and crews were assembled in a large room on the "second deck" of the pier, as it was nautically termed, and submarine exercises were gone through.
>
> In the afternoon, units practiced just outside the harbor by chasing one of our own submarines, both on the surface and submerged. If a submarine was not available another chaser answered the purpose as a noise maker to give the listeners practice. When finally a number of boats and crews were thought to be sufficiently equipped and trained they were sent down to Bermuda under convoy of ocean-going tugs or battleships. The first detachment left about March 20th and the second at the end of the month.[22]

As the commanding officer of *SC-128*, Chambers was in the group that departed New London in March, 1918, "at the end of the month." The chasers from his group, which was headed for the subchaser base at the Greek island of Corfu,[23] was actually the third detachment heading overseas, the first having left New London in February. Chambers described subchasers in detail, including the submarine detection devices his crew had been trained to use:

> Amidships are the listening devices. These are the S. C. and M. B. tubes. They are inverted T's with ears at each end of the horizontal. Sound is transmitted to these ears from the water and follow tubing to the listener, who wears a stethoscope head apparatus. When this lower part is turned perpendicularly to the bearing of the sound, the noise is transmitted binorally [sic], of the same intensity in each ear, or centered.[24]

The simple listening devices that Chambers mentioned, the SC-and MB-tubes, required the listener to lower and rotate the vertical section of the "T," which passed through the hull, such that the pair or line of multiple sensors could turn below the keel. When the direction of the sound source was determined, and the bearing transmitted to the flagship of the hunting group, the SC-or MB-tubes were pulled up against the hull and secured within a protective housing (shown on page 249). Once the bearings were plotted, the chaser unit sped to the location indicated by the plotting device, and the process repeated. When the submarine was determined to be below or near the flagship, depth charges, had this been in the war zone, would be dropped from the three vessels in the unit. This was the scenario the subchaser units practiced—over, and over, and over—until, as Chambers mentioned, "a number of boats and crews were thought to be sufficiently equipped and trained," and were sent overseas.

To respond to the German submarine commanders' penchant for stealth, more than acoustics was necessary. Lieutenant Junior Grade (LTJG) William W. Nutting, who was involved with naval construction, described a different technology these submarine chasers would carry across the Atlantic:

TRAILING WIRE

> Still another detection device with which the S.C.'s were equipped was called the 'Trailer," the purpose of which was to detect the presence of a submerged submarine when lying idly on the bottom as was frequently their custom. No type of listening device would help in such a case and so the trailer was designed to establish an electrolytic action and ring a buzzer in the pilot house when contact was made with the steel hull of the submarine.[25]

Early in the war, U-boat commanders realized that they could rest their submarine on the bottom to avoid detection by the hydrophones used by allied vessels—a non-acoustic approach was needed. With no sounds emanating from the sub, the hunters could only assume that the submarine had escaped the limited range of the hydrophones or had, as was certainly a possibility, settled onto the bottom. Unable to detect the U-boat, the listeners would abandon their search.[26] The submarine, however, listened with its own hydrophones as the noisy hunters faded into the distance, and after time had passed, would surface and resume their course.

It was in November, 1917; *U-62*, under the command of Ernst Hashagen, had bottomed at a depth of 150 feet one night near the southern coast of Britain to avoid detection. In his memoir, Hashagen described their night, listening to British ships patrolling overhead. But *U-62* remained quiet, and there were no telltale sounds coming through the hunters' hydrophones;

the ships moved on. Prior to surfacing, *U-62*'s coxswain listened with their hydrophones; the ocean above them was quiet. The submarine surfaced in the pre-dawn darkness and proceeded beyond the English Channel, charging her batteries. At sunrise, *U-62* submerged to periscope depth and patrolled quietly for its next unsuspecting target.[27]

This common evasive tactic registered with the civilian engineers who were faced with developing submarine detection technology. In the United States, where listening devices dominated the efforts, this tactic was certainly recognized as a problem. The mission of the Navy's Special Board on Antisubmarine Devices was "to further the development of any apparatus or device which would assist in the detection of enemy submarines . . . Most of the devices developed through the agency of the special board were based on the principal of detection through the water of the noises given off from the submarine." But the Special Board also recognized that "[a] second fundamental problem was that of detecting a 'silent' submarine, either lying on the bottom or operating at its most silent speed, which rendered detection by sound almost impossible."[28]

Dr. Ernest Merritt, at the Experimental Station in New London, had been involved throughout the war with the problem of detecting a bottomed submarine. One device, produced by Western Electric Co., was referred to as a "trawling apparatus" and later the "trailing wire," intended for installation on subchasers. A length of phosphor-bronze wire, weighted at its end, was lowered from a reel mounted near the stern and dragged across the bottom. When the wire crossed over a submarine, contact between the steel hull and the wire caused a small electrical current to pass along the wire to a receiver mounted in the pilot house. The current would trigger a buzzer, which alerted the crew that contact was made.[29] There were several variations of the trailing wire developed in New London. A typical subchaser installation is shown on page 213.

During the summer of 1917, when the New London scientists worked from the submarine base, Merritt produced a general test plan for each day's activities. At this time, the station's vessel *Thetis* (SP-391) provided the platform for installation of the rudimentary devices being evaluated. One of the devices scheduled for testing was the trailing wire, as Merritt described in a test plan that included *Thetis* and the submarine *G-4*, on August 28, 1917: "The 'Thetis' and G-4 will sail at 11 o'clock and proceed to a point about a mile and a half north of Race Rock. Both should be provided with rations for lunch." The plan for that day would begin with a series of acoustic tests presided over by Max Mason, who was anxious to continue his development of the modified Walzer listening device, followed by tests of the trawling apparatus. Merritt continued:

> [After completing the acoustic tests,] G-4 will proceed to some point where the depth is as much as 60 feet. She will submerge and lie on the bottom for 30 minutes. During the time that she is on the bottom everything should be stopped if possible, except the gyro compass and its generator. The G-4 will put up a telephone buoy and the dory of "Thetis" will lie alongside this buoy and keep in communication with the G-4
>
> The "Thetis" is to pass over the G-4, one or more times, dragging behind her, weighted wires, intended to touch the G-4 and indicate her presence. For a portion of the time, the "Thetis" will lie over the G-4 at rest, making certain tests. The G-4 will be careful to notify the observer in the dory before coming up and if the telephone should fail to act properly, signal by six strokes on the submarine's bell before starting to come up, the signal being repeated several times.[30]

Safety of all the vessels participating in the experimental work was always of concern, and communication was essential. The buoy mentioned in Merritt's test plan was carried as an emergency device. In the event a disabled submarine became stranded on the bottom, the crew would release the buoy, showing her position and allowing contact between the sub and a rescue vessel. U.S. submarines were also outfitted with a signaling bell, which could be used while submerged for communicating with surface ships as well as other submarines as shown installed on *E-1*, page 148.

Additional tests of the trawling apparatus were made throughout the following week, and the results passed to Commander McDowell in Merritt's weekly report. During that week, the submarine *D-1* joined *G-4* in the testing.

> A test was made on August 31, to see whether it was practicable to detect a submarine lying on the bottom by dragging with a copper wire and copper sinker, contact with the submarine to be indicated electrically by the e.m.f. developed in the circuit copper—iron of hull—sea water. The first two trials, with the D-1 submerged at 60 feet were successful. In each case, contact was indicated definitely by a bell operated through a relay.[31]

The trawling apparatus, or trailing wire device, was among technologies brought to England in December, 1917, by Captain Leigh and a

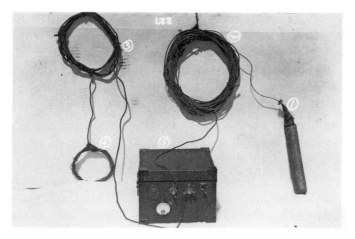

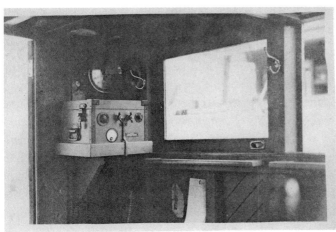

Top and Middle: *The cabling and weight of the trailing wire, with the electronics box installed in the pilot house.* (Hayes Family Archive) Bottom: *The cable drums and weights for a pair of trailing wires on the aft deck of a subchaser.* (Courtesy Todd Woofenden)

team of engineers, representing the various devices thus far developed at Nahant and New London. After Captain Leigh's team had apparently successfully detected, tracked, and attacked a U-boat, the trailing wire was towed in the area and when contact was made, a buoy was set to mark the location. The following morning, a second trawl again indicated the presence of the U-boat, and all were confident that they had destroyed the submarine. That confidence, however, was later disproved when records indicated that no U-boats were sunk during that time. (See chapter 16 for the complete story.)

By early 1918, the trailing wire was ready for service overseas. Ensign Hilary R. Chambers, who left New London at the end of March on *SC-128*, mentioned the trailing wire among the devices carried on subchasers: "There are also two large drums of copper wire that can be trailed over the stern. By means of an electric attachment a bell rings in the chart house when this wire comes in contact with the metal of a submarine lying on the bottom."[32] Trailing wire components, as described by Ensign Chambers, are shown on the previous page.

For the tenacious U-boat, there would be no escape, whether stalking yet another merchant ship or quietly hiding on the bottom. By the spring of 1918, the Allied navies carried many new technologies to locate, track, and destroy the relentless predator.

The trailing wire was not the only piece of electronic technology developed at Nahant and New London, though likely the simplest. The civilian and military staff of the various experimental stations, under the direction of the Special Board on Antisubmarine Devices, raced to bring a variety of recent scientific discoveries and technological marvels to the Navy. The civilian staff—most having been college professors—readily participated with their naval colleagues in aircraft, under the sea in submarines, and on the sea, working under conditions expected when these vessels crossed the Atlantic.

The chaser crew on *SC-253* trained at New London throughout the winter and spring, experiencing the brutal winter winds on Long Island Sound. Her commanding officer, Ensign George Wallace, often carried civilian scientists, whom he referred to as "Long Hairs," during experimental trials. With little prior sea time, chaser crews and the Long Hairs who joined them were not prepared for the seas riled up by the March winds. "In those days," as Wallace recalled, "few of us had our sea stomachs, and many a seaman locked arms with a civilian inventor or two over the rail."[33] Max Mason wasn't the only crazy American who crossed the Atlantic—subchaser crews would venture out in their 110-foot wooden vessels onto a remorseless ocean, bound for uncertain encounters with an invisible enemy.

Friday night [submarines] are going to operate in Block Island
Sound in the afternoon, and along towards sundown, a group
of probably 8 Chasers are going to take up a blockade across the
Sound between Race Rock and Montauk Point. The chasers are
all equipped with K-tubes. The SC-6 will be equipped with "MF"
and "MB" [tubes] and the D-3 will follow the Chasers. There
will be six submarines trying to get through. The Chasers will be
equipped with radio telephone and blinker sets. . . The SC 6 and
SC 19 will have lightless signals.

—Ernest Merritt, April 10, 1918[1]

I n the spring of 1918, a simulated blockade of the entrance to Long
Island Sound would find a group of eight subchasers outfitted with
multiple submarine detection systems, the chasers operating across an
approximately sixteen mile wide area between Race Rock and Montauk
Point. In this tactical exercise, six submarines were to attempt to pass undetected beneath the "blockade," gaining entry through the deep water channel into the Sound, which was a principle route for ships heading from New
York to Europe. Note that the blockade was to begin "towards sundown."
The chasers were to listen on their K-tubes, a standard device carried by
chasers en route to the war zone. One of the chasers, *SC-6*, would use the
more sophisticated MB-and MF-tubes.

The sixteen mile blockade meant that there could be nearly two miles between each vessel, providing gaps through which a submarine might quietly
pass. For a group of chasers listening for submarines, it was essential that
any submarine contact made by one of the chasers be quickly transmitted
to other chasers. Communication between the chasers was to be primarily
via radio telephone; as a backup, the blinker sets could transmit Morse code
signals between vessels. At night, an enemy submarine on the surface could
intercept the radio signals, thus having direct knowledge of the activities
of the hunting groups, and if close by, the bright lights of the blinkers were

certainly visible. There was, however, one more piece of newly-developed technology— "lightless signals"—being tested for night operations. *SC-6* would be in direct contact with *SC-19,* both of these vessels having been assigned to the experimental station. Their primary mission was exclusively for experimental work, though *SC-6* would soon find itself hunting U-boats off America's coast.

The tactical exercise above was described by Ernest Merritt to the Special Board on Antisubmarine Devices at a meeting on April 10, 1918. Whether the submarines managed to evade the subchaser blockade is not among the papers in Professor Merritt's archives, nor was there any mention of the success of the various technologies including the lightless signals. Everything being tested and evaluated was handled as highly classified information. Even after the war, only vague references to this were published. A caption to an illustration in the 1921 book *War Work of the Bureau of Standards* made this perfectly clear:

> This [infrared signaling] system is the most secret of all means of conveying messages and has been developed to a practical point. It is impossible for the enemy to detect and intercept such messages.[2]

The problem, according to Admiral Griffin in *The History of the Bureau* (1922), was to find "a means for signaling at night between vessels of a hunting group and between different vessels in convoy, without the possibility of detection by an enemy." Few details were mentioned by Griffin, other than a communication device had been developed "utilizing invisible light rays which had a range of about 5 miles in the type adopted for smaller vessels," likely referring to subchasers.[3] Griffin's "invisible light" was in the infrared range. Ultraviolet waves were dismissed after experiments were conducted at the Bureau of Standards, which emphasized that "radio-telegraphy and telephony can be detected and interfered with, but the device for the secret transmission of intelligence by means of invisible thermal radiations, while still in its infancy, stands unique . . ."[4]

While the Bureau of Standards was involved with investigating both ultraviolet and infrared transmit and receive devices, the most successful system was one developed by Theodore W. Case, working at the Naval Experimental Station. Case graduated from Yale in 1912, and eventually established the Case Research Laboratory with his father Willard in Auburn, New York. He had been experimenting with substances which created an electrical current when subjected to light, eventually finding that thallium sulfide was sensitive to infrared waves, well beyond that visible to the human eye. In 1917, Case joined the staff in New London, where he began work on adapting a

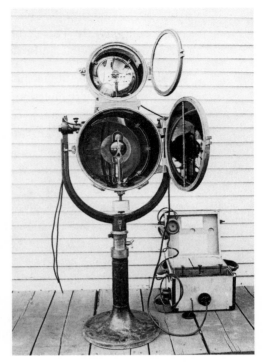

Left: *One of the Infrared (IR) signaling devices developed at the Naval Experimental Station. The dots and dashes of Morse code sent with infrared light were converted to electronic pulses for the signalman to hear.* Right: *Another IR signaling device.* (Hayes Family Archive)

vacuum tube he developed containing thallium sulfide, which he called his "Thalofide Cell," to a signaling device; the electrical current from the cell producing audible dots and dashes.[5] Now able to send those Morse code dots and dashes between vessels, a signalman on *SC-6*, for example, could send messages throughout the night to *SC-19* regarding the location of one of those submarines attempting to enter Long Island Sound.

Case was eventually able to transmit voice messages across his infrared system. Those employed at his laboratory in Auburn were warned that their work "was of a secret nature and would do grievous injury to the United States Government and its Allies in the present war if it should become known. Doing so would constitute a form of treason to the United States Government."[6]

MORE INVISIBLE WAVES

[T]he seaman in charge of the pigeons had made pets of them and fed them too well. . . . a 'C' class submarine tried to report by carrier-pigeon, to find that they had been so over-fed by their keeper that they could not fly. They fell into the sea, and were rescued with considerable trouble and risk."[7]

This story by British submariner Lieutenant Commander Kenneth Edwards (1939) emphasized the need for submarine-to-shore communication. A submarine's mission was often to covertly enter an enemy's waters hundreds of miles from home and gather intelligence about their naval activities. With a very limited ability to communicate with its home port, a submarine had to depend on a technology that dates back thousands of years to the Egyptian and Persian empires—the carrier pigeon. Navies of the twentieth century consisted of massive fleets of dreadnaughts, battleships and destroyers, and now submarines. Rapid communication between vessels and with shore was necessary for success in a naval engagement, which may span great expanses of ocean far from the chain of command at the Admiralty in London. A new technology was needed, one which would not require a submarine to carry a supply of bird seed.

On land, telegraphy across many miles of wire was well established during the nineteenth century, providing a valuable link among field commanders during the Civil War. Morse code, a system of dots and dashes representing letters and numbers, became a dependable post-war method of communicating information along wires that stretched across and between countries. Passing messages over a wire must have been a strange concept at first, but there was a physical link between the sender and the receiver. To anyone, even a visionary scientist, the concept of sending the same information through thin air across hundreds of miles would have been laughed at as an absurdity, worthy of nothing more than a chapter in a Jules Verne novel.

It wasn't until the pioneering work of Guglielmo Marconi, Nikola Tesla, and Heinrich Hertz in the 1880s and 1890s that a wireless system of transmitting those same dots and dashes using "Hertzian waves" was developed. Marconi patented his device in 1897, operating in a portion of the electromagnetic spectrum at frequencies well below those associated with light, specifically radio waves. Within a few years, wireless systems became a common feature on board ships. When the Titanic struck an iceberg in 1912, the distress signal was transmitted, not by an employee of the Cunard Line, but by a member of the Marconi International Marine Communications Company.

During the winter of 1902 to 1903, Frederick Stockbridge, author of *Yankee Ingenuity in the War* (1920), spent time with Marconi at his transatlantic wireless station at Cape Breton, Canada. The incredible feat impressed Stockbridge, who declared that the "inventor's imagination had projected itself so far beyond the bounds of anything with which the world was familiar that his dream savored of the supernatural," later jokingly cautioning Marconi with the story of "Salem's famous witchcraft trials and executions."[8]

The United States Navy was quick to see the importance of Marconi's invention and rushed to incorporate wireless technology throughout the fleet. Germany was no different. As the stalemate along the western front continued, and submarine warfare became a significant element of German strategy, wireless communication between a U-boat on patrol and its home port became a common practice. The German penchant for engaging in frequent messaging while at sea, however, made their operations vulnerable. Transmitting a wireless message was easily intercepted, and as "direction finding" technology improved, the general whereabouts of a submarine could be determined.

There was soon an even more significant addition to the world of wireless communications. On December 24, 1906, another scientist and inventor, Reginald Fessenden, a competitor of Marconi, successfully broadcast his voice over hundreds of miles to ships at sea from his transmitting station near Boston.[9] No longer was it necessary to use Morse code, although that system continues to this day. Very early in the war, a short range naval adaptation of Fessenden's wireless radio, produced by Western Electric Company, was installed on subchasers. The Navy, through the Bureau of Steam Engineering, had long recognized the need for rapid communication "in connection with a concerted attack by destroyers or other small craft in close formation," this several years before the concept of subchasers was considered.[10]

The wireless telephone system used by the Navy remained a tightly guarded secret. The story of a German spy operating in New London in 1917 is in chapter 14, which also includes a directive from the Special Board on Antisubmarine Devices to the Naval Experimental Station staff regarding the need for secrecy. These concerns continued throughout the war, with reminders sent to the experimental station staff, as with this one from June 12, 1918:

> Several instances have occurred when persons attached to this Station, (both officers and civilians) have been overheard in public places discussing features of the work underway.

This morning two civilians and one officer are reported as having discussed in a street car the question of changes in MB tubes.

Attention is called to the dangerous results which might accrue from any conversations in public places on any subject pertaining to National Defense work and all personnel attached to this Station will conduct themselves accordingly.[11]

A telephone school was established on the grounds of the station, in the building adjacent to the dogleg pier jutting into the Thames River (see the plan view of the Station, page 139). Wireless operators who had qualified in standard Morse code telegraphy at the Navy's Harvard Radio School in Cambridge, Massachusetts (not associated with the university), continued their training in anticipation of an assignment with a chaser unit.

After the war, and while a student at Stanford University, Ensign James Bean, who had attended the Harvard Radio School, wrote a lengthy description of the school in 1920, which survives as a manuscript at the Submarine Force Library and Museum in Groton, Connecticut.

After leaving Harvard Radio School, those who were sent to the Radio Telephone School at New London were given a four weeks intensive course in vacuum bulbs and radio telephone sets. Defects were purposely placed in the laboratory sets and the students were required to find and remedy such defects as a part of their examination.[12]

Radio telephones, a new technology and in limited supply, were provided to subchasers, where rapid, accurate communication between each vessel in a hunting group was essential. Thus these little vessels were given precedence over the much larger ships. Aircraft, however, were soon outfitted with this same technology.[13] Most naval ships were equipped with the Marconi wireless and depended on the operator's proficiency in Morse code. As the war progressed, destroyers and battleships also received the radio telephones, and with them an increasing need for qualified operators. Ensign Bean:

All submarine chasers and most of the larger naval vessels carry radio telephone sets so it was essential that operators assigned to these boats be thoroughly familiar with maintenance and repair as well as with the operation of telephone (radio) sets and spark sets. Three to six operators were assigned to each of the larger vessels.[14]

Because of the tactical importance of a system that could readily operate ship to ship up to ten miles, radio repair facilities were established at the subchaser bases at Queenstown, Plymouth, and at Corfu in the Mediterranean. Around one thousand of these radio telephone sets were built, and "were of inestimable value in the antisubmarine campaign."[15]

A Force to be Reckoned With

> The presence of a body beyond our reach can be detected by intercepting some form of energy radiating from the body or the presence of some field of force surrounding the body . . .[16]

In his 1920 report "Detection of Submarines" presented to the American Philosophical Society, Harvey Hayes began the discussion with two physical phenomena that were considered as solutions to Germany's unrestricted predation by their U-boats. Hayes distinguished acoustic "energy radiating from the body" from "some field of force surrounding the body," which he then explained: "The steel shell of the submarine must be surrounded by a magnetic field, due to polarization induced by the earth's magnetic field and also due to such permanent polarization as it may have taken on during construction."[17] In order to take advantage of the "steel shell of a submarine," another bit of scientific magic was necessary.

For millennia, the lodestone was one of nature's inexplicable mysteries, simply looked upon as a magician's curiosity. Its eventual use as a rudimentary compass led to a whole new era of maritime navigation and, subsequently, to theories about the Earth's magnetic field. Early in the nineteenth century, experiments demonstrated the relationship between magnetism and electricity, whereby an electric current passing through a coil of wire created a magnetic field around the coil. Conversely, a magnet passing through or across the coil induced a measureable electric current. A German submarine searching for its next target could be a 250-foot-long, 2,000 ton magnet moving through the ocean. It was now up to the scientists and engineers to develop a large enough coil, either a single one or several lying on the bottom at the entrance into a strategic harbor. If a U-boat crossed the coil, the electric current would trigger an audible alarm or a visual indication on an instrument known as a galvanometer for an observer on shore.

Submarine detection devices known as Bragg Indicator Loops (chapter 4), designed around this new technology called electromagnetics, had already been in use by the British and French when America entered the war. By 1918, similar devices were developed by the staff at New London working with Western Electric Company engineers, one of which is described in the next chapter. The detection range of these magnetic loop installations was very short when compared to acoustic detection. Yet, if a submarine, having perfected its silent running tactics, slowly approached a harbor, acoustic listening devices might not detect its transit. There was no amount of silencing, however, that would shield a U-boat from being detected if it passed over or near one of these coils. The effectiveness of this idea had been demonstrated during the war at shore installations along the English Channel and the Orkney Islands to the north (chapter 4).

From the point of view of the hunter, these magnetic detection loops were stationary defensive systems, operating often in conjunction with shore stations where listeners manned their acoustic devices. There was still the possibility of developing an offensive system using electromagnetics for detecting a submarine from a vessel actively hunting from the surface. The motivation, as with the trailing wire, was to locate a U-boat which was attempting to hide by sitting on the bottom, shutting down all noise-producing machinery. If discovered, the U-boat would be an easy target for a barrage of depth charges.

Thousands of concepts for tackling the submarine problem were submitted to the Navy by private citizens and from many American industries, finding their way to members of the National Research Council and the Naval Consulting Board. Most were wishful thinking and of little value; these were quickly filtered by the staffs of the experimental stations in New London and Nahant. At New London, those few considered potentially worthy of further consideration landed on the desk of Ernest Merritt, who had been assigned the primary responsibility to review the various ideas related to electromagnetic detection; he was at the same time developing his own device. Admiral Griffin (1922), highlighted two of these suggestions, giving few details due to the sensitive nature of the technology:

> Prof. [Vannevar] Bush, of the American Radio & Research Corporation, started investigations upon a magnetic method of detection of a quiet submarine early in 1917, and went to New London with the apparatus where a number of tests were conducted.
>
> Mr. B. G. Lamme, chief engineer of the Westinghouse Electric & Manufacturing Co., and a member of the Naval Consulting Board, undertook investigations upon the detection of submarines at rest, shortly before the United States declared war, and developed an experimental device at Pittsburg, Pa. After exhaustive tests over a period of several

months, the final product was brought to New London for further development and tests under actual sea conditions.[18]

The decision to proceed with an evaluation of any submarine detection idea was the responsibility of the Special Board on Antisubmarine devices, based also on the backgrounds of the staff and physical resources available at the experimental stations. Once that decision was made, Special Board secretary Commander C. S. McDowell expected periodic briefings. While many individual experiments were attempted with each system, Merritt's assignment was to eventually run comparison tests between two or more of these electromagnetic detectors, once each had demonstrated its potential. In the Merritt archive papers, his correspondence with McDowell emphasized his own design, although he certainly gave credit to systems that performed as well as or nearly as well as his.

> Prof. Merritt reported that a test was held on Monday [June 10] with balanced coils. The same submarine [*G-3*] was used as had been arranged for testing Mr. Bush's apparatus. The submarine submerged to 51 feet, and at that depth the loudness was very great. A great deal of time was spent in seeing how far [Merritt] could go off to one side to try to get the effect of crossing in different directions. . . . Said that he could get the submarine at 100 feet on both sides. Could not get it at 200 feet. The limiting range is somewhere between the two.[19]

By mid-June, Merritt's "balanced coil" device was ready for testing. The system consisted of two wire coils; one located fore and the other aft under the hull of the station's test vessel, *Thetis* (SP-391). An electric current was run through each coil, and when the test ship ran across or near the submarine hull, the magnetic fields would be affected and an additional electrical current imposed on the coil. As the vessel approached, the current increased, as did the loudness of a speaker which the operator was listening to. The two coils, fore and aft, would indicate when the ship had approached, passed across or near, and then left the submarine. The hunter did not have to pass directly over the submarine, and the tests thus determined how far the vessel could transit from the target and still hear the tone; in the case above, between 100 and 200 feet.

The minutes of that June 12 meeting also mentioned another test being planned for "Mr. Bush's apparatus," adding that: "Prof. Bush expects to make a preliminary test in 20 fathoms of water tomorrow. Said that the last few days had been spent in getting 'bugs' out of the installation." I wonder if that is where the phrase "getting the bugs out" originated, having heard and used those words frequently during my career.

There was no description of the Bush apparatus, but two weeks later, in a memo to McDowell, there were still those "bugs" that had to be fixed. His system had been installed on *SC-21*, and the last mention of this apparatus occurred when this chaser was involved with tests scheduled for October 4.[20]

Throughout June and July, Merritt continued testing his own balanced coil system on *Thetis*, improving its efficiency. Each experiment included the submarine *G-3* on the bottom at different depths, the data recorded on a chart showing the location of *G-3* and the transit paths of *Thetis*, as reported at the end of June: "Test #194, June 25, 1918 . . . Test of Balanced Coil Detector for locating submarine on the bottom."[21]

By August, Merritt was satisfied with what he had learned about his design, now officially designated as the AD-tube. He had also installed one of his systems on *SC-250*, and in an August 22 memo to McDowell, he anticipated shipping a system to England as soon as the next tests on *SC-250* were completed.[22] A typical data plot is shown on the facing page.

Those tests would require another three weeks, but when Commander McDowell was assigned to antisubmarine duty in the war zone, Merritt was able to report to McDowell's successor, Captain J. R. Defrees (see group photo page 144), that "a set for use on a 110 ft. wooden chaser has been built and sent abroad with Commander McDowell's party." Merritt noted that tests with *SC-250* were run in rough seas outside Montauk in order to simulate the conditions that would be encountered overseas.[23]

By the end of August, Merritt could switch his attention to comparison tests between his AD-tube and other designs. The British had already been experimenting with an electromagnetic system, referred to as the Mark IV Search Gear, which was on Merritt's list of potential systems to test. The standard Mark IV was comprised of two electrodes towed at a set distance apart, measuring what was referred to as "stray current" created between the electrodes when passing in the vicinity of a submarine sitting on the bottom. Merritt had immediately realized that this appeared to be a much less complex system than the balanced coil AD-tube. Yet, as soon as the engineers in New London got their hands on one of these systems, several modifications were included, hoping to improve its performance. Tests in September "confirmed the results from abroad." Merritt continued:

Left: SC-250 *underway on Long Island Sound where the electromagnetic submarine detection data (below) was collected and plotted.* (Merritt Papers, Cornell University)

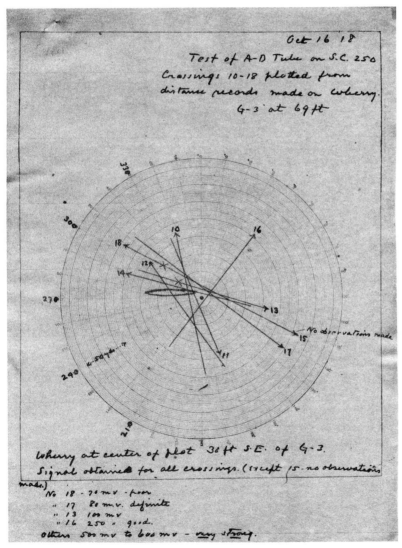

The signal was definite enough to determine accurately the proper time to drop a depth charge. . . Experiments on the use of one or both electrodes on the hull will be pushed, for there would appear to be a great advantage in getting the signal early enough so that a depth charge could be dropped on the first crossing and without the necessity of further maneuvering.[24]

As with all of these technologies, secrecy was at the forefront. There was pressure to get detection systems to the front as soon as they had been evaluated and deemed practicable. Germany was equally anxious for any information that would enable them to design materials and methods to counter each device. The Mark IV Search Gear had already been in use around Britain. Concerns had been expressed about Germany taking steps to counter this detection method, which Merritt had conveyed in a September 19 memo to the current secretary of the Special Board, Captain J. R. Defrees:

[I]t would be easy for the Germans to take steps which would so greatly reduce the stray currents utilized by the Mark IV method. . .and that it is a strong argument for proceeding with all possible rapidity with the installation of some form of Mark IV search gear, so that we may get all possible benefit from this extremely simple method before the Germans have had time to make changes.[25]

At least four promising systems were being considered by Merritt, who, while devoting much of his effort to his AD-tube, was determined to provide the Navy with the best system. No one knew that the war would end soon, and the efforts by all the civilian and military staff at New London and elsewhere continued around the clock. In a memo to Captain Defrees dated November 2, titled "Short Range Methods of Detection," Merritt summarized the results of tests completed in October, with recommendations for continued work.

Merritt included the towed electrodes used with the British Mark IV system, his AD-tube balanced coils, the "Bush Electromagnetic Method," and the "Lamme Method," which he noted "looks promising as a method for use on destroyers." Few details about these last two were found in the Merritt archive. In this November memo, however, he expressed concern that in the future, the enemy might be able to "eliminate stray currents," which the Mark IV type system relied on, or "by building his submarines of non-magnetic material or by devising some means of demagnetizing an iron submarine."[26] A century later, these insights are still being considered in submarine designs, with hull coatings, degaussing procedures, and even non-magnetic titanium hulls.

The goal of all of the development work by the Special Board on Anti-submarine Devices underway in New London and Long Island Sound, and other test facilities during 1917 and 1918, was sending vessels to the war zone equipped with new technologies to defeat the U-boat. Yet by the spring of 1918, submarine detection by air, off ships, or from shore took on an unanticipated urgency when *U-151* arrived off America's coast on May 15. Five additional submarines would follow.

On the morning of May 21st, a month and three days since our departure from Kiel, the water turned a dirty gray blue. We sounded and found a depth of thirty-five metres. We had reached the coast . . . Here was the Western hemisphere where our serious work was to begin.

We waited for nightfall. Even then we would have taken a chance of being rammed in the dark if it had not been for the unsuspecting cooperation given us by the Americans themselves. Far from the scenes of the war, they blissfully kept their ships' lights burning during the night, just as in days of peace.

—Frederick Körner to Lowell Thomas,
in *Raiders of the Deep*, 1928[1]

U-151, the first U-boat to arrive along the east coast. (NHHC NH 111050)

An officer aboard *U-151* described their arrival off the Atlantic coast after a month-long transit. His crew was ready to begin their mission; first to lay mines within the entrance to Chesapeake Bay, then north to Delaware Bay. Once that was completed, *U-151* was to use a new device designed to cut trans-Atlantic cables running out from New York; then remain along the coast to intercept and sink any vessel considered of mercantile or naval value. After the war, Lowell Thomas searched out many of Germany's U-boat veterans and recorded their stories in his book *Raiders of the Deep* (1928). Thomas was unable to contact the commander of *U-151*, Heinrich von Nostitz und Janckendorff, but did locate the submarine's boarding officer Fredrick Körner. "He got out his diaries," according to Thomas, "and filled in with bits of vivid description—an epic, a comedy of the raiders of the deep in American waters."[2] Körner continued:

> At six-thirty in the evening we came to the surface and steered toward Cape Henry. Soon we made out the lights of Cape Henry and Cape Charles and then the Cape Charles [lightship]. . . The moon behind us lighted everything [and we] could easily have been seen from shore. Any watcher with a strong pair of night glasses might have observed an interesting sight on our deck as our men brought up the mines and made them ready for launching.[3]

The United States seemed unaware that their coast was about to become vulnerable to the same predation as was a daily occurrence in the waters around Europe. The year before, on April 28, 1917, Admiral Sims sent a dispatch to the Navy Department from London regarding intelligence about German mine-laying submarines. "Of the thirty-four mine U-boats two for some days were not located, and the Admiralty was on the point of informing us of the probability of their being en route to the United States when their whereabouts was discovered. [adding that it is] the Admiralty's belief now that at present none are likely to be sent over . . ."[4] A year later, on May 1, 1918, in another dispatch, Admiral Sims passed on the latest intelligence:

> Admiralty Informs me that information from reliable agents states that a submarine of the *Deutschland* type left Germany about nineteenth April to attack either American troop transports or ships carrying material from the States. . . It is thought that the submarine is taking a northern route across the Atlantic, average speed five knots.[5]

There had always been some concerns at the Navy Department about the possibility of submarines crossing the Atlantic, particularly with the availability of large, long-range mine-laying *Deutschland*-type cruisers. It wasn't until March 6 when the Chief of Naval Operations (CNO) approved a "plan of defense against submarine attack in home waters." The intent was to maintain the flow of troops and supplies from the Atlantic seaboard and not overreact to unsubstantiated reports of U-boat operations. The comprehensive CNO directive to naval districts included the following: "War warnings not to be given unless presumed to be authentic."[6]For some reason, Admiral Sims' dispatch on the first of May apparently hadn't created enough concern to have been treated as a war warning. As a result, Germany's "unrestricted submarine warfare" arrived at the entrance to Chesapeake Bay three weeks after Sims' dispatch, as *U-151* completed its first task without interruption. Körner described the relief the crew felt:

> We listened that night with the keenest interest to the radio news from Arlington, Virginia. First came the weather reports, then warnings against wrecks and icebergs, then stock-exchange quotations, sports news, boxing, baseball, and finally—music to our ears—'No submarine. No war warning.' Our mine-laying had been entirely unobserved.[7]

Admiral Sims' next dispatch came on May 15, a week before *U-151* began its deadly work in Chesapeake Bay; his estimate that at least one submarine would arrive soon after the twentieth was rather accurate, as was his suggestion as to where to expect a mine field:

> Information contained in this cable is given me by the British Admiralty . . . There appears to be a reasonable probability that the submarines in question may arrive off the United States any time after May twentieth and that they will carry mines. English experience indicates the favorite spot for laying mines to be the position in which merchant ships stop to pick up pilots. For instance, for Delaware Bay the pilots for large ships are picked up south of the Five Fathom Bank Light Vessel. This in our opinion is one of the most likely spots for a submarine to lay mines.[8]

Delaware Bay was, in fact, *U-151*'s next target. Fredrick Körner:

> We ran submerged to keep out of the way of traffic. With the earpieces of our under-water microphone on my head, I listened to the bell and we maneuvered the boat until the tolling sound was of the same loudness in each ear. That meant we were steering straight toward it, or in other words, through the narrow channel [to Delaware Bay]. A good place to lay the rest of our mines.[9]

As described to Lowell Thomas, within a week of arriving off Chesapeake Bay, *U-151* had laid two mine fields at strategic shipping points. Körner apparently was also the listener on board *U-151*, and with the help of the Five Fathoms Bank lightship bell, guided his U-boat into Delaware Bay, where the rest of her mines were placed. On May 28, she was off the south coast of Long Island, in sight of the Fire Island lighthouse where her next mission was cutting trans-Atlantic cables running out from New York harbor. Using their cable-cutting mechanism dragged along the bottom, Körner later learned that one cable to Europe and one to South America had been severed. Then, it was off to hunt ships around Nantucket, Boston, and the Gulf of Maine.[10]

Admiral Sims continued to send dispatches about the latest information available from their intelligence sources . . . much too late, however, as *U-151* was well into her mission by the time Sims' next dispatch arrived: "*June 4, 1918*—It is practically certain that there is but one submarine on the Atlantic coast, which is probably U-151." A second dispatch sent on June 7 described *U-151* as a "converted mercantile submarine of the Deutschland type," with a compliment of eight officers and sixty-five men. Sims included details about her armament, which included "two 22 pounders one machine gun six torpedo tubes 4 bow 2 stern," adding that *U-151* likely carried twelve torpedoes and forty mines.[11]

Admiral Sims continued to provide updates throughout the summer and into October. The following are a few examples:

June 29—Second cruiser at sea. At present off west coast of Ireland. Her field of operations not yet known. Can not reach longitude of Nantucket before July fifteenth.

July 5—Enemy cruiser submarine outward bound, reported July 4 about 45 N. 30 W. proceeding southwesterly.

July 24—Admiralty has received reliable information indicating U-156 is intended to operate in Gulf of Maine but if foggy there to shift operations off Delaware.

August 1—It is considered probable by Admiralty that a new mine-laying type submarine on its way to the American coast . . .

August 7—We feel so certain that mine-laying submarine will operate in Vineyard Sound and Nantucket Sound August10 that counter measures in mining are recommended.

August 9—Admiralty informs that two converted mercantile type submarines will probably leave Germany middle of August for American coast. One of them will probably lay mines east of Atlantic City and Currituck. The other off St. Johns, Newfoundland, Western bay, Newfoundland and Halifax. These submarine estimated to reach American waters about second week of September.[12]

U-151 was a lone wolf. Her mission in American waters had been successful, and on the first of July, *U-151* left the coast, continuing to harass shipping in the North Atlantic while heading back to Germany. Two more submarines, *U-156* and *U-140*, arrived in July, joined by *U-117* in August. All three left the coast on September 1. The unarmed mercantile submarine *Deutschland*, which had visited New London and Baltimore in 1916, returned to America as *U-155* (shown on page 68) on September 8, now with the firepower commensurate with her sister U-boat cruisers. Three weeks later, on September 29, *U-152* arrived off the east coast. With the end of the war becoming apparent, Germany recalled these last two submarines, and on October 20, both began the nearly month-long return.

Considering the advance notice provided by Admiral Sims, and in particular his suggestion as to the probable targets, it is difficult to understand the lack of preparedness. While there was no apparent sense of urgency, the Navy was certainly aware of the possibility that U-boats would become actively engaged along the east coast, as far north as Newfoundland and Nova Scotia and south into the Caribbean. It wasn't until February of 1918 when the Navy Department (CNO) appointed a special board tasked to formulate a plan of defense, should submarines appear off America's coast. The following are excerpts from the board's understanding of the threat:

> The Germans have completed a number of cruising submarines of
> large radius and large capacity, and these may be used on our coast
> with a view to divert some of our military activity away from European
> waters. . . A division of four submarine cruisers, each armed with 6-inch
> guns, 36 mines, and 16 torpedoes, and capable of at least one month's
> activity on our coast, may appear in American waters without warning. . .
> They will employ mines, guns, torpedoes, and bombs. Their principal
> activities may be expected to be directed against the main shipping
> centers—Halifax, New York, Hampton Roads, and the Florida Straits.[13]

With such a vast coastline, the assumption had been to concentrate resources at strategic locations, including "Chesapeake, New York, Long Island area, Boston . . ."[14] Certainly Chesapeake Bay, with the port of Baltimore, was a likely target, and protection from submarines entering the bay must have been on the minds of the naval and civilian staffs of the experimental stations. Their mission from the start was to develop defensive antisubmarine measures.

Professor Ernest Merritt was responsible for electromagnetic detection devices at the Naval Experimental Station. On March 30, the New London staff received a memo from Commander McDowell listing activities underway at other facilities; included were recent endeavors from abroad, one of which mentioned the use of magnetic loop detection. McDowell's memo also contained Merritt's handwritten annotation regarding the magnetic loop along the margin:

> A report of Feb.22 by W.H. Brag [sic] on LOOP TESTS OFF BOLOGNE is transmitted by letter of March 4th by Capt. Leigh. This appears to be a recent application of method outlined in an early B.I.R. report. [and in Merritt's hand] The method is that recommended by our magnetic committee in spring of 1917. It was this report of its use abroad that led to my being asked to design the cable for the Chesapeake Bay.[15]

The successful development in Britain of the Bragg Loop and it deployment in the English Channel and the Orkney Islands are described in chapter 4. Merritt was involved with the original scientific team, which comprised the initial staff in New London, where he brought his interest in electromagnetic detection. On April 22, 1918, Merritt sent his first status report to McDowell, titled "Cable loop installation for the protection of the entrance to Chesapeake Bay:"[16]

> Not having a chart at hand, I have estimated the width of the channel to be protected as ten miles. If this is correct, 50 miles of cable will be sufficient to make a loop in the shape of a "W" as indicated in Figure 1 [a hand-drawn sketch provided at the end of Merritt's memo].
>
> If we assume that a submarine of the "D" type moves at right angles across the cable 100 feet above it at a speed of 2 miles per hour, the maximum emf. developed will be approximately 10 micro-volts, and if a galvanometer is used whose resistance is the same as that of the cable so that the total resistance is 1000 ohms, the maximum current will be 10^{-8} amperes. Leeds and Northrup make two types of galvanometer either of which would have the required [sensitivity].

A "loop" was not necessarily circular, but only required that there be a continuous circuit from land to the sea bottom and returning to the land-based observation station where the operator would view the induced current on a galvanometer. Merritt later suggested using a telephone receiver and amplifier to provide the operator with an audible tone rather than watching a meter. Each leg of the "W" configuration was intended to extend across the width of the channel; thus, a submarine would cross the "loop" four times if transiting into the bay, providing four opportunities for the observer to detect and report the transit path.

Merritt provided McDowell with estimates about how the loop would perform if a D-type submarine was used for tests of the proposed installation. He continued to supply design updates to McDowell throughout May. In a memo dated May 31, Merritt mentioned the need to eliminate external land-based "disturbances in the Cape Henry loop installation," which may indicate that the Chesapeake Bay loop was in operation.[17] If so, it was a week late. By May 31, *U-151* had already set a mine field near Cape Henry, where the loop was to be installed. *U-151* had also placed mines at the entrance to Delaware Bay, and at the end of May, was on its cable cutting mission off New York. There were no more references to the loop installation by Merritt, as its operation had likely been turned over to the local naval district forces.

In addition to the magnetic loop installations, the experimental stations at Nahant and New London were actively involved with shore-based acoustic listening stations, which had been successfully operated by the British as early as 1915. This technology had been developed at Nahant in 1917, and underwent further testing at New London as well. The British stations included a single hydrophone in a bottom-mounted frame, whereas the improvements made here included a three-hydrophone triangular frame based on the K-tube device carried on subchasers, which provided a reasonably accurate direction of the sound. Listener training had already been established at New London in the fall of 1917 for U.S. naval enlisted men, with one installation reaching into the harbor from shore on the west side of the harbor entrance at Ocean Beach.

Shore-based listening stations were among the many recommendations made by the board established by the Navy Department in February, 1918, to create a submarine defense plan. The board's report, approved by the Chief of Naval Operations on March 6, included specific reference to shore stations:

> Establish listening stations at the entrance to Chesapeake Bay, New York, and the east end of Long Island Sound. If these stations prove effective and are needed, to extend the system to other important localities.[18]

In April, in response to the board's recommendations, "All coastwise shipping bound to or from New York, proceed via Long Island Sound, keeping to the northern shore, and travel by night or day as far as New London." Additional instructions for shipping included use of Buzzards Bay, Cape Cod

Canal, or Vineyard Sound, all tempting hunting grounds for a submarine predator.[19]

For the Second Naval District, which included New London, the waters near the entrance to Long Island Sound were critical. The training exercise described at the beginning of chapter 21 was likely done in response to this possibility; six submarines were to attempt to enter the Sound, protected by eight subchasers equipped with listening devices. The eastern tip of Fishers Island was the perfect location to listen for a submarine lurking just outside the Sound, and the installation of a shore station (shown on the following page) would augment the mobile listeners on subchaser hunting groups.

Ensign James Bean, who had attended the hydrophone school in New London, made a specific reference to the need for shore stations in a manuscript document he wrote after the war.

> The subject of permanently located deep sea apparatus was taken under consideration but the most successful type was developed at Nahant. Such apparatus was planted at the ends of Long Island Sound and at the mouths of the most important harbors. . .The operator on duty could locate any vessel attempting to make the harbor and communicate the position to the skipper of a sub-chaser . . .[20]

In a meeting held by Commander McDowell in New London at the Naval Experimental Station on September 1, the discussion included one of those "important harbors" being Cape Henry. Not only was there mention of the condition of the magnetic loops, but there had also been an installation of an acoustic listening post, which had apparently been in operation for some time. An inspection of the tripods revealed that the microphones "were overgrown with seaweed, but it did not seem to affect them at all."[21] The entrance to Chesapeake Bay was well covered that summer, as was the entrance to Long Island Sound.

The cruiser submarines, however, had an additional mission beyond laying mine fields—sinking ships whenever and wherever some unlucky crew would cross a U-boat's path. An enemy submarine with long range operational capability could appear and disappear anywhere along the east coast. The Navy emphasized a defensive posture at strategic locations, yet also ensured a maximum degree of mobility. Mobility meant scouting from the air, patrolling on the sea, and stationing submarines in the vicinity of principal shipping points. Troop transports and mercantile vessels carrying war materials to Europe needed escorts through designated shipping routes. That summer and into the fall, every avail-

Top: *Tripod listening device being lowered to the bottom along the Fishers Island coast. An electrical cable from the three hydrophones ran to a shore station* Bottom: *where the listener was able to determine the direction of a submerged submarine. (*Hayes Family Archive*)*

able destroyer, subchaser, and SP-class converted yacht that remained in U.S. waters was assigned to antisubmarine duty, most carrying listening devices. Commander McDowell had also suggested that the Fire Island Lightship be outfitted with listening capability.[22] All of this was included in the March recommendations by the Navy Department's special board for homeland defense; those associated with naval aircraft, convoy escorts, lightships, and subchasers are provided below:[23]

That air scouts should patrol the convoy's intended course out at least to the 50 fathom curve and as far beyond as circumstances permit . . .

That Naval Air Service, in addition to assisting the escort of convoys, may contribute materially to the locating of submarines by air scouting off our coast, including the use of kites and dirigibles, especially between Nantucket Shoals and Cape Hatteras.

That, in addition to harbor and inshore vessels, there should be a force of destroyers and of submarines ready to act upon information of hostile submarines near our coast.

That immediate steps be taken to install on board all outside lightships on the Atlantic Coast radio and listening equipment and that, upon the appearance of a hostile submarine in American waters, all submarine signal bells be stopped . . . [note that this order was not implemented soon enough, as *U-151* used the Five Fathom Bank lightship bell to navigate into Delaware Bay.]

A force of 30 submarine chasers each, based on New York and on Hampton Roads, will be needed for convoy escort and listening service.

That convoys should be preceded to the 50 fathom curve by four submarine chasers equipped with listening attachment.

That the antisubmarine escort should consist of submarine chasers armed with depth bombs and guns up to 3-inch caliber.

That provision should now be made for forces to be available where likely to be needed, to detect and locate enemy submarines, to act upon information of their whereabouts, and to be capable of attacking a submarine if encountered.

These excerpts were selected to emphasize the significance of subchasers to the Navy's response to U-boat incursions along the American coast, and thus the importance of the listeners and their submarine detection devices. In practice, subchasers were assigned to accompany destroyers in hunting groups actively involved with antisubmarine patrols and training.[24] The USS *Jouett* (DD-41) was stationed at the submarine base in Groton, and had been assigned to support the nearby Naval Experimental Station. By June, there were twenty-four chasers in the *Jouett* group, including one of the chasers, *SC-6*, which had been heavily involved in operational testing of the latest antisubmarine devices.

When the reality of U-boats along the east coast became evident, *Jouett* brought her chasers to Norfolk, Virginia, for troop transport convoy duty. *SC-6* was joined by *SC-214* and *SC-253*, and formed *Jouett's* tactical group. The commanding officer of *SC-253*, Ensign George Wallace, described his experiences during that summer.

> We three boats joined fifteen others, which, with the destroyer *Jouett*, made up the Special Anti-submarine Force. During June we operated out of Norfolk and had the honor of convoying over 400,000 troops on four separate convoys two-thirds of the way to Bermuda—and not without a brush with a submarine. . . . After leaving the troopships we would scout back to port. Many were the lifeboats and the wrecks we sighted, and one night for six and a half hours [we] chased a Hun. Of course we could not see him, but we heard him, and if we had not run out of gas I think we would have got him.[25]

There was only one submarine, *U-151*, operating along the U.S. coast in June when the listener on *SC-253* detected the submerged predator. Todd Woofenden, in his *Hunters of the Steel Sharks* (2006), provides brief accounts of additional encounters between chasers and a U-boat off the coast of America, some detected by listeners and some based on sightings, including *SC-241* operating off Nova Scotia.[26] Another chaser, *SC-294*, rescued survivors of a Norwegian sailing ship, the bark *Stifinder,* en route from New York to Australia. Sunk by *U-152* on October 13, (shown on the following page), the lifeboat with eleven of the crew was spotted on the 28th.[27]

America's homeland antisubmarine effort may seem extensive, considering that no more than three U-boats were active along the entire eastern seaboard at the same time, and those three were here together for only three weeks in August. At other times, only one or two were here. Nonetheless, a long list of vessels damaged or sunk appeared in the Navy's 1920 summary: *German Activities on the Atlantic Coast of the United States and Canada*, published by the Navy Department's Office of Naval Records.[28] Only seven hit mines, including the armored cruiser USS *San Diego* (ACR-6), which sank as a result, and the battleship USS *Minnesota* (BB-22), severely damaged but later repaired. The naval cargo ship USS *Ticonderoga* was one of fourteen ships torpedoed and lost.

U-boat alongside the Norwegian bark Stifinder. *The crew was set adrift before*
U-152 *sank the ship (inset).* (NHHC NH 110771 and NH 110772)

The vast majority, seventy-nine, were sunk or damaged by gunfire or
by bombs placed by a boarding party. Surprisingly, of those one hundred
U-boat victims, only one of many anchored lightships that would seem to
be sitting ducks, the Diamond Shoal Lightship, was sunk by gunfire off Cape
Hatteras on August 6 by *U-140*. It is also hard to imagine why certain other
vessels were targeted. On August 10, *U-117* attacked a fishing fleet near
Georges Bank east of Cape Cod, sinking nine of these tiny unarmed vessels.[29]
Submarine warfare along the United States coast was finally over when the
last two German submarines, *U-152* and *U-155*, were recalled on October
20; both arrived at their base in Kiel, four days after Armistice.

The massive deployment of vessels, aircraft, as well as shore based defensive measures undoubtedly minimized the U-boat offensive, which did
little to slow down the transport of troops and supplies to the war zone.
Their goal had also been to create enough concern among the public that
American destroyers in Europe would be recalled. Throughout 1918, in
spite of the numbers of ships and subchasers involved in homeland defense,
American antisubmarine efforts rapidly expanded around the British Isles,
along the west coast of France, past Gibraltar, and into the Mediterranean
and Adriatic Seas. There was plenty of work ahead for the listeners.

Chapter 23 America Eastward to the War

On April 30th [1917], I received a message from Admiral Jellicoe asking me to come to the Admiralty. When I arrived he said that the projected study of the convoy system had been made and he handed me a copy of it. It had been decided to send one experimental convoy from Gibraltar. The Admiralty, he added, had not yet definitely decided that the convoy system should be adopted, but there was every intention of giving it a thorough and fair trial.

—Admiral William S. Sims, "The Victory at Sea," 1919-1920[1]

With America's entry into the war on April 6, 1917, this country was no longer neutral and was subject to the same predation by German submarines as all the other participants. It was a very large ocean over which any naval or mercantile vessels would need to cross. Admiral William S. Sims arrived on the 9th of April, and immediately entered into discussions with the British Admiralty, in particular with Admiral John R. Jellicoe, about the submarine problem. To Sims, an obvious first step was to implement the convoy system.

Many defensive and offensive measures had been tried by the Admiralty attempting to minimize the deadly efficiency of the U-boat. Hundreds of mercantile vessels were converging on the British Isles and France, and past Gibraltar into the Mediterranean with food, fuel, and war materials—all targets scattered across waters within the war zone, most unprotected and with few defenses. Limited use of convoys had been implemented for local, short range commercial shipping where, according to Admiral Jellicoe, the "protection of the vessels employed in the French coal trade was entrusted largely to trawlers . . ."[2] Colliers and trawlers were slow moving and well-suited for coastal escort partnerships. That was not the case, however, if the intent was convoying ships across many hundreds of miles of open ocean.

Unrestricted submarine attacks on unarmed commercial vessels was a new mode of warfare, and the concept of using convoys on the shipping lanes far out at sea against this hidden predator was not immediately favored either by the Admiralty or by many merchant ship captains. "The speed of a convoy was the speed of the slowest ship, and vessels that could easily make twelve or fourteen knots were obliged to put on the brakes, much to the disgust of their masters."[3] The advantage of a convoy became apparent immediately after the Admiralty's experimental convoy from Gibraltar arrived without incident at its English destination on May 20. The following day, "the British Admiralty, now entirely convinced, voted to adopt the convoy system for all merchant shipping."[4]

Soon, vessels eagerly departed from distant ports with the anticipation that they would assemble at a specified longitude and latitude far from the war zone, where it was assumed the U-boats would not venture. As groups of ships gathered, they were met by an escort of naval ships—typically destroyers although other armed vessels, which Admiral Sims referred to as "dollar-a-year" converted yachts, were also enlisted for escort duty.[5]

The convoy then proceeded along prescribed routes, often determined by intelligence as to the current position of U-boats. The process was reversed when leaving the coast; individual ships assembled at departure points; destroyers then escorted the convoy to the designated "safe" location far out on the open ocean. As these outbound merchant vessels dispersed toward their destinations, the escorts waited for incoming ships to arrive and form a convoy heading into the war zone. This process was well understood by U-boat commanders, who patrolled these routes hoping for a convoy encounter.

Throughout 1917, when the convoy system championed by Admiral Sims became a common practice, listening devices had not been added to the ocean convoy escorts. Offensive measures were simply by brute force—and luck. A well-guarded convoy presented a risky venture for any U-boat that happened upon such a large group of tempting targets. Yet for a submarine captain anxious to increase his tally of tonnage sunk, it was often worth the risk.

In Admiral Sims' estimation, a "destroyer could usually sink the submarine whenever it could get near enough; it was for the underwater boat, however, to decide whether an engagement should take place." There were many unfortunate U-boats that found themselves unable to submerge deep enough to avoid being rammed by a fast-approaching destroyer, or could not maneuver out of the area once depth charges were dropped over its last position. Yet, once having avoided destruction during the initial encounter,

One of Admiral Sims' "dollar-a-year" converted yachts, USS Harvard *(SP-209), stands by while receiving survivors from the British steamer* Trelissick, *torpedoed off the northwest coast of France by* UC-72 *on July 15, 1917. (Courtesy Marist College; Lowell Thomas Archive)*

"the submarine still possessed that one great quality of invisibility which made any final method of attacking it such a difficult problem."[6]

Germany's Admiral Reinhard Scheer, whose submarines easily picked off hundreds of merchant vessels in the early years of the war, recognized the advantages of the convoy system. "The practice of gathering considerable numbers of British merchantmen together and convoying them added greatly to the difficulties the U-boat encountered in achieving success; these ships were protected according to their size and value either by light craft or by bigger warships."[7] Scheer provided an example of these difficulties, with excerpts from the log of *U-82*, commanded by Lieutenant Commander Hans Adam:

> September 19, 1917, 3:19 P.M.—I shot past the bows of this steamer towards steamers 4 and 5. Steamer 4 I hit. Steamer 2 had hoisted a red flag, which was probably to announce the presence of the boat; for several torpedo-boats make for the steamer. As there was no chance of firing from the only remaining usable tube (stern tube) I dived. The destroyers dropped about 10 depth charges; one burst pretty near the stern.

4:45 P.M.—Rose to surface. I try to come up with the convoy again, as it is still to be seen. But a destroyer forces me under water again.

6:37 P.M.—Rose to surface. Two destroyers prevent me from steaming up. Owing to heavy seas from S.E. it is impossible to proceed south so as to get ahead of them. . . Therefore gave up pursuit."[8]

While *U-82* successfully torpedoed one of the steamers in the convoy, there would be no second shot. The escort destroyers immediately engaged in a relentless pursuit, and after a near miss from the depth charges, *U-82* decided that it was best to leave the convoy without further harassment.

There was no perfect solution to U-boat predation. Industrious captains, once a convoy was sighted, found ways to take on at least one vessel. This from Admiral Sims: "The submarines would follow for days in the track of convoys, looking for a straggler. . . and for this reason one destroyer at least was often detached from the escorting division as a rear guard. In this connection we must keep in mind that at no time until Armistice was signed was any escort force strong enough to ensure entire safety."[9]

As America sailed eastward bringing hundreds of thousands of troops to Europe, convoy protection took on a new urgency. "A convoy of four or five large troopships would be surrounded by as many as ten or a dozen destroyers," as Admiral Sims recalled. He emphasized that a transport ship could carry four to five thousand troops, which would serve to replenish the daily loss of three to four thousand men on the Western Front. While the losses were a staggering number, the nearly daily arrival of thousands of men at the ports of France kept the ground war from turning in Germany's favor. It was essential, then, to maintain the uninterrupted passage of American convoys, which Sims estimated averaged about three per week.[10]

Admiral Sims stressed that "one of the greatest protections which a ship possesses against submarine attack is unquestionably high speed." To be used as transports, ships were required to run at twelve knots, while a U-boat, which had to remain submerged to avoid the escort destroyers while launching a torpedo, were typically limited to about eight knots. When at sea, the tactical maneuvers of transports also contributed to their becoming difficult targets. "Like all convoys, the troopships began zigzagging as soon as they entered the danger zone; and this in itself made it almost impossible for a submarine to get its bearings and take good aim."[11]

Commercial vessels in convoy, having passed through the danger zone where long-range cruiser submarines hunted, once again dispersed as each vessel headed for its intended port. Although this final portion of their transit was relatively short, the UB-class boats were designed for coastal operations and found plenty of cautious, but vulnerable targets. Most of the destroyers were off with another convoy heading out, and the independent vessels now had to rely on coastal patrol craft and aerial spotters.

> [Admiral Sims] described the dangers in which these ships were involved owing to the fact that the groups were obliged to break up after entering the Channel and the Irish Sea, and thus to proceed singly to their destinations. . . .The circumstance that our seaplanes, perched high in the air, could see the submarines long before they had reached torpedoing distance, and could, if necessary, signal to a destroyer for assistance, made them exceedingly valuable for this kind of work.[12]

Aircraft played an important escort role for convoys and individual vessels, but were restricted by their limited range and need to remain close to their land-based airfields. Admiral Sims credited what he referred to as "aerial hunters of the submarine" as having "great value in escorting convoys [and] even a single airship not infrequently brought a group of merchantmen or troopships safely into port." According to Sims, "all dirigibles had wireless telegraph and wireless telephone; as soon as a submarine was 'spotted,' the news was broadcast [to] every offensive warship which was anywhere in the neighborhood."[13]

When General John J. "Black Jack" Pershing sent the first soldiers of his American Expeditionary Force to France in June of 1917, troop and mercantile convoys were escorted by naval ships, principally destroyers, which continued to rely on a brute force response to a U-boat. Throughout 1917, the option was to chase it, ram it, and if that failed, drop depth charges and simply hope they were on target. As Sims noted, "the submarine still possessed that one great quality of invisibility which made any final method of attacking it such a difficult problem."[14] By 1918, that quality of invisibility acquired as the U-boat submerged was rapidly replaced by a lethal vulnerability—submarines were incredibly noisy.

Germany Understood the U-boat's Vulnerability

All the participants—belligerents on both sides—were taken by surprise at how effective the submarine had become, and that the outcome of a world war could hinge on this new form of naval warfare. Germany, at the turn of the century, had considered the submarine as a novelty with only limited use for coastal defense. When it became apparent that the High Seas Fleet, after the battle of Jutland, would remain bottled up at bases in Germany, emphasis turned to the submarine. Mine laying capability was an important element in Germany's submarine strategy with the introduction of the small "UC" boats, which were built throughout the war, and conversion of some coastal UB-class boats as minelayers. U-boat construction rates increased with emphasis on long-range capability, including converting the unarmed mercantile submarine *Deutschland* to a combatant naval vessel, *U-155*, and building additional vessels of the same design.

Efforts by Britain and France to exploit the distinct sounds of a transiting U-boat began within months of the sinking of the British armored cruisers *Aboukir, Cressy,* and *Hogue,* on September 22, 1914, by *U-9*. The Hawkcraig Admiralty Experimental Station in the Firth of Forth, under the command of Captain C. P. Ryan, successfully applied the hydrophone, a new technology made from a microphone housed in a waterproof case, as a listening device. His early designs were able to detect the unique sounds of a submarine and distinguish them from the myriad of underwater sounds from other vessels, but less adept at determining direction. Improvements continued to be implemented in Ryan's designs plus those of the Admiralty Board of Inventions and Research. With America's entry into the war, additional scientific, engineering, and naval minds tackled the numerous technologies being tested and, ultimately, by the beginning of 1918, implemented in vessels designed specifically for antisubmarine operations.

Germany understood, as a technology oriented culture, that the Allies would not rest until they had perfected antisubmarine devices based on the U-boat's vulnerability. But it was the degree of emphasis on listener training by Britain and America which would make the difference once the technology entered the struggle. How well the listeners performed, and how well German submarines could frustrate the technology, would determine who would take command of the undersea battlespace. As Lloyd Scott (1920) noted:

> [W]hen the listening devices and patrol work became active, the submarine found an unsafe game inshore and began to work farther and farther out to sea. . . .As our listening devices increased in accuracy and sensitiveness, the Germans did everything possible to quiet and reduce all noises that a submarine might give out.[15]

There should be no surprise that Germany would be concerned with submarine detection efforts, which Britain and France had begun developing soon after the first unrestricted U-boat campaign had commenced in 1915.

While these early listening devices were somewhat effective, once the U.S. began improving detection capabilities and tactics, Germany responded to the challenge. The Navy's Office of Naval Intelligence published information from a German submarine manual, which outlined the "Procedure When Pursued With Hydrophones:"

> The reduction to a minimum of the sounds caused by your own boat is an effective protection. (a) Connect the vertical rudder and hydroplanes for hand working. (b) Stop your ballast and trimming pumps. Use compressed air in lieu. (c) Let your main motors run at the lowest possible number of revolutions . . . The submarine must, however, stop frequently to listen, even at the risk of not increasing her distance from the enemy so rapidly. . . When attacked and forced to submerge, a submarine may (a) Attempt to escape by proceeding at maximum speed (b) Proceed at slow speed. (c) Proceed slowly, stopping and balancing occasionally to listen, or to synchronize with stops of hunting units (d) Bottom (in water 40 fathoms or less) (e) Anchor submerged.[16]

It was more than a tactical issue for Germany, and measures to minimize the sounds from their submarines were underway at U-boat bases. The Navy's civilian engineers working under the Special Board on Antisubmarine Devices were very aware of German efforts at submarine silencing. Again, from Lloyd Scott (1920):

> It is understood that the Germans tested each submarine at various speeds, in order to determine at what speed the least vibration and noises occurred. This having been determined, the vessel navigated at that speed when it suspected the presence of vessels with listening devices aboard.[17]

In his memoir *U-boats Westward* (1931), Ernst Hashagen, commanding officer of *U-62*, described the conditions U-boat crews faced during the last twelve months of the war, resulting from the technological improvements brought to bear by the Allies. The German response to these new tactics and technologies confirmed the suspicions expressed by Scott and the Special Board. Hashagen:

> Only from the end of 1917 were defensive measures [by the Allies] effectively applied under water, in the form of barrage nets, depth-charges and hydrophones. . . .At this time we commenced, before

our U-Boats went on active service, to "listen-in" to our own craft. At Travemünde they underwent an "audibility" course. With this end in view, the U-Boat, travelling under water, was listened to through submarine telephones. First of all, the engines and pumps normally used in under-water cruising were put into use, and then one by one shut off, to see when the least noise was heard. All the results were then combined on a schedule at the end of the course. Every boat had her technical melody. Out there at the front it was *vital* that one should sing no unnecessary tune to the destroyers and submarine-chasers.[18]

British hydrophone flotillas, American subchaser units, and allied destroyers constantly patrolled known U-boat operating areas, listening for the distinct sounds of a transiting submarine. The silencing efforts described by Hashagen became a crucial U-boat survival tactic. Listeners on board subchasers had discovered that one of the "tricks [employed by] enemy submarines to escape detection," as told by Ray Millholland in *The Splinter Fleet of the Otranto Barrage* (1920), "was accomplished by running their electric motors, while submerged, at two different speeds."[19] Millholland then described how submarine commanders learned and implemented this technique:

This "silent running speed" was very carefully determined for each submarine before it was allowed to make its first hostile voyage. In the engine room of one captured submarine I saw a notice posted over each tachometer, stating that one motor was to be run at seventy-five revolutions per minute and the other at ninety revolutions when the order for silent running was given. This difference in speed of the two revolving shafts had the faculty of neutralizing the vibrations of one propeller with those of the other and rendering them inaudible to us.

Knowing our preference for seeing oil and air bubbles rising to the surface after we had gone to great pains to bomb a submarine, the accommodating U-boat commanders would squirt out a discharge of oil, and if they felt very accommodating, would release some compressed air. Then while we were still religiously bombing the spot where the oil showed on the surface, the sub would go into silent running and slip away. . .[20]

As mentioned above, Ernst Hashagen pointed out how the sounds generated by a submerged U-boat underway made the submarine vulnerable, referring to every submarine having its own "technical melody," emphasizing that U-boats "should sing no unnecessary tune."[21] Modern submarines also have their own specific "melody." Known as a submarine's "signature" by acousticians, highly sensitive sensors have been able to distinguish the subtle differences between vessels in a particular class and, at times, specific submarines that—as with Hashagen's U-boats—hope to "sing no unnecessary tune."

The scientific staff in New London was likewise concerned that the captain of a U-boat being pursued would certainly have several escape options available to him. The silent running techniques would most likely be used if the U-boat had not yet been detected. The assumption by the American designers and tacticians, however, was that once discovered, a U-boat would rely on speed and maneuvering; the reasoning explained by Max Mason:

> A carefully tuned up submarine running at its predetermined most
> silent speed made very little noise and could be heard at most but a few
> hundred yards. The "silent speed" was, however, very low, from two-thirds
> of a knot to a knot and a half, and such low speed made the submarine
> very liable to destruction by depth charges. The submarine commanders
> usually attempted to escape by higher speed, in which case the sound
> from their engines became much greater, with a great increase in range of
> detection. A submarine running at four knots could be accurately located
> under favorable weather conditions at two thousand yards . . .[22]

In December, 1917, Captain Leigh and a contingent from the naval and civilian staff of the Nahant and New London experimental stations had sailed to England to demonstrate the new listening devices (see chapter 16). The Navy's Special Board on Antisubmarine Devices was ready, after only six months, to provide the first of a growing list of submarine detection capabilities, including the 110-foot wooden-hulled submarine chaser with a crew that featured well-trained listeners. These fast-moving vessels were outfitted primarily with their K-tube (shown on pages 129-130) and the binaural SC-tube. Others carried the electrical MB-and MF-tubes.

THE SUBCHASERS CROSS THE ATLANTIC

The first subchasers left New London on February 24, 1918. The recent book *Hunters of the Steel Sharks: The Submarine Chasers of WWI* by Todd Woofenden (2006) includes an archive of letters, documents, and photographs by Ensign (later Lieutenant) George S. Doyle, commanding officer of *SC-93*, one of the first chasers to make the Atlantic crossing. Author Woofenden is the grand-nephew of LT Doyle. Excerpts from many of the letters Doyle wrote home throughout his time on *SC-93* make the book a great tribute to the versatility and perseverance that dominated all of the chaser crews.

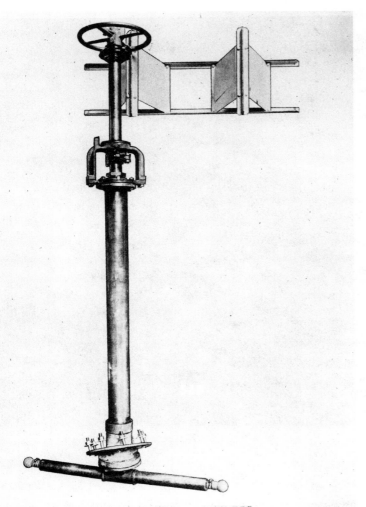

Left: *SC-tube assembly as installed through the hull of a subchaser.* (Hayes Family Archive)
Bottom Left: *When underway, the SC-tube was raised into the streamlined housing.* (Courtesy Todd Woofenden)

SCC—FORM 1, COMPLETE.   ½ Scale

Subchaser listener with his SC-tube and stethoscope. He would pass the target bearings to the pilot house through the speaking tube on his left. Also on his left is a K-tube compensator. (Sims, 1919-1920)

The Atlantic crossing involved three legs: New London to Bermuda; Bermuda to the Azores; Azores to Gibraltar. From there, the chasers in this first group were heading to the Greek island of Corfu to participate in what was termed the Otranto Barrage in a narrow passage into the Adriatic Sea. Antisubmarine efforts were building in intensity there in order to restrict U-boats from the Albanian naval base at Durazzo from entering the Mediterranean. It was a difficult trip for the chasers and their crews, as described by Admiral William S. Sims:

> The men and officers indeed presented what at first seemed to be almost as hopeless a spectacle as the vessels themselves. . . .for the greater number [of them], that terrible trip on that icy ocean, with the

thermometer several degrees below zero and with no artificial warmth on board, represented their first experience at sea. Yet there wasn't the slightest sign of whimpering . . ."

The early 80-foot subchasers which we built for Great Britain and France crossed the ocean on the decks of ocean liners; but all of the 110-footers crossed the ocean under their own power . . . almost constantly tossed upon the waves like pieces of cork."

The unexpected sea qualities which the subchasers displayed, and the development of listening devices which made it possible to detect all kinds of sounds underwater at a considerable distance, immediately laid before us the possibility of direct offensive operations against the submarine.[23]

With the final work of the chasers waiting on the other side of the ocean, the following is a brief summary of the crossing. Along with the above comments by Admiral Sims are a few memories of Ensign Hilary R. Chambers, Jr., commanding officer of *SC-128*, and Chief Machinist Mate Ray Millholland, chief engineer on *SC-124*.

New London to Bermuda

Ensign Hilary R. Chambers (*SC-128*):

> In this second detachment was a division of six chasers all built at the Norfolk Navy Yard, numbered 124 to 129 inclusive. The 124 was commanded by Mr. Kelly ("Red"), Lieutenant (J.G.), who was the only regular naval officer in the division. All the other officers were Reserves, and their only experience of this character was the trip from Norfolk, Va., to New London, Conn. . . . a certain four striper (naval captain) on board one of our battleships, who, when told the Reserves admitted their experience, or rather lack of it, said 'Well, may God help them.'
>
> At last, at six o'clock on the evening of March 31, 1918, the convoy got under way.[24]

Chief Machinist Mate Ray Millholland (*SC-124*):

> It was a bitterly cold winter day . . . [W]e left New London, bucking the drifting ice of the Thames River, and fearful of smashing our paper-shell bows and wrecking our propellers. At dusk we were just off Block Island, straggling along in something of a formation with twenty-odd other chasers.

Seasickness struck every one of us violently; there was no relief, except to hang a bucket around our necks and go on tending the engines between retching convulsions.

Nobody slept, and everyone was sick as a dog. . . .The storm seemed to know our destination, for it blew just as enthusiastically on the fourth day as it had done that first night.

For the first few days at Bermuda, the war was still a vague, remote idea, but the arrival of a large convoy of American troopships, battle tugs, armed yachts, and a fleet of cargo ships, broke the illusion.[25]

Chambers:

There was a ten-day stay here during which time everything was overhauled and examined, for our next run was to be of twelve days. Some chasers needing it were put in dry dock. Supplies were procured, not at the navy yard but at an American base on a nearby island, where storehouses had been built and there were large caves for the storage of gasoline.[26]

BERMUDA TO THE AZORES

Chambers:

While we remained at Bermuda the first detachment of chasers went on to the Azores and shortly we followed them. Our convoy consisted of thirty chasers, ten ocean tugs, one submarine, one battleship, one transport, and a converted yacht. The chasers sailed in formation so as to protect the three big ships. There was a scout line of chasers flanking and astern, and behind them came the tugs. We expected to be in submarine-infested waters when we got near the Azores, and so our instructions were most explicit.[27]

Millholland:

Whose brilliant mind conceived the idea of providing each subchaser with a fuel storage capacity of only twenty-four hundred gallons, I do not care to know, nor at this date will I indulge in useless criticism; but the most childish acquaintance with arithmetic should have told the man that a chaser, which burns six hundred gallons of fuel per day, could not make a voyage of fourteen days without refueling several times at sea.[28]

The refueling business at sea was far from being a joke, especially as our turn alongside the tanker always came in nasty weather. . . .The tanker, steaming along at six knots, would toss over heavy lines which we secured to our aft towing bits and the three-inch gun mount forward. The strain on the hull of a chaser, plunging along and tethered to a big tanker, is almost incalculable. I saw one gun and mounting snatched from the deck of a chaser when the strain became too much for the steel bolts to hold it down.[29]

Chambers:

There was always one unit of chasers standing by to prevent submarine attack while the others were refueling.

We sailed along, however, making such repairs as we could till the twelfth day out we sighted the Azores amid great rejoicing. As we formed column to enter the harbor large crowds were seen on the shore and faint sounds of cheering were heard. . . .Preparations were immediately made for trips ashore to see the hot springs and other sights of the island, among which not the least of interest was the celebrated gambling club which was open to officers.[30]

Millholland:

[T]hese Portuguese were slow to appreciate the almost limitless capacity of Americans to suffer overcharging and shortchanging. The sellers of wine and liquors woke up to the existence of the charming phenomenon that a thirsty Yankee sailor drinks first and asks price only after his volumetric efficiency has been reached.[31]

Chambers:

While at Ponta Delgada a general overhaul was carried on and necessary repairs made.[32]

AZORES TO GIBRALTAR

Chambers:

After about two weeks in Ponta Delgada, all pay having been spent ashore, thirty chasers and the *Leonidas*, an old survey ship, with a tanker shoved off for Gibraltar. . . .Without further undue incident Gibraltar was sighted on the morning of the fifth day.[33]

Subchasers at Ponta Delgada, Azores, awaiting the next leg of their journey to the war. (NHHC NH 95227)

Millholland:

> No guns were visible from the harbor, . . .Nets, booms, submarine defenses of every device protected the shipping that huddled under the shadow of the Rock. Enemy submarines hung about, out of gun-range, like hungry wolves.[34]

> After only a few days at "the Rock," Ensign Chambers found one of those hungry wolves close at hand: "One morning the signal of 'submarine outside the harbor' was hoisted at the flagstaff of the port control office. . . ." For the chasers at Gibraltar, which had been in New London only six weeks earlier, the chase was on.[35]

CHAPTER 24 LISTENERS AT THE FRONT AND ARMISTICE

We built nearly 400 of these little vessels in eighteen months; and we sent 170 to such widely scattered places as Plymouth, Queenstown, Brest, Gibraltar, and Corfu. Several enemy submarines now lie at the bottom of the sea as trophies to their offensive power; and on the day that hostilities ceased, the Allies generally recognized that this tiny vessel, with the "listening devices" which made it so efficient, represented one of the most satisfactory direct "answers" to the submarine which had been developed by the war.

—Admiral William S. Sims, "The Victory at Sea," 1919-1920[1]

Admiral William S. Sims, writing his war memoir during 1919 and 1920, heaped praise on the vessels and the crews who manned them. "Who could ever have thought that a little vessel displacing only sixty tons, measuring only 110 feet from bow to stern, and manned by officers and crew, very few of who had ever made an ocean voyage, could have crossed more than three thousand miles of wintry sea, and proved one of the formidable enemies of the submarine?" Yet, as Sims pointed out, there had been no perfect solution to the submarine problem: "A depth charge, fired from the deck of a destroyer, was a serious matter for the submarine; still the submarine could avoid this deadly weapon at any time by simply concealing its whereabouts when in danger of attack."[2]

From the beginning, a submarine's vulnerability lay in its engines, propellers, pumps, and valves, each creating distinctive sounds that a well-trained listener could recognize from among all the natural and man-made noises that filled the not-so-silent sea. This book has focused on that vulnerability. Sims put it bluntly: "In our struggle against the German [submarine] campaign we were deprived of one of the senses which for ages had been absolutely necessary to military operations—that of sight. We were constantly attempting to destroy an enemy we could not see."[3] Hunting the U-boat blindly was simply a matter of hit or miss. The listeners would enable the hunters to take aim.

There was nothing certain about the hunt when the listeners put on their headphones, and Germany was not going to make it easy—nor was Mother Nature. "It is on official record," according to Lieutenant H. W. Wilson, RNVR, "that a certain ship belonging to one of our great allies chased a sperm whale—I forgot how many miles. The chase was by hydrophone . . . and did not become visual until many miles had been run, when the hydrophone experts were reluctantly compelled to admit that their legs had been pulled . . . [and] state the fact that the sperm whale faithfully reproduced the sound of a U-boat running on electric motors throughout the entire chase." Wilson did not reveal which of the great allies, as he put it, had "their ears tweaked," but most likely one of the American listeners had been duped.[4] In 1918, the Office of Naval Intelligence published a similar encounter. The following are a few excerpts:

> At 4:30 p.m. [September 6, 1918], while on patrol, suspicious sounds were reported by listeners on two boats and an excellent fix was obtained at 70° magnetic, distance 1000 yards. A moment later a large whale broke the surface at this position. The unit was about to proceed on running hunt when listeners on sub-chaser *86* reported a new suspicious sound. . . . At times during the chase, the whales first picked up at 4:30 were seen in directions different from those of the sound we were tracking. . . . The listeners on sub-chaser *84* were very sure that the sound heard was that of a damaged submarine or one running very slowly. . . . The listeners on sub-chaser *86* considered the sound to come from whales at all times during the chase and never conceded the presence of a submarine. The sound heard is described as similar to that made by a trawler or other very slow-moving propeller.[5]

The ONI report emphasized the difficulties interpreting the sounds heard: "The chase is an excellent example of the complications which the difference of opinion among listeners may raise. . . . All of the listeners have heard submarines both in training and in actual contact with the enemy." The training all listeners received, British or American, included recordings made of submarines on the surface and submerged. Then, after many hours of experience at sea, the listeners became adept at distinguishing the sounds of a submarine. That opportunity would soon come.

One morning the signal of 'submarine outside the harbor' was hoisted at the flagstaff of the port control office. At once, the English motor launches and destroyers started out, and the chaser officers were called for a conference.[6]

As described in the previous chapter, Ensign Hilary R. Chambers, commanding officer of *SC-128*, arrived at Gibraltar in the third convoy of chasers from America, his group eventually heading for the chaser base on the Greek island of Corfu. The officers who were called to that conference were all filled with enthusiasm at the prospect of their first encounter with a U-boat. Just after arriving, Chambers told of having a conversation "with British motor launch officers who had thrilling tales to relate of submarine encounters just outside the harbor." This was not a training exercise on Long Island Sound, and the chaser crews were ready for their first real test, which Chambers described in his memoir *United States Submarine Chasers in the Mediterranean, Adriatic and the Attack on Durazzo* (1920):

[A] submarine discovered and bombed by aircraft had taken refuge on the bottom in a cove on the Spanish coast east of the rock. The area involved was immediately divided into sectors, one for each unit of chasers. The S. C.'s 127, 128, and 129 were given the cove itself. . . . When we were off the rock we laid our course straight for our positions, and when their trailing wires were let out, to drag parallel to the coast, stopping at intervals to listen with the S. C. tubes. We continued dragging the rest of the day and listened during the night. Then the next morning dragging was resumed until 128 got contact and reported it. Turning, she went back over the spot, which had been buoyed, where she got it again. The contact was of such long duration, though broken at intervals, that permission to bomb was requested. The request was not complied with but the 127 and 129 came within hail, and on lowering their listening devices a submarine was heard under way. Trailing wires were immediately secured and a chase began.[7]

The subchasers continued their pursuit for two hours, their listeners keeping in contact. The U-boat, however, ran a zigzag course, making it difficult to obtain a definite fix on its location, eventually eluding the chasers. The U-boat had employed tactics her captain had undoubtedly practiced, initially sitting quietly on the sea bottom listening to the hunters on the surface. Yet, in spite of the escape of that U-boat, the chasers were able to use their listening gear as well as the trailing wire, and were ready for more submarine hunting.

Beginning in February, groups of chasers headed from New London into the Atlantic Ocean. In addition to assignments in the Mediterranean, many from the initial crossings were assigned to the naval base at Plymouth, England, arriving in May. Beginning with their tactical training in New London, hunting units consisted of three chasers. More of these antisubmarine vessels arrived in June and by August 11, after the last of the Plymouth chasers were on station, twenty-two units had been formed. Ten days later, thirty of those chasers were reorganized into ten hunting units and assigned to the destroyer base at Queenstown, Ireland.[8]

Nine chasers in the first group from New London had been assigned to a newly established chaser base on the Greek island of Corfu. Admiral Sims had ordered the chasers to participate in the Otranto barrage, where the British and Italians had been attempting to restrict German and Austrian submarines based in the Adriatic from entering the Mediterranean. "In the spring of 1918 I therefore sent Captain Leigh to southern Italy to locate and construct a subchaser base in this neighborhood. After inspecting the territory in detail, Captain Leigh decided that the Bay of Govino, in the island of Corfu, would best meet our requirements."[9] By the time the detachment of chasers arrived on June 4, malaria was rampant at Govino, and a small bay, which the chaser crews named "American Bay,"[10] was selected as an alternative.

On the 5th of June, twenty-one additional chasers arrived, with Ensign Chambers on *SC-128* and Chief Millholland on *SC-124* (shown on page 268). That convoy included the support ship assigned to the Corfu chasers, USS *Leonidas* (AD-7). Their entire trip took more than nine weeks; much of that included stops for repairs and replenishment at Bermuda, the Azores, Gibraltar, and a final stop at Malta. Thirty-six chasers made up the Corfu detachment, the last of which arrived on June 19. They were organized into two squadrons of six hunting units. *SC-124* became the lead, or flagship, of Unit A, while *SC-128* was assigned to Unit B.[11] Chief Ray Millholland was later assigned to *SC-225*.

The summer of 1918 saw over one hundred of these vessels distributed among three naval bases in areas where submarine warfare continued to create the biggest threat to an Allied victory. Admiral Sims summarized the tactical mission of the subchasers throughout the war zone:

Destroyers and other patrol boats kept track of the foe pretty well so long as he remained on the surface; the business of the subchaser, we must remember, was to find him after he had submerged. The Commander-in-Chief on shore sometimes sent a radio that a German had appeared at an indicated spot, and disappeared beneath the waves; the chasers would then start for this location and begin hunting with their listeners. Aircraft which sighted submarines would send similar messages; convoys that had been attacked, individual ships that had been torpedoed, destroyers which had spotted their prey, only to lose track of it as soon as it submerged, would call upon the chasers to take up the battle where they had abandoned it.[12]

As this book has emphasized, there were listeners trained in New London who were assigned to a variety of vessels, including the chasers, but they also served on destroyers, armed yachts, and submarines. Likewise, British listeners, trained at several facilities within the war zone, served on motor launches, drifters, trawlers, and destroyers, as well as many shore stations. It is impossible to relate all the stories told by listeners' encounters with U-boats. What follows are a few samples documented during and soon after the war.

The descendants of Fred George Bankson, who served on *SC-177*, have preserved his diary from his service with Subchaser Detachment One, Base 27, at Plymouth, England. *SC-177* was the lead chaser of the hunting unit, which also included *SC-143* and *SC-148*. These chasers were among the first to arrive in May, 1918. The diary has been transcribed by the family to a web site, referenced here, where the text (and the excepts below) retained the sentence structure and spelling as appeared in the diary. The following are extracts related to U-boat encounters. The daily diary entries began on October 1, although the following earlier account appeared on the first page.

May 30, 1918
   On drifting patrol 15 miles South of St. Catherin's light, Isle of Wight, the [U.S. destroyer] Aylwin had been circling vicinity for two hours, after dusk had just gone out of Hydrophone range when an enemy submarine broke water within two boat's lengths of starboard quarter of S.C. #143. Evidently ballast tanks had been blown without using propellers, which started when conning tower was up, promptly reported by "C" tube listener on #143, which fired Y-gun immediately before getting underway. Submarine was distinctly visible to all hands

on deck of the #143. On starting 143 dropped two more charges from stern, ordering #177 to stand by, but not to move. #143 circled and stopped, at once reporting that submarine was approaching her starboard beam on the surface close aboard, apparently being unable to dive. When within estimated range "Y" gun was again fired by 143 underway, and another charge, set 50 ft., dropped from stern across estimated course of enemy. Submarine submerged—night dark—143 anchored. S.C.#177 drifted so that one boat would be near submarine whatever it did. Tubes down, and for an hour listened to hammering and other sounds, like fuses blowing out, from submarine. Also heard his anchor chain pay out. Then S.C. #177 anchored. After getting very accurate cross bearings, #177 attacked estimated spot with four charges, silencing all sounds. The next day 177 and 143 stayed on spot until relieved by Div. 2, which stayed in the vicinity for two days. The morning of May 31, USS AYLWIN coming up laid a bomb barrage on a large oil patch nearby. Position was buoyed, but tide carried buoy under. Depth 40 fathoms. No evidence, except oil.

During this encounter, Bankson referred to the destroyer USS *Aylwin* (shown on page 48), having "laid a bomb barrage" where the submarine was suspected of having settled onto the sea bottom. Destroyers and chasers were outfitted with Y-gun projectors, which could lob depth charges over the area in hopes of finishing off the submarine predator. Bankson then continued with his log, where the following encounter began on October 10:

At Scilly Is. all day, very quiet, 9:30 PM underway to patrol certain area, very rough sea.

Oct 11

Listening all day, 11:30 PM heard U-boat running, got good fix on him when he stopped, heard him 4:00 AM Oct 12, got underway and dropped 3 bombs and good bye—Fritz—

Oct 19

Underway, running patrol, this morning got a radio that sub was around Lizzard's Head light, nothing seen of him, returned to Plymouth that night.

Oct 26

Running patrol till 10:00 AM, then drifting patrol till 5:00 PM of Lizzard Head, drifting 14 miles off Land's End, got underway 10 miles off Scilly Is. 8:00 PM, general quarters till 10:00 PM, sub seen at 11:30

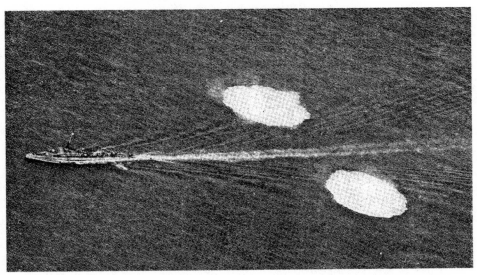

Depth charge firing sequence from a Y-gun: (1) Sailor arms the depth charge and sets the depth; (2) Firing lanyard ready to pull; (3) The two depth charges in the air (NHHC NH 52675, 52676, and 123844); (4) The depth charges detonate while the destroyer speeds away. (Sims, 1919-1920)

PM and we had general quarters till 11:00 AM Oct 27 when we heard Fritz get underway, then we got underway and circles him till 2:00 PM, then got cross bearings on him and dropped 12 cans of T.N.T. on the poor little Fritzies, sub reported badly damaged.

Oct 28

Plymouth at 8:00 AM, got more cans and turned in reports of sub, then we got credit from Admiral of base for our good work.[13]

Todd Woofenden, in his *Hunters of the Steel Sharks*, provides many accounts of the subchaser hunting units operating from Plymouth, Queenstown, and Corfu. His descriptions are drawn from a series of war diaries associated with subchaser detachment one (Base 27 at Plymouth), subchaser detachment two (Base 25 at Corfu), and subchaser detachment three (Base 6 at Queenstown). The U-boat encounters of *SC-177* from Bankson's personal diary closely follow the detachment one war diary accounts in *Hunters of the Steel Sharks*. The war diaries are in the naval records collection at the National Archives, Washington, D. C.

BRITISH LISTENERS

It can't be forgotten that British vessels also carried a variety of listening devices. Crews had trained extensively with their own hydrophone flotillas, which, by 1918, included American devices as well as much improved British versions (see page 264). The following three accounts of listeners operating around Britain and at Gibraltar are from Gibson and Prendergast, in *The German Submarine War 1914-1918* (1931):

> [O]n January 28—the hydrophones of the Granton trawler *W. S. Bailey* detected a submarine off the Firth of Forth, evidently trying to wait for the passing of the Scandinavian convoy. As soon as the enemy's sound was located, depth-charges were put over. Hours passed. No wreckage floated to the surface to denote possible injury. No sound of motors was heard. Then in the moonlight the hull of UB 63 (Gebeschus) emerged; the periscope was seen to be distorted at an angle of forty-five degrees. Depth-charges were again put in, this time by the trawler *Fort George*, and the wrecked U-boat disappeared for ever.[14]
>
> In the spring of 1918, motor launches equipped with hydrophones were established at Gibraltar, in the Aegean, and in the Otranto Straits. The Gibraltar unit drew first blood. In the early hours of April 21 the

ML 413, lying off Almina Point, heard the sound of fast-running propellers coming up out of the west. Switching on her lights to avoid a collision, she espied a submarine rapidly moving east. The U-boat altered course sharply, crossed the bows of the motor launch barely ten yards distant, and dived. ML 413 swung round, followed up the wake of the submarine, and put over two depth-charges. After the disturbance had subsided, she listened on her hydrophones. The little vessel heard nothing. As day broke the sea around was seen to be covered with oil. Upon the greasy Lagoon there floated four pieces of woodwork and part of a steel lined mahogany door, pitted with steel splinters. Thus terminated abruptly and decisively the career of UB 71 . . .[15]

On August 8 the Torbay hydrophone unit (consisting of the old destroyer *Opossum* and 7 ML's) located a submarine 4 miles south by west of Berry Head; and so thoroughly did they lard the area with depth charges, that the UC 49 (Kukenthal) then and there passed out of existence.[16]

Torbay and Berry Head are located east of Plymouth along the southern coast of England, facing out into the Channel. The Office of Naval Intelligence reported on a coordinated attack by several American subchasers and a British destroyer, HMS *Roebuck*, which occurred on September 6, 1918. The supposition was that the U-boat was sunk, but the crew survived the initial attack. Several listeners reported that they heard "sounds like rifle or revolver shots near this position on tubes," referring to the SC-tubes carried on the subchasers, then: "Three [shots] first, followed by 22. Heard simultaneously on [chasers] *137* and *41*."[17]

HUNTING *U-53*

[A]s soon as the chasers and British hunting vessels became active here [southern end of the Channel], the Germans abandoned this field of operations. This was the reason that the operative area of the Plymouth detachment was extended. Some of the chasers were now sent around Land's End and up the north Cornish coast, where colliers bound from Wales to France were proving tempting bait for the U-boats; others operated further out to sea, off the Scilly Islands and west of Brest. In these regions their contacts with the submarine were quite frequent.[18]

Admiral Sims described the summer of 1918, when one of the most sought-after U-boats, *U-53*, was operating south of the British Islas, within

British motor launch stops to listen for a U-boat. With his hydrophone lowered over the side, the listener adjusts his headset. (Courtesy Marist College; Lowell Thomas Archive)

range of the American chasers. Two years earlier, in September 1916, *U-53* (shown on page 67) had paid an unanticipated visit to Newport, Rhode Island. Her visit was unlike that of the mercantile submarine *Deutschland*, ostensibly on a commercial run to neutral America in July. After a brief stay in Narragansett Bay, *U-53* headed back to Germany, passing within sight of the Nantucket Lightship and sinking British, Dutch, and Norwegian vessels (see chapter 7). From Admiral Sims:

> About the middle of August, 1918, we discovered that the *U-53* was operating in the Atlantic about 250 miles west of Brest. At the same time we learned that two German submarines were coming down the west coast of Ireland. We picked up radio messages which these three boats were exchanging; this made it quite likely that they proposed to form a junction west of Brest, and attack American transports, which were then sailing to France in great numbers. Here was an opportunity for the subchasers. The distance—250 miles to sea—would be a severe strain upon their endurance, but we assigned four hunting units,

twelve boats in all, to the task, and also added to this contingent the destroyers *Wilkes* and *Parker*. On the morning of September 2nd, one of these subchaser units picked up a suspicious sound. A little later the lookout on the *Parker* detected on the surface an object that looked like a conning tower . . . The *Parker* put on full speed, found an oilslick where the submarine had evidently been pumping its bilges, and dropped a barrage of sixteen depth charges. But had these injured the submarine? Under ordinary conditions there would have been no satisfactory answer to this question; but now these little wooden boats came up, advanced about 2000 yards ahead of *Parker*, stopped their engines, put over their tubes and began to listen. In a few minutes they conveyed the disappointing news to the *Parker* that the depth charges had gone rather wild, that the submarine was still steaming ahead, and that they had obtained a 'fix' of its position. But the *U-53*, as always, was exceedingly crafty. It knew the chasers were on the trail; its propellers were revolving so slowly that almost no noise was made; the U-boat was stealthily trying to throw its pursuers off the scent. For two and a half hours the chasers kept up the hunt, now losing the faint noise of the *U-53*, now again picking it up, now turning in one direction, then abruptly in another. Late in the afternoon, however, they obtained a 'fix,' which disclosed the welcome fact that the submarine was only about 300 yards north of them. In a few minutes four depth charges landed on this spot.[19]

The subchaser continued to listen, but heard nothing. Radio signals from other U-boats attempting to contact *U-53* were intercepted, but there was no response, the assumption being that the submarine had been sunk. After a week had passed, radio operators at last heard a transmission from *U-53* as she passed north of Scotland, heading home. "[I]t apparently had as many lives as a cat, for it was able, in its battered condition, to creep back to Germany. . . a voyage of more than a thousand miles. The subchasers, however, at least had the satisfaction of having ended the active career of this boat . . . two months before the armistice."[20]

SUBMARINE LISTENERS ON USS *L-9*

On January 11, 1918, after a cold month spent at the naval base in Norfolk, Virginia, the USS *L-9* headed eastward along a path across the Atlantic which the subchasers would soon follow—first to Bermuda, then the crossing to the Azores. *L-9* and six of her sister L-class submarines were bound for Bantry Bay in a fjord at the southwestern end of Ireland where they joined a flotilla of British E-, H-, and L-class submarines. To avoid confusion with the British L-class, the American submarines were designated "AL" boats (a group of these are shown on page 1). In his memoir *Take Her Down* (1937), T. B. Thompson, executive officer of *L-9* during the war, related that the Germans recognized how effective submarines had been at attacking their U-boats, and "kept their underwater craft out of any areas where they thought Allied subs might be." Thus, the Allied boats "performed two vital roles: an offensive one of attacking U-boats and a defensive one of patrolling focal areas off important seaports to keep the U-boats away . . ."[21]

Thompson related an incident during their first patrol off the west coast of England near where the Bristol Channel enters the Irish Sea: "All day long the L-9 cruised back and forth in her area. . . At frequent intervals the officer of the watch ran up his periscope, [and] took a careful look all around the horizon. . . A man at the listening gear constantly swept the ocean depths for the distant throb of propellers . . ."[22] And then:

'High-speed propellers, close aboard, bearing 290,' reported the listener.

'Left. Hard left. Steady on one two zero,' calmly ordered our Skipper. Gradually the intent of his order gripped us. He was trying to ram the U-boat, submerged.

'Steady on one two zero, Sir,' came the quiet reply from the quartermaster at the steering lever.

'Propellers getting closer. Drawing ahead, Sir. Bearing three three zero. Drawing rapidly across the bows,' advised the listener.

'Come right. Come right hard,' ordered our Commander and the quartermaster repeated back:

'Propellers dead ahead. Dead ahead, Sir. Very close, Sir.'

'Stand by to ram.'

Four short words. We braced ourselves. Breaths came fast and hard. The manifold man made the sign of the Cross.

'Propellers drawing away to starboard.'

'Keep coming right. Hard right.'

So, for nearly an hour, the Skipper played blindman's buff down in the ocean depths as he tried to ram the slower but zigzagging U-boat, with certain death the price of success . . . the listener reporting propellers sometimes nearer, sometimes farther . . .

The U-boat continued running at her full speed of around 9 knots and drew slowly away, although the L-9 could make eleven. But we had to slow the motors to allow the listener to hear accurately.[23]

It was a close call for *L-9*—anxious to put an end to a predator before it could sink any more merchant vessels—even at the risk of being sunk in the encounter. This U-boat slowly moved on. There was no record of which U-boat was involved, so there is no way to know if it continued its mission of unrestricted submarine warfare, or was lost to one of the many other Allied attempts to destroy each German submarine that ventured out to sea.

THE OTRANTO BARRAGE

The several lines of patrolling vessels extended about thirty-five miles; there were vessels of several types, the whole making a formidable gauntlet, which the submarine had to run before they could get from the Adriatic to the Mediterranean. First came a line of British destroyers; it was their main duty to act as protectors and to keep the barrage from being raided by German and Austrian surface ships—a function which they fulfilled splendidly. Next came a line of trawlers, then drifters, motor launches, and chasers, the whole being completed by a line of kite-balloon sloops.[24]

The Otranto Barrage, which included numbers of American chasers, as Admiral Sims described, created a dangerous passage into the Mediterranean for U-boats stationed at several bases in the Adriatic. "Practically all these vessels," according to Sims, "were provided with the American devices; and so well did these ingenious mechanisms function that it was practically impossible for any submarine to pass the Otranto barrage in calm weather without making itself heard."[25] Submarines would routinely wait for storms in the area, hoping that the increased ambient noise would mask the sounds from their propellers.[26]

ARMISTICE ON THE HORIZON

The listeners, both British and American, remained busy on the barrage throughout the final months of the war. "From July, 1918, until the day of the Armistice, our flotilla at this point kept constantly at work; and the reports of our commanders show that their sound contacts with the enemy

Subchaser SC-124 with SC-127 and SC-125 while on duty in the Adriatic. (NHHC NH 195164)

were very frequent." Admiral Sims then noted it was only when Austria surrendered and an armistice was signed with that country on November 4 that American officers learned from officers in the Austrian navy that the chasers "were responsible for a mutiny in the Austrian submarine force." Sims described the effect on morale:

> Two weeks after [the subchasers'] arrival it was impossible to compel an Austrian crew to take a vessel through the straits, and from that time, until the ending of the war, not a single Austrian submarine ventured upon such a voyage. . . There was practically no case in which a submarine crossed the barrage without being bombed in consequence; the morale of the German crews steadily went to pieces, until, in the last month of the war, their officers were obliged to force them into the submarines at the point of a pistol.[27]

German submarines operating in the Atlantic were recalled on October 21, including the two still along the eastern seaboard of the United States. An attack on the Austrian naval base on the Albanian coast at Durazzo on October 2nd[28] also led to the mutiny and eventual surrender by Austria, with the additional loss of the submarine bases at Pola (now Pula, Croatia) and Cattaro (today Kotor, Montenegro). German U-boats were either already in the Mediterranean or bottled up in the Adriatic without a base;

in desperation, as many as were able attempted their escape by way of Gibraltar. According to Gibson and Prendergast (1931):

> As they neared the Straits of Gibraltar, each boat essayed the passage independently. Hartwig, who was in U 63, relates that the Straits were swarming with hunters: destroyers, torpedo-boats, patrols, submarine-chasers, gunboats, sea-planes—all massed in an attempt to prevent U-boats from passing.[29]

Additional chasers, which had crossed the Atlantic not expecting the war to end, were in the Azores en route to Plymouth; seven were sent to Gibraltar to intercept U-boats attempting to pass through the straits.[30] One of these chasers, *SC-253*, arrived in time to see HMS *Britannia* sinking just west of Gibraltar, having been torpedoed by *UB-50*. Ensign George Wallace recalled those last days:

> We were ordered to Gibraltar—rush. . . Austria, just having made peace meant that German subs had no base nearer than Germany, and every one in the Mediterranean had to pass through the Straits to get home. . . .We made Gibraltar just in time to see the last of the torpedoed British battleship 'Britannia'—to see the destroyer 'Parker' miss destruction by about 6 feet and take up the hunt ourselves immediately. I certainly admire the Hun's nerve. After stealing through the Straits he hung around awhile and got a battleship.
>
> And then the Armistice—a stirring race to port, a shift to shore clothes and a shave, and the finest, craziest time of the whole war. We lay in Gibraltar for a month and a half—every one bent on doing the same things—as little work as possible and having all the fun there was. There were trips to Africa and others to Spain—to Algeciras, where there is the daintiest hotel in all Europe—afternoon tea with the 'limies,' at the Grand or Cecil, and many evenings of related experiences.[31]

The war was over, and the job of the listeners turned to celebrating the success. I doubt for most sailors, however, that tea was the drink of choice. Although many of the overseas chasers soon returned home, others faced a variety of fates. Several were assigned to mine sweeping operations, while others participated in an expedition past Norway and into the Russian arctic. For those being sold, all armaments were removed as well as the submarine detection devices. The last of the chasers finally returned home, arriving at Staten Island, New York, on November 19, 1919.[32]

Cold War submarine USS George Washington *(SSBN 598) underway.* (Courtesy General Dynamics Electric Boat)

[W]e had shown a skeptical world that even the wide expanse of the Atlantic was not enough to keep us from a super-raid to the coast of far-off America. To those who can see into the future, surely this is a warning of what later wars may bring.

—Frederick Körner to Lowell Thomas,
in *Raiders of the Deep*, 1928[1]

After the war, Lowell Thomas interviewed Fredrick Körner, an officer aboard *U-151* during her raid along America's Atlantic coast in May, 1918 (chapter 22). Körner was unequivocal about the future "when submarines will think no more of a voyage across the Atlantic than they do now of a raid across the North Sea. . . . America's isolation is now a thing of the past."[2]

Unprecedented in the carnage at sea and in the trenches, this four-year conflict among the world's nations had been dubbed The Great War. Millions of young men in uniform had died as did countless civilians; those who managed to endure and survive must have believed that this surely had been a war that would end all wars. That would prove to be a forlorn hope.

Of all the twentieth-century technologies brought onto and above the battlefields and at sea, none had the same potential to have won the war for Germany and the Central Powers as did the submarine. Fredrick Körner was right—submarine warfare had gone far beyond its origins as a novelty suitable only for coastal defense; there were many admirals who understood this from the beginning. Admiral William S. Sims, who commanded the U.S. naval forces in Europe throughout the war, praised the efforts of American and European scientists who successfully labored throughout the war to develop new antisubmarine technologies. He recognized, however, that it was not enough:

> Until it is possible for our naval forces to set out to sea, find the enemy that was constantly assailing our commerce, and destroy him, it was useless to maintain that we had discovered the antisubmarine tactics which would drive this pest from the ocean for all time."[3]

Certainly more had to be done before there was any hope of driving "this pest from the ocean." But how effective were these new technologies which Allied scientists and engineers had provided to naval antisubmarine forces? An assessment was made soon after the war by Admiral Robert S. Griffin, Chief of the Bureau of Engineering, writing in 1922:

> It has been unofficially estimated by those in a position to form such an estimate that the destruction of six, and possibly seven, enemy submarines was due to the use of American antisubmarine devices.[4]

That number may possibly be optimistic after a hundred years of archival research by those who may now be in a better position "to form such an estimate."[5] But in this new undersea battlespace, there was more to success than the numbers game.

> *The Value of the Submarine Sound Detector as an Instrument of Warfare* is not to be measured by the number of "U-boats" that by its aid have been located and damaged or sunk but rather by the resulting curtailment of their radius of operation and the effect on the morale of the officers and crews. The U-boat in operation was never safe after the perfection of the submarine detector.[6]

When Naval Experimental Station scientist Harvey Hayes used the term "perfection" in reference to submarine detection devices, he may have been a bit optimistic. What was evident to military strategists, however, was the importance of enlisting the minds of those scientists and engineers who worked side by side with naval officers and enlisted to put theory into practice. There were other devices being actively experimented with throughout the war, yet didn't involve "listening" to the sounds of a submarine, or even that lovesick mermaid.

A Future Rooted in the Past

The work of the Station in the development of antisubmarine devices should continue even after peace is declared with the idea of obtaining such devices as will make it extremely difficult for submarines to be used in the future in the way in which they have been used by the enemy in this war.[7]

On November 9, 1918, two days before Armistice, Ernest Merritt explained to the Special Board on Antisubmarine Devices his belief that research into submarine detection devices should continue after the war. Merritt mentioned one technology which showed potential: "Echo methods whether using waves above the audible range or, if practicable, longer waves." The concept had been studied among the Allies' scientific establishments, but was not ready for operational use before Armistice. The idea had been considered exceptionally promising, and thus handled as a classified technology:

The confidential nature of the work prevents a detailed account of the progress made . . .[8]

That was in 1922. Admiral Griffin, who may have believed that Germany could rise again as a threat to Europe, was cautious not to reveal details of these "echo methods" of submarine detection. U-boats, when discovered operating in shallow water, often settled to the bottom and remained quiet, providing the "listeners" with nothing to hear and hoping the hunters would give up the chase.

A great deal of effort at the Naval Experimental Station had been devoted to what Griffin referred to as "detection of submarines at rest." Much of the technology, however, relied on the application of electromagnetic fields, which would indicate when the hunter on the surface passed over or very near to a large metallic object—a submarine, for example. Experimental work, much of which was accomplished in Long Island Sound, showed promise, but the detection range was typically no more than two hundred feet. (See chapter 21.) Surely, there must have been a better solution.

As far as this country is concerned, the starting point was a conference in Washington, D. C., 14-16 June 1917. This was a big affair, sponsored by the National Research Council, at which delegates from England and France told a group of American scientists and engineers of the progress that had been made in meeting the German submarine menace."[9]

Walter Guyton Cady, physics professor at Wesleyan University in Middletown, Connecticut, had been invited to attend the June conference in Washington, D. C. (chapter 12). Prior to this, Cady had been considering the possibility of transmitting short duration pulses of high frequency sound through the water which, likely, would strike an object—a U-boat for example—then recording the time it would take for the sound pulse to return as an echo to a receiving device. Knowing the speed of sound in water, the distance or range to the targeted submarine, Cady understood, could be readily calculated.

Cady's interest was immediately piqued when the French delegates described the work of Professor Paul Langevin, who had left the *Collége de France* and was working for the French Ministry of Inventions at Toulon.[10] Langevin had been experimenting with the "piezoelectric" properties of quartz crystals, where an alternating current of electricity will cause a crystal to expand and contract (mentioned in chapter 5). This effect was found to be an efficient means to send those pulses of sound through the water; soon the American scientists were hard at work, hoping to expand on Langevin's experimental efforts. Cady had become associated with a group of scientists at Columbia University, headed by Dr. M. I. Pupin.

This concept, which relied on very high frequency sound pulses, was initially referred to as "supersonics," but later changed to "ultrasonics." In either case, the frequencies being considered were on the order of 30,000 to 100,000 Hz [cycles per second], well above the audible range of the human ear. "The most promising results in underwater ultrasonics," according to Cady, writing years later, "were achieved by the Columbia group, with which I cooperated from September 1917 until the end of the war."[11] Cady continued:

The tests at Columbia were made in a large tank. By the early part of 1918, the apparatus was ready for long-range testing, and the group went to the Navy Yard in Key West, Florida, where for several weeks the Gulf of Mexico served as a "tank." Among those associated with us at various times were Commander Houghton (England) and Lieutenant Abetti (Italy). [Houghton and Abetti are pictured on page 192]
After our return to the north, the tests were continued at the newly

organized Naval Experimental Station at New London, Connecticut, where some echo tests were made in the harbor.[12]

During a department meeting at the Naval Experimental Station, held on June 5, 1918, and chaired by Commander McDowell of the Special Board on Antisubmarine Devices, McDowell expressed hope that the efforts of Professor Pupin and his Columbia University team would soon show good results. Pupin was expected to bring his apparatus to New London on the 11th.

That signals can be sent which are directional and that range up to five miles is expected. In addition to that, is in hopes of getting good results in sending signals out and getting an echo back. Also getting an echo back in case the submarine goes to the bottom thereby getting direction."[13]

The system Pupin was bringing was also being considered for installation on a submarine, either *G-1* or G-2. McDowell then added: "This apparatus can be used for secret signaling," the idea being that unless U-boats were outfitted with high frequency receivers, supersonic dot-dash pulses would not be detected. There was no further mention at this department meeting of Professor Pupin and his Columbia team, which included Walter Cady, likely due to the highly sensitive nature of this specific series of tests.

At a technical meeting held on July 21, there was mention of the assembly of additional experimental apparatus including a "large power outfit for operating a large quartz sender." Of interest was a brief mention of some related work underway at the "New London Harbor Lighthouse," but no details were provided at that meeting.[14]

In the meantime, experimental work underway at San Pedro, California, was also producing important results. A nearly twenty-page report by Harris J. Ryan and Leonard F. Fuller was provided to the station on August 1, titled: "Quartz Supersound Source Projector: To determine essentials required for the design and construction of a supersound source projector of ample size required for trials at sea." They had observed a phenomenon, which was poorly understood at the time, but continues to be a design issue with the most sophisticated sonar systems in modern fleets—cavitation:

[W]hen the supersound was turned on, one would perceive in a few seconds the presence of many fine bubbles suspended against buoyancy in the water . . . They were driven or drawn toward each other and coming in contact would form a single larger bubble. . . . The liberation of the air from the water by the supersound in the foregoing fashion was, during the rest of the present work, a real help in exploring supersound fields, estimating the magnitude of their intensities and in making initial studies of supersound absorptions and reflections.[15]

What was misunderstood in 1918 was that the bubbles were not caused by "the liberation of air." When the vapor pressure within the liquid exceeded the local pressure field in the vicinity of the vibrating source, it was water vapor that formed bubbles (water molecules will change from a liquid to a gaseous state, either under heat or reduced pressure). The observers saw these tiny bubbles coalescing into larger ones, which, as is the case with cavitation, "broke and disappeared" once the bubbles moved away from the vibrating surface and into an ambient pressure field that exceeded the vapor pressure, causing the cavitation bubbles to collapse.

Cavitation was also observed by Professor Robert W. Wood of Johns Hopkins University. Wood, who also attended the June 14 conference in Washington, was commissioned a major and assigned to the Board of Inventions in Paris. He observed Langevin's experiments at Toulon, commenting about these bubbles: "[With] the frequency adjusted for resonance the narrow beam of supersonic waves shot across the tank causing the formation of millions of minute air bubbles and killing small fish which occasionally swam into the beam."[16]

Much had yet to be learned about echolocation as an effective submarine detection tool, but the groundwork was being laid by the Allies. According to Walter Cady, Langevin in France had created a projector which could transmit a high frequency pulse five miles, and by late 1918, had been able to receive an echo from a submarine at a range of about one mile.[17] During this same time, British Board of Inventions and Research (BIR) scientist R. W. Boyle had also been investigating echolocation using quartz transmitters, having limited but encouraging success by the summer of 1918.[18]

In America, research at New London continued. On September 1, it was announced at an experimental station technical meeting that a high-powered transmitter had been installed "at the Lighthouse in New London Harbor and experiments for range will be made this week." What made these experiments unique and important for future echolocation devices was that "[it] *was thought that the nature of the bottom would have considerable effect on results, and inasmuch as there was no theory covering it, it would have to be worked out by experimentation.*"[19] Oceanographic research related to underwater acoustics became an intense priority during the Cold War as sonar became an essential antisubmarine technology.

By mid-October the war was winding down, but the search for the best possible submarine detection devices continued. Scientists and engineers on both sides of the Atlantic were learning more about the complexities associated with echolocation. Unfortunately, neither the French, nor the British, nor the American devices were ready for use when Armistice was signed on November 11, 1918.

A conference on supersonics had been held in Paris between October 19 and 22, attended by British, French, and American naval scientific representatives. Professor J. H. Morecroft of Columbia University, who had worked on supersonic devices with Professor Pupin, attended as did the American associate scientific attaché in Paris, Kart T. Compton. Gary E. Weir (1997) described that meeting, adding comments made by Compton about issues affecting underwater sound transmission: issues that would lead to scientific measurements of the ocean environment throughout the twentieth century:

> They not only described in great detail the performance of the Langevin device but also demonstrated a heightened appreciation of the properties of the ocean that affect undersea sound transmission. In the course of American experiments in underwater signaling, Compton "noticed, as have all those who have been engaged in listening under water, great irregularities in transmission due certainly to the influence of the water medium." He went on to discuss the viscosity of the water, its temperature, the presence of marine life and debris, and the effect of bubbles on sound transmission.[20]

Compton was writing in 1918, but he and other scientists were aware of the complex nature of sound transmission through the water and the significant work that had to continue. As Ernest Merritt had recommended two days prior to Armistice, one priority should be: "Echo methods whether using waves above the audible range or, if practicable, longer waves." Those "longer waves" would increase the detection range, enabling echolocation to become a primary antisubmarine warfare tool during World War II, and even more so during the Cold War. Detection capabilities improved as the science of sound propagation in the sea became a priority among the civilian and military research institutions. "Oceanography," as Weir pointed out, "had quickly become indispensible to modern ASW."

"MODERN ASW" IN A NUCLEAR AGE

> The stakes were high—Soviet submarines prowled in a real battlespace and it would take real data and real science to maintain the advantage. . .
> It would be the intellectual risk takers and the physical risk takers—those

Cold Warriors walking the halls of the U.S. Navy Underwater Sound Lab—who would quietly enter that real battlespace, gathering scientific data needed to create the tools for a Cold War strategy.[21]

We—a Cold War generation of civilian scientists, engineers, technicians, and machinists—walked in the footsteps, literally, of those risk takers from the Great War. It was the Naval Experimental Station in 1917. Fifty years later, in June 1967, this twenty-one-year-old graduate engineer entered the gates to that same Fort Trumbull waterfront. As I looked toward Long Island Sound from a fifty-year-old wooden pier jutting out into the Thames River, I had no idea of the antisubmarine warfare legacy created along these same paths during the War That Did *Not* End All Wars. It wasn't until after a long career that I could fully comprehend how crucial their efforts had been to curtailing the relentless German U-boats, so instrumental in winning that devastating war. A century has now passed, and as I grew more familiar with how tirelessly my civilian predecessors had struggled, I was driven to write their story.[22]

A book like this would never have been possible without access to the written legacies of individuals from a long-departed generation who had an impact on the course of history. It is *their* voices readers will hear as they read this book.

First and foremost, I owe a special expression of gratitude to a retired coworker, Bernie Cole. It was during a chance meeting with Bernie when I first learned of the Naval Experimental Station. His step-grandfather, Harvey C. Hayes, was one of the Station scientists who walked the same paths along the New London waterfront that Bernie and I and many of our U.S. Navy Underwater Sound Laboratory Cold War colleagues walked a half-century later. Hayes had the foresight to save nearly two hundred photographs from his time at New London, which are now a family archive. Immediately after the war, Hayes published a summary of the technologies developed at the Station in the *Proceedings of the American Philosophical Society*.

It is essential that I acknowledge Harvey Hayes and many others who contributed so much to history, represented herein by individuals from both sides of the Great War. Their contributions to this book are found in documents, reports, interviews, and memoirs written during and shortly after the war. The specific sources are detailed in the bibliography.

First, my thanks go to the late Charles F. Horne, editor of the seven-volume *Source Records of the Great War,* published in 1923, from which I quote much of the political intercourse between America and Germany. Voices from the top include America's Admiral William S. Sims' memoir, "The Victory at Sea," serialized in *The World's Work: A History of our Time* between 1919 and 1920, later published in a single volume; and Britain's Admiral John R. Jellicoe, who published *The Crisis of the Naval War* in 1921; from the other side of the conflict is Admiral Reinhard Scheer's memoir, *Germany's High Sea Fleet in the World War* published in 1920.

Much of this book, however, relies on the voices of members of the civilian staff at the Naval Experimental Station, who worked 24/7 to develop the complex technologies needed to end the destruction brought by Germany's submarine predators. The establishment and inner workings of the Station come from the 1919 article "New Opportunities in Science" written by Robert Millikan in the journal *Science*. Additional insight comes from Millikan's 1950 autobiography, wherein he describes much of his antisubmarine work during World War I. Harvey C. Hayes has already been mentioned, but much is also drawn from an article by his colleague Max Mason, "Submarine Detection by Multiple Unit Hydrophones," serialized in *The Wisconsin Engineer* between February and April, 1921.

I am indebted to the archival staff at Cornell University's Carl A. Kroch Library, Division of Rare and Manuscript Collections, where the papers of Ernest George Merritt (#14-22-46) are held. These documents and his photo album give details of the day-to-day testing of listening technologies used on surface vessels and aircraft, hunting for simulated U-boats represented by American submarines from their nearby base in Groton, Connecticut.

It is also necessary to acknowledge the stories told by naval personnel who brought these U-boat hunting technologies to the war, many having received their training at New London. I am indebted to Wendy Gulley, archivist at the Submarine Force Library and Museum in Groton, where the 1918 hydrophone class notes of Ensign James Bean, along with other of his manuscript documents, are held. Published accounts of individuals who served on American subchasers include the memoirs of Lieutenant (JG) Hilary R. Chambers, Ensign George Wallace (as told to Lieutenant (JG) William Nutting), Chief Machinist Mate Ray Millholland, and the diary of a petty officer aboard *SC-177*, Fred G. Bankson. My deepest appreciation goes to Todd Woofenden and his recent book, *Hunters of the Steel Sharks: The Submarine Chasers of WWI* (2006), which chronicles the wartime experiences of Ensign George S. Dole, the twin brother of Woofenden's grandfather, while commanding officer of *SC-93*.

From the perspective of German submariners, two sources stand out and need to be acknowledged here. Ernst Hashagen, commanding officer of *U-62*, wrote a memoir, *U-boats Westward*, which was translated and published in America in 1931. The second source, *Raiders of the Deep* (1928), was written by American war correspondent Lowell Thomas, who returned after the war and interviewed German submarine officers. I also thank John Ansley, archivist at Marist College, where a collection of Lowell Thomas's World War I photos resides.

Finally, I want to acknowledge and thank Tim Straw, who labored through the entire manuscript and made valuable suggestions. I also extend my thanks to the many individuals who read and commented on portions of the text, and to Bonnie Beatrice and others who helped assemble the many historical photos, providing visual images to accompany the voices from the past.

Preface

1. David Bushnell, "General Principles and Construction of a Sub-marine Vessel," in *Transactions of the American Philosophical Society* (1799), p. 303.

2. For insights into Bushnell's engineering talents see Roy Manstan and Frederic Frese, *TURTLE: David Bushnell's Revolutionary Vessel* (Yardley, PA: Westholme, 2010).

3. John Wilkins, *Mathematical Magick: or the Wonders that may be Performed by Mathematical Geometry* (London: Ric. Baldwin, 1691 [1648]), chapter 5, pp. 178-90.

4. See Alex Roland, *Underwater Warfare in the Age of Sail* (Bloomington & London: Indiana University Press, 1978), pp. 18-26, for a discussion of Cornelius Drebbel and his submarine and underwater explosives. Roland also discusses concepts for a submarine vessel proposed in the last quarter of the sixteenth century, yet it is most likely that Drebbel's submarine was the first to be built and operated underwater.

5. A contemporary account of Bushnell's Turtle is in David Humphreys, *An Essay on the Life of the Honorable Major-General Israel Putnam* (Middletown, CT: Moses H. Woodward, 1794 [1788]), pp. 111-17.

6. Manstan and Frese, *TURTLE*, p. 30.

7. Bushnell, "General Principles," p. 305.

8. Manstan and Frese, *TURTLE*, p.293, appendix c, quoting from a November 9, 1775, letter by Bushnell's mentor, Benjamin Gale, to Silas Deane, a Connecticut representative to the Continental Congress.

9. Ibid., pp. 88-90.

10. Ibid., p. 174. The scientific principles Bushnell relied upon were essential to convince skeptics and supporters, as Manstan and Frese note, p.24: "[I]t was through scientific argument that Bushnell was able to convince his most ardent champion, Benjamin Gale. In a letter to Benjamin Franklin, Gale wrote a lengthy description of Bushnell's 'machine for the Destruction of Enemy Ships.' Gale emphasized that 'it is Constructed with Great simplicity, and upon Principles of Natural Philosophy.' Gale's entire letter is found in appendix b, p.289-91.

11. Ibid., chapter 22 ("September, 6, 1776: The Turtle Sets out on Its Mission") and chapter 23 ("The Next Day: Why the Turtle Mission Failed").

12. Francis M. Barber, *Lecture on Submarine Boats and their Application to Torpedo Operations* (Newport, RI: U.S. Torpedo Station, 1875), p. 30.

13. For a history of the activities at the U.S. Navy Underwater Sound Lab and its successors, see Roy Manstan, *Cold Warriors: The Navy's Engineering and Diving Support Unit* (Bloomington, IN: AuthorHouse, 2014).

14. Ibid., pp. 183-4.

15. William S. Sims, "The Victory at Sea," in *The World's Work* (New York: Doubleday, Page & Co., 1919-1920), vol 39, p.360.

16. Ernst Hashagen, *U-boats Westward*, (New York: G.P Putnam's Sons, 1931), p.215. The "electric fingers" Hashagen referred to are described in chapter 20. See the section titled "Trailing Wire."

Introduction

1. Rudyard Kipling, *Sea Warfare* (Annapolis: Naval Institute Press, 2002 [Facsimile reprint of 1916 edition]), p.95.

2. Ibid., p. 12.

3. Charles F. Horne, *Source Records of the Great War* (National Alumni, 1923), vol. 3, p. 56.

4. Sims, "The Victory at Sea," vol 39, p.357.

5. George W. Melville, "The Submarine Boat: Its value as a Weapon in Naval Warfare" in *The Annual Report of the Smithsonian Institution for the Year Ending June 30, 1901 (Washington:* Government Printing Office, 1902), p. 727.

6. V. E. Tarrant, *The U-Boat Offensive 1914-1945* (Annapolis: Naval Institute Press, 1989), pp. 161, 163-64 .

7. John Moore, *Jane's Fighting Ships of World War I* (New York: Military Press, 1990), pp. 124-27.

8. Tarrant, *The U-Boat Offensive*, p. 76.

9. This passage and the account that follows are from Ray Millholland, *The Splinter Fleet of the Otranto Barrage*, (New York: Readers' League 0f America, 1936), pp.167-72.

10. Sims, "The Victory at Sea," vol 39, p.352.

11. The number of civilian scientific staff at the end of the war is from John Merrill, *Fort Trumbull and the Submarine* (Avon, CT: Publishing Directions, 2000). The naval staff, which rose from 200 at the beginning of 1918, to 700 by the end of the war, is from Robert S. Griffin, *History of the Bureau of Engineering, Navy Department, During the World War* (Washington: Government Printing Office, 1922), p. 55.

Chapter 1

1. Reinhard Scheer, Admiral, *Germany's High Sea Fleet in the World War* (London: Cassell and Co., 1920), p. 33.

2. Ibid., p. 33.

3. Ibid., p. 34.

4. The British version, including the aftermath, is documented in Admiral John R. Jellicoe, Viscount of Scapa, *The Grand Fleet 1914-1916: Its Creation, Development and Work* (New York: George H. Doran, 1919), chapters 12-15, pp. 304-414. For the German point of view, see Scheer, *Germany's High Sea Fleet*, chapters 10-11, pp. 133-202.

5. Robert Fulton, *Torpedo War and Submarine Explosions*, facsimile reproduction [New York: William Elliot, 1810; ed. Herman Henkle (Chicago: The Swallow Press, 1971)] p. 4.

6. Ibid., p. 8.

7. H. W. Dickenson, *Robert Fulton Engineer and Artist His Life and Works* (London: John Lane, 1913) pp. 284-88.

8. William Wizard, "Plan For Defending Our Harbor," *Connecticut Courant* (Hartford, CT: September 9, 1807), p.1. [original emphasis]

9. Colt's sketch, which attributes the submarine to Halsey, is in Roland, *Underwater Warfare in the Age of Sail*, p. 140. During the 1840s, Colt experimented with, and attempted to sell Congress, the idea of remotely detonated, tethered sub-surface mines, portrayed in Philip Lundeberg, *Samuel Colt's Submarine Battery* (Washington: Smithsonian Institution Press, 1974). Lundeberg also relates (p. 22) Colt's interest in the reports of a submarine used during the War of 1812, which inspired Colt to visit New London, Connecticut, and other nearby towns.

10. Mark Ragan, *Submarine Warfare in the Civil War* (Cambridge, MA: Da Capo Press, 2002).

11. Jack Bell, *Civil War Heavy Ordnance* (Denton, TX: University of North Texas Press, 2003), pp. 471-96.

12. Naval Torpedo Station, "Notes on Movable Torpedoes," (Newport, Rhode Island, n.d. (c. 1875)), bound with "Torpedo Vessels in Naval Engagements," "The Italians on the Harvey System," and "Description of the Luppis-Whitehead Submarine Projectile or Fish Torpedo," pp. 1-33.

13. Ibid., p.5, original brackets.

14. Francis M. Barber, *Lecture on the Whitehead Torpedo* (Newport, RI: U.S. Torpedo Station, 1874), pp. 1-39.

15. Ibid., p. 19.

16. Ibid., p. 32.

17. For the history of John P. Holland and his submarine developments, see Richard K. Morris, *John P. Holland 1841-1914: Inventor of the Modern Submarine* (Annapolis, MD: United States Naval Institute, 1966).

18. Scheer, *Germany's High Sea Fleet*, p. 341, Scheer's parenthesis. Note that the torpedo is referred to by various spellings other than that referred to by Scheer, including Schwartzkopf and Schwarzkopf.

19. Ibid., p. 341.

20. John Rushworth Jellicoe, *The Crisis of the Naval War* (New York: George H. Doran, 1921), p. 7.

21. Martin E. Trench, et al. *The Naval Torpedo Station* (Newport, RI: Training Center Press, 1920), pp. 1-37.

22. Ibid., pp. 15-22.

23. Ibid., pp. 27-29.

24. Scheer, *Germany's High Sea Fleet*, p. 261.

25. Ibid., p. 261.

26. Jellicoe, *The Grand Fleet*, chapter 7 "German Mines and Submarines," pp. 221-48.

27. Ibid., p. 229.

28. Ibid., p. 226. An account of the ramming of a surfaced submarine is on p. 230.

29. Ibid., p. 245.

30. The offensive and defensive technologies employed by Britain against Germany's U-boats can be found in Chris Henry, *Depth Charge: Royal Navy Mines, Depth Charges & Underwater Weapons 1914-1945* (South Yorkshire, UK: Pen & Sword Military, 2005) and Dwight R. Messimer, *Find and Destroy: Antisubmarine Warfare in World War I* (Annapolis, MD: Naval Institute Press, 2001).

31. Jellicoe, *The Crisis of the Naval War*, pp. 49-50.

32. Ibid., p. 62.

33. Charles Domville-Fife, *Submarine Warfare of Today* (Philadelphia: J. B. Lippincott, 1920), p. 70, original emphasis.

34. Ibid., p. 79.

Chapter 2

1. H. W. Wilson, *Hush or the Hydrophone Service* (London: Mills & Boon, 1920), p. 5.

2. See Willem Hackmann, *Seek & Strike: Sonar, antisubmarine warfare and the Royal Navy 1914-1954* (London: Her Majesty's Stationery Office, 1984), pp. 21, 23, for Ryan's career path in the Navy.

3. Lowell Thomas, *Raiders of the Deep* (Garden City, NY: Doubleday, Doran & Co., 1928), p. 3.

4. Harvey Hayes, "Detection of Submarines," in *Proceedings of the American Philosophical Society*, vol. 59, no. 1 (1920), p.5. See Hackmann, *Seek and Strike*, pp. 63-64 for a discussion of the resonant "tuned" hydrophones used by the Germans. A discussion of resonant vs. non-resonant hydrophones during the war is also found in Griffin, *History of the Bureau*, pp. 64-65.

5. Hayes, "Detection of Submarines," p5. Hayes became a leading scientist at the Naval Experimental Station in New London, CT, working on hydrophone-based submarine detection systems.

6. Ibid., p. 43.

7. Submarine Signal Company remained actively involved in submarine detection technologies for a half century, eventually becoming a component of Raytheon Corporation, where sonar development continues into the twenty-first century.

8. Hackmann, *Seek and Strike*, pp. 45-46.

9. Roy M. MacLeod and E. Kay Andrews, "Scientific advice in the War at Sea, 1915-1917: the Board of Invention and Research" in *Journal of Contemporary History* (1971), vol 6, no. 2, p. 5, quoting from an article by H. G. Wells from *The Times* [of London], June 11, 1915.

10. Richard Walding, "Bragg and Mitchell's Antisubmarine Loop" in *Australian Physics*, vol. 46, no. 5, (September/October 2009), p. 140, quoting a letter by H. G. Wells published in *The Times*, June 11, 1915.

11. MacLeod and Andrews, "Scientific advice," p. 5, quoting Professor J.A. Fleming in *The Times*, June 12, 1915, and Sir Philip Magnus in *The Times*, June 15, 1915.

12. Ibid., pp. 4-9.

13. R. H. Gibson and Maurice Prendergast, *The German Submarine War 1914-1918* (London: Constable and Co., 1931), p. 24.

14. Ibid., pp. 23-28, for a discussion of the controversial decision within Germany between 1913 and 1914 to undertake the first submarine war on shipping, and the divisions within the British Admiralty over this possibility.

15. MacLeod and Andrews, "Scientific advice," p. 9. quoting from the *Balfour Papers*, British Museum, 49712, June 26, 1915.

16. Ibid., p. 7, quoting from the British Public Records Office, Admiralty 116/1430, August 19, 1915.

17. Ibid., pp. 5, 10.

18. Walding, "Bragg and Mitchell," p. 143.

19. Wilson, *Hush*, p. 7.

20. A naval "drifter" was a small vessel similar to a commercial fishing vessel, but outfitted for naval support. Many were supplied with listening devices.

21. Wilson, *Hush*, p.6.

22. A table of shore stations installed between 1915 and 1918 is provided in Hackmann, *Seek & Strike*, p. 65.

23. Ibid., p. 23.

24. Wilson, *Hush*, pp. 5-6.

Chapter 3

1. Jellicoe, *The Crisis of the Naval War*, p. 65.

2. Wilson, *Hush*, p. 7.

3. Ibid., p. 27.

4. Ibid., pp. 26-27.

5. Ibid., p. 30.

6. Ibid., p. 8.

7. Ibid., p. 32. While *B-3* may have been considered "obsolescent," another submarine of that class, *B-11*, was a assigned to operations in the Mediterranean. On December 13, 1914, *B-11* proved herself a capable war fighting vessel, having entered the Dardanelles, where she spotted and torpedoed the Turkish battleship *Messoudieh*. Other B-class submarines performed admirably during the war.

8. MacLeod and Andrews, "Scientific advice," p. 29. This submarine was likely *UB-26*, which was eventually scuttled by the French near La Havre.

9. Domville-Fife, *Submarine warfare*, p. 76.

10. A. B. Feuer, *The US Navy in World War I: Combat in the Sea and the Air* (Westport, CT: Praeger Publications, 1999), p. 38, also mentioned in Griffin, *History of the Bureau*, p. 54.

11. Jellicoe, *Crisis of the Naval War*, p. 67.

12. Ibid., pp. 65-66.

13. Wilson, *Hush*, p. 10.

14. MacLeod and Andrews, "Scientific advice," p. 20, quoting from an article titled "A Tribute to A.B. Wood," in *Journal of the Royal Naval Scientific Service*, July, 1965.

15. See A. B. Wood, "Reminiscences of Underwater-Sound Research, 1915-1917." *Sound: Its Uses and Control*, 1, 3, (May-June 1962), pp. 8-17, for Wood's account of his activities as a member of the BIR at Hawkcraig. This is an important source for material on British scientific research. Wood (pp. 16-17) included an account of an attempt to train sea lions to listen for the sounds of a U-boat.

16. MacLeod and Andrews, "Scientific advice," p. 21, quoted from the *Fisher Papers*, at St. Andrews University Library, 1209, Bragg to Fisher, May 12, 1916.

17. Ibid., p. 21, quoting from the *Fisher Papers*, at St. Andrews University Library, 1192, Wood to Rutherford, March 22, 1916 (original parentheses). See also Wood, "Reminiscences," p. 16 for more details about the move of BIR scientists from Hawkcraig to the Admiralty Experimental Station at Parkeston Quay, Harwich.

18. MacLeod and Andrews, "Scientific advice," p. 22, quoting from the Bureau of Invention and Research, Minutes, March 24, 1916.

19. Wilson, *Hush*, p. 122.

20. Ibid., p. 123.

21. Hackmann, *Seek and Strike*, pp. 60-61. See also Messimer, *Find and Destroy*, p. 116 and George Muhlhauser, *Small Craft* (London: John Lane Co., 1920), pp. 250-52.

22. Wilson, *Hush*, p. 9.

23. Hackmann, *Seek and Strike*, pp. 61-62. See also Messimer, *Find and Destroy*, pp. 115-16.

24. Hackmann, *Seek and Strike*, p. 62.

25. Wilson, *Hush*, p. 10. Elie lies at the northeast entrance to the Firth of Forth.

Chapter 4

1. Griffin, *History of the Bureau,* p. 69.

2. Wilson, *Hush*, p. 6.

3. See Hackmann, *Seek & Strike*, pp. 65-66 for the distribution of shore station locations from 1915-1918.

4. Domville-Fife, *Submarine Warfare of Today*, p. 184.

5. See chart in William S. Sims with Burton Hendrick, *The Victory at Sea* (New York: Doubleday, Page & Co., 1920), p. 286.

6. Hashagen, *U-Boats Westward*, p. 128.

7. Ibid., p. 218.

8. Hackmann, *Seek & Strike*, pp. 64-68, discusses the process of detection from shore stations, and what he refers to as shore-controlled mine fields. U-boat losses during 1918, which include those lost in the Dover mine fields, are listed in Tarrant, *The U-Boat Offensive*, pp. 75-76.

9. Hashagen, *U-Boats Westward*, p. 128.

10. Jellicoe, *Crisis of the Naval War*, p. 96.

11. Walding, "Bragg and Mitchell," p. 140.

12. Ibid., pp. 140-45, for the account of Alexander Mitchell's experiments with the use of electromagnetic loops.

13. Locations included Oxcars, Elieness, and the small island of Inchcolm, according to Hackmann, *Seek & Strike*, pp. 65-66.

14. Walding, "Bragg and Mitchell," pp. 141-42.

15. Griffin, *History of the Bureau*, p. 70-71.

16. See Hackmann, *Seek & Strike*, pp. 65, regarding the Stanger Head shore station installation, and Walding, "Bragg and Mitchell," p. 144, regarding the magnetic loops at Scappa Flow, which resulted in the sinking of *U-116*.

17. Gibson and Prendergast, *The German Submarine War*, p. 327.

Chapter 5

1. Domville-Fife, *Submarine Warfare*, pp. 76-77.

2. Ibid., pp. 54-55.

3. Ibid., pp. 57-58.

4. Ibid., p. 59. An account of the meeting between the British representative and Sutphin is also in William W. Nutting, *The Cinderellas of the Fleet*, (Jersey City, NJ: The

Standard Motor Construction Co., 1920), pp. 14-17. See also http://www.naval-history
.net/WW1NavyBritishMLs.htm for additional information about the British motor
launches.

5. Moore, *Jane's Fighting Ships of World War I*, pp. 68-79, 124-7. See also Sims,
"The Victory at Sea," vol. 38, p. 604.

6. Domville-Fife, *Submarine Warfare*, p. 135.

7. Rodengen, *The Legend of Electric Boat* (Ft. Lauderdale, FL: Write Stuff Syndicate, 1994), pp. 58.

8. Domville-Fife, *Submarine Warfare*, pp. 10-11.

9. Gibson and Prendergast, *The German Submarine War*, p. 255n1.

10. Domville-Fife, *Submarine Warfare*, pp. 74-75.

11. Hashagen, *U-Boats Westward*, p. 139.

12. Robert Yerkes, ed., *The New World of Science: Its Development During the War*
(New York: The Century Co., 1920), chapter 3, "Contributions of Physical Science"
by Robert Millikan, see pp. 41-42.

13. Hackmann, *Seek and Strike*, p. 78 and MacLeod and Andrews, "Scientific
advice in the War at Sea," p. 6. Langevin also considered magnetostriction as a
potential method of transmitting sound through the water, finally preferring the
use of piezoelectric crystals.

14. For an excellent summary of Langevin's work with piezoelectricity and his
involvement with submarine detection system development see Hackmann, *Seek
and Strike*, pp. 77-83.

15. MacLeod and Andrews, "Scientific advice," p. 12.

16. Griffin, *History of the Bureau*, pp. 50-51.

17. Hackmann, *Seek and Strike*, p. 83.

Chapter 6

1. The text of the German notification is from http://www.firstworldwar.com
/features/lusitania.htm

2. Thomas, *Raiders of the Deep*, p. 95.

3. See Horne, *Source Records*, vol. 3, pp. 187-94 for an account from the British
law court as reported by Lord Mersey, presiding judge. For the full report, which
was issued on July 17, 1915, see "1915: Mersey Inquiry report" at: http://www
.rmslusitania.info/

4. Thomas, *Raiders of the Deep*, p. 97.

5. Ibid., p. 98. See also, Horne, *Source Records*, vol. 3, pp. 194-95, for Collector
of the Port Dudley Malone's testimony.

6. Thomas, *Raiders of the Deep*, p. 82.

7. Ibid., pp. 107-08.

8. American Association for International Conciliation, "Documents Regarding the
European War, Series No. IX, Official Correspondence Between the United States and
Germany" in *International Conciliation*, No. 94, (New York, September, 1915), p. 30.

9. Ibid., pp. 30-32.

10. Ibid., pp. 14-18, 30-32.

11. Horne, *Source Records*, vol. 3, pp. 196-97.

12. Ibid., 201-03.

13. According to the inquiry held soon after, documented in the July 17, 1915 Mersey Report, 286 women and 94 children were lost. See "1915: Mersey Inquiry report" at: http://www.rmslusitania.info/

14. Scheer, *Germany's High Sea Fleet*, p. 232.

15. Horne, *Source Records*, vol. 3, p. 203.

16. Scheer, *Germany's High Sea Fleet*, p. 232. Note that *Lusitania* sank on May 7, not May 8 as Scheer indicated.

Chapter 7

1. Horne, *Source Records*, vol. 4, p. 91.

2. Ibid., p. 91.

3. Ibid., p. 95.

4. Horne, *Source Records*, vol. 6, pp. 89-90.

5. Horne, *Source Records*, vol. 4, p. 98-99.

6. Ibid., pp. 100-101.

7. Gibson and Prendergast, *The German Submarine War*, p. 96.

8. Ibid., p. 95.

9. Ibid., p. 95.

10. Navy Department, *German Submarine Activities on the Atlantic Coast of the United States and Canada* (Washington: Government Printing Office, 1920), P. 15.

11. Ibid., pp. 16-17.

12. Horne, *Source Records*, vol. 4, p. 277.

13. Ibid., pp. 278-79.

14. Ibid., p. 280.

15. Navy Department, *German Submarine Activities*, pp. 18-23.

16. *U-53* and the Nantucket Lightship were within sight of Cape Cod and Nantucket Island.

17. Opened in 1878, Race Rock Light still sits at the entrance to Long Island Sound and is listed on the National Register of Historic Places.

18. Navy Department, *German Submarine Activities*, p. 18.

19. Scheer, *Germany's High Sea Fleet*, p. 261. Note in Gibson and Prendergast, *The German Submarine War*, p. 103, the authors discuss the increased endurance of *Deutschland* and the loss of her sister ship *Bremen*, which "left for Norfolk, Virginia, but she never reached her destination."

Chapter 8

1. Lloyd N. Scott, *Naval Consulting Board of the United States*, (Washington: Government Printing Office, 1920), p. 9.

2. Melville, "The Submarine Boat," p. 719.

3. Manstan, *Cold Warriors*, pp. 16-17.

4. Theodore Roosevelt, "American Preparedness" in *The New York Times Current History: The European War*, Vol. 4, July-September, 1915 (New York: New York Times, 1917), pp. 840-41.

5. See Scott, *Naval Consulting Board*, pp. 286-88, for the entire letter from Daniels to Edison, excerpts from which are also provided in the following paragraph.

6. Ibid., pp. 9-11.

7. Ibid., pp. 13-15.

8. National Research Council, *Third Annual Report of the National Research Council* (Washington: Government Printing Office, 1918), pp. 1-2.

9. Daniel Kevles, *The Physicists* (New York: Alfred A. Knopf, 1978), p. 109. Emphasis is Kevles'.

10. Ibid., P. 106.

11. Ibid., P. 109.

12. Ibid., p. 111.

13. George Ellery Hale's effort to bring the Academy's offer to President Wilson is in Kevles, *The Physicists*, pp. 109-12, and Helen Wright, *Explorer of the Universe: A Biography of George Ellery Hale* (New York: E.P. Dutton & Co., 1966), pp. 287-89. For additional information regarding the initial interactions between President Wilson and the establishment of the National Research Council, see Robert A. Millikan, *The Autobiography of Robert A. Millikan* (New York: Prentiss Hall, 1950), pp. 124-35.

14. Millikan, *Autobiography*, pp. 125-26.

15. Ibid., p. 126.

16. Scott, *Naval Consulting Board*, p. 37

17. Rexmond Cochrane, *Measures for Progress: A History of the National Bureau of Standards* (Washington: Government Printing Office, 1974), p. 159. For additional information see Scott, *Naval Consulting Board*, pp. 37-51.

18. Scott, *Naval Consulting Board*, pp. 42-43.

19. Millikan, *Autobiography*, p. 134.

20. Ibid., p. 137.

21. Ibid., p. 165. Emphasis is Millikan's.

22. Ibid., p. 135

Chapter 9

1. Scheer, *Germany's High Sea Fleet*, p. 218.

2. American Association for International Conciliation, "Documents Regarding the European War," No. 94, (September, 1915), pp. 4-13, includes correspondence from August, 1914 to April, 1915, between American Ambassador James W. Gerard in Berlin and Secretary of State William Jennings Bryan regarding discussions about what constitutes "contraband" according to Prize Law as understood by Germany. Additional Insight into Germany's position through February 1915, with examples of shipping sunk, are in Horne, *Source Records*, vol. 3, chapter 3 "The U-boat War on Commerce," pp. 40-64.

3. The tonnage is a reference to the displacement of a vessel, or the weight of the water which the vessel's volume displaces when afloat (or fully submerged in the case of a submarine). It is a measure of the vessel's buoyancy—when the weight of a vessel exceeds the weight of the water displaced, (i.e. while filling with water after the hull was penetrated by a torpedo or mine), it will sink. A small merchant ship may only displace a few hundred tons; a cargo ship may range from 2,000 to 5,000 tons; while an ocean liner may displace 10,000 tons. A WWI battleship may be 15,000 tons, a destroyer 1100 tons, a subchaser 75 tons, and an L-class submarine sent overseas would displace about 600 tons surfaced and nearly 800 tons submerged.

4. See Tarrant, *The U-Boat Offensive*, pp. 148-49 for statistics regarding tonnage losses due to U-boat predation.

5. Gibson and Prendergast, *The German Submarine War*, p. 140.

6. Scheer, *Germany's High Sea Fleet*, p. 247.

7. Ibid., pp. 248-52 for Holtzendorff's memorandum to the Kaiser in its entirety.

8. Horne, *Source Records*, vol. 5, pp. 8-11 for Bethmann-Hollweg's Reichstag address in its entirety.

9. Ibid., p. 10.

10. Scheer, *Germany's High Sea Fleet*, p. 219.

11. Horne, *Source Records*, vol. 5, p. 14.

12. Ibid., p. 14.

13. Ibid., p. 14.

14. Ibid., pp. 2-5.

15. Ibid., p. 6.

16. See Horne, *Source Records*, vol. 5, pp. 42-47 for what was referred to as "The Zimmermann War Scheme." This section also includes Japan's immediate reaction to Germany's proposal, calling the idea "repugnant to our sense of honor."

17. Article, "Sure U-Boats in Gulf of Mexico," *The Day*, April 6, 1917, front page.

18. Horne, *Source Records*, vol. 5, p. 107. President Wilson's address to Congress on April 2, 1917 is provided on pages 107-17.

19. Ibid., p. 108.

20. Ibid., p. 109.

21. Ibid., p. 110.

22. Ibid., pp. 123-24.

23. Ibid., p. 116-17.

Chapter 10

1. Sims and Hendrick, *The Victory at Sea*, p.7.

2. Horne, *Source Records*, vol.5, pp7-8.

3. For accounts of Sims' voyage to England, see Liam Nolan and John Nolan, *Secret Victory: Ireland and the War at Sea 1914-1918* (Cork, Ireland: Mercier, 2009) pp. 167-69; Sims and Hendrick, *The Victory at Sea*, pp. 3-7; Josephus Daniels, *Our Navy at War* (Washington, D.C.: Pictorial Bureau, 1922), p. 40. The story of Sims' crossing the Atlantic reached as far as New Zealand, "Admiral's Incognito Adventures—Secret Mission in England" in the *Auckland Star*, Vol. 50, Issue 137 (June 10, 1919), p.5.

4. Daniels, *Our Navy at War*, p. 36.

5. Ibid., pp. 38-39.

6. Ibid., p. 41.

7. See chapter 9, note 3 for a discussion of a vessel's tonnage.

8. See Gibson and Prendergast, *The German Submarine War*, pp. 160-64 regarding the effectiveness of U-boats after unrestricted submarine warfare was instituted.

9. Sims and Hendrick, *The Victory at Sea*, p. 7.

10. Robert A. Millikan, "A New Opportunity in Science" in *Science*, vol 50, No. 1291 (September 26, 1919), p. 287.

11. Ibid., P. 287. Note that Painlevé became Prime Minister of France in September 1917; headed the Ministry of Inventions when the European scientific mission to America was organized.

12. Scott, *Naval Consulting Board*, p. 52.

13. David R. Woodward, *Trial by Friendship: Anglo-American Relations, 1917-1918* (Lexington, KY: University Press of Kentucky, 1993), pp. 44-68, chapter 3, "The Balfour Mission and Americans Abroad."

14. Scott, *Naval Consulting Board*, pp. 52-53.

15. Burton J. Hendrick, *The Life and Letters of Walter H. Page* (Garden City, NY: Doubleday, Page & Co., 1923) vol 2, chapter 22, "The Balfour Mission to the United States" n.p., see letters dated 27 April, 1917, and 4 May, 1917. Search "Diaries, Memorials, Personal Reminiscences" and then "Page, Walter": http://wwi.lib.byu .edu/index.php/

16. Melville, "The Submarine Boat," p. 737.

Chapter 11

1. Griffin, *History of the Bureau*, p. 47. See also Scott, *Naval Consulting Board*, p. 68.

2. Submarine Signal Company's British patent No. 10,463 (1904) for an "Improved Method for Producing Sound Vibrations in Water Applicable to Marine Signaling."

3. Hammond V. Hayes, *Submarine Signaling: An Address by Hammond V. Hayes, Ph.D., August 30, 1920* (Boston: Submarine Signal Company, n.d.), n.p.

4. Griffin, *History of the Bureau*, p. 47.

5. Ibid., p. 47.

6. Scott, *Naval Consulting Board*, p. 67.

7. Ibid., p. 68.

8. Ibid., p. 69.

9. Ibid., p. 70. A similar list of physics-based issues was suggested by Charles F. Thwing, *The American Colleges and Universities in the Great War* (New York: MacMillan, 1920), pp.121-22: "The detection of the presence of a submarine is a definite physical problem . . . What lines of attack are open? Not many. The submarine in motion emits certain sounds; can they be heard? It is a solid body; can one obtain an echo from it? It is made of iron; can this fact help through some magnetic action?"

10. Scott, *Naval Consulting Board*, pp. 68, 74-75. For additional details about the association of H. J. W. Fay, vice president of Submarine Signal Co., and the Naval Consulting Board, including correspondence with Secretary of the Navy Daniels, is in H. J. W. Fay, *Submarine Signal Log* (Portsmouth, RI: Raytheon Company, 1963), pp. 18-22.

11. Gerald W. Butler, *Nahant's Naval Secrets* (Nahant, MA: Nahant Historical Society, 2012), p.14.

12. Griffin, *History of the Bureau*, p. 48.

13. Scott, *Naval Consulting Board*, p. 75.

14. Griffin, *History of the Bureau*, p. 49.

15. Thwing, *American Colleges and Universities in the Great War*, p. 115.

16. Scott, *Naval Consulting Board*, pp. 50-51. See also Cochrane, *Measures for Progress*, p. 159 regarding the Council of National Defense mandates for the Naval Consulting Board and the National Research Council.

17. Scott, *Naval Consulting Board*, p. 52.

Chapter 12

1. Millikan, "A New Opportunity in Science," p.288. An excellent summary of the initial work of the National Research Council and the European scientific mission to America, including this quote from Rutherford, are in Yerkes, ed., *The New World of Science: Its Development During the War*, chapter 3, "Contributions of Physical Science" by Robert Millikan, see pp. 34-40.

2. Wright, *Explorer of the Universe*, pp. 294-95.

3. E. H. Richardson, ed., *The Official Bulletin*, vol.1 (June 11, 1917), p. 1.

4. Ibid. (June 21, 1917), p. 1.

5. Millikan, "A New Opportunity in Science," p.287.

6. Richardson, *The Official Bulletin*, vol.1 (June 8, 1917), p. 5.

7. Ibid. (June 21, 1917), p. 1.

8. Scott, *Naval Consulting Board*, pp. 82-83.

9. Millikan, *Autobiography*, p. 154.

10. Hayes, "Detection of Submarines," p. 9.

11. Scott, *Naval Consulting Board*, p. 75.

12. H. A. Wilson, "The Theory of Receivers for Sound in Water," in *The Physical Review: A Journal of Experimental and Theoretical Physics*, vol. 15, no. 3, (1920), 178-205. Professor Wilson, who was a founding member of the scientific team assigned to the Naval Experimental Station in New London, was instrumental in defining the physics behind binaural submarine detection, and his work became the basis for designs of detection devices using multiple sensors. He published his theoretical analyses of binaural submarine detection soon after the war.

13. Scott, *Naval Consulting Board*, p. 75-76. See also Kevles, *The Physicists*, pp. 122-23. William Coolidge was a prolific inventor, and his portable X-ray tube found its way to battlefield hospitals along the Western Front. See the Edison Tech Center web site at http://edisontechcenter.org/coolidge.html

14. Only the C, SC, MB, MF, and MV devices included a length of tubing for the transmission of sound, while all the other devices incorporated various hydrophone designs, which converted sound waves to electrical signals received by the listener's headphones.

Chapter 13

1. Scott, *Naval Consulting Board*, p. 74.

2. Millikan, "A New Opportunity in Science," p. 288.

3. Scott, *Naval Consulting Board*, p. 75.

4. Millikan, "A New Opportunity in Science," p. 288.

5. Millikan, *Autobiography*, pp. 145, 161-62.

6. Ibid., p. 154

7. Millikan, "A New Opportunity in Science," p. 288.

8. Hayes, "Detection of Submarines," pp. 20-21. See also Millikan, *Autobiography*, p. 154, and Hackmann, *Seek & Strike*, p.55.

9. Millikan, "A New Opportunity in Science," p. 289.

10. Millikan, *Autobiography*, p. 163.

11. T. B. Thompson, *Take Her Down* (New York: Sheridan House, 1937), p. 56.

12. Contemporary discussions of the acoustics associated with the New London scientists can be found in Hayes (1920), "Detection of Submarines;" Mason (1921), "Submarine Detection by Multiple Unit Hydrophones;" and Wilson (1920), "The Theory of Receivers for Sound in Water."

13. Griffin, *History of the Bureau*, p. 51.

14. Millikan, *Autobiography*, p. 163.

15. Ernest Merritt archive (Cornell University, Accession number 14-22-46 b3), letter from Robert Millikan to Merritt dated July 25, 1917. Subsequent documents will be referred to as Merritt archive.

16. Article, "Harvey Hayes, Formerly of Oneonta Submits Design to Government," *Oneonta Daily Star*, December 27, 1917.

17. Article, "Prof. Hayes Summoned to Leave Swarthmore and Complete Device," *Oneonta Daily Star*, December 28, 1917.

18. Article, "Swarthmore Inventor Called By U.S. To Finish U-Boat Device: Prof. H. C. Hayes, College Physicist, Perfecting Device to Defeat Submarine—To Work in Secret Laboratory," from unidentified newspaper c. December 1917 in the Harvey Hayes family archive.

19. Horne, *Source Records*, vol. 5, p. 111.

Chapter 14

1. Merritt archive, memorandum from Commander Stirling to Merritt, July 9, 1917.

2. Ibid., Merritt report to Commander McDowell, July 23, 1917.

3. See Max Mason, "Submarine Detection by Multiple Hydrophones" in *The Wisconsin Engineer* (February-April, 1921), pp. 76-77: "The use of this principle was proposed by the author at a meeting . . . [with] representatives of the U.S. Navy on July 3, 1917. An instrument [the trombone device] was at once designed and constructed in the physical laboratory of the University of Wisconsin and tested with successful results at Madison on July 17, and at New London on July 30."

4. Merritt archive, Merritt report to Commander McDowell, July 30, 1917.

5. Ibid., Merritt letter to Experimental Station researcher Professor H.A. Bumstead, August 4, 1917.

6. Ibid., Robert Millikan letter to Professor Bumstead, August 1, 1917

7. Butler, *Nahant's Naval Secrets*, chapter 1 "World War I," pp. 11-59. This is an excellent summary of the contributions of the staff at what Butler referred to as the Nahant Antisubmarine Laboratory, well illustrated with photographs and drawings.

8. Kevles, *The Physicists*, p. 122.

9. Griffin, *History of the Bureau*, p. 55.

10. Merritt archive, test plan for USS *Margaret* operations, August 23, 1917.

11. Thompson, *Take Her Down*, p. 59.

12. Ibid., p. 60.

13. Butler, *Nahant's Naval Secrets*, pp. 25-26.

14. Merritt archive, letter from Robert Millikan to Merritt, July 12, 1917.

15. Ibid., letter, Millikan to Merritt, July 19, 1917.

16. Kevles, *The Physicists*, p.123.

17. Merritt archive, letter from Commander McDowell to Merritt, August 15, 1917.

18. Griffin, *History of the Bureau*, p. 56.

19. Merritt archive, letter from Merritt to Robert Millikan, September 24, 1917.

20. Millholland, *The Splinter Fleet*, p. 43. Because of the need to provide fast communication between the three chasers that operate in concert during the hunt, the radiotelephone was a priority technology, as described in Griffin, *History of the Bureau*, p.71: "This radiotelephone was similar, in general, to that developed for aircraft, and the development of the two was carried on at the same time, but the radiotelephone was in satisfactory operation on submarine chasers before it was adopted for aircraft."

21. Ibid., pp. 43-46.

Chapter 15

1. Sims, "The Victory at Sea," vol. 38, p. 490.

2. Ibid., pp. 491-93.

3. Ibid., p. 494.

4. Tarrant, *The U-Boat Offensive*, pp. 47, 53, 56; also Jellicoe, *Crisis of the Naval War*, p. 51.

5. James Bean, manuscript "The Naval Experimental Station at New London, Conn" (n.d., c. 1920), p. 2. This manuscript is available at the Submarine Force Library and Museum in Groton, CT.

6. Ibid., p. 2.

7. Jellicoe, *Crisis of the Naval War*, p. 40.

8. Ibid., p. 49.

9. Millikan, "A New Opportunity in Science," pp. 288-89: "This group worked under the authorization of the Secretary of the Navy and with the heartiest cooperation from the Navy Department, although it was first financed by private funds obtained by the National Research Council. In the course of a few months, however, when it had demonstrated its effectiveness it was taken over by the Navy, which spent more than a million dollars at that place."

10. John Merrill, *Fort Trumbull and the Submarine* (Avon, CT: Publishing Directions, 2000), p. 28. See also Kevles, *The Physicists*, p. 123; the $300,000 dollars was provided to the Special Board on Antisubmarine Devices, which was a change of heart by Secretary of the Navy Josephus Daniels who, previously, was unwilling to provide any funds to the scientists at work in New London.

11. Griffin, *History of the Bureau*, pp. 54-55.

12. Ibid., p. 54.

13. Thwing, *American Colleges and Universities in the Great War*, p. 118.

14. Millikan, "A New Opportunity in Science," pp. 291-92.

15. Millikan, *Autobiography*, p. 164.

16. Griffin, *History of the Bureau*, p. 56.

17. Ibid., p. 49. In September, 1918, Commander McDowell was transferred to U.S. naval headquarters in London to continue the antisubmarine work in the war zone. He was replaced as Special Board secretary by Captain J. R. Defrees; see Griffin, *History of the Bureau*, p. 59.

18. Ibid., p. 54.

19. Ibid., p. 59.

20. James Bean, manuscript "Notes from the Hydrophone School" (September 10, [1918]). Bean's hydrophone school class notes are available at the Submarine Force Library and Museum in Groton, CT.

21. Bean, "Naval Experimental Station," p. 4.

22. James Bean, manuscript "War-time Naval Radio Instruction" (Stanford, 1920), pp. 3-10. This manuscript is available at the Submarine Force Library and Museum in Groton, CT.

23. Ibid., p. 16.

24. ECHO, "Whannel Was At Fort Trumbull During World War I," vol. 11, No. 8, March 11, 1955. pp. 1-2.

25. Thompson, *Take Her Down*, p. 98.

26. Ibid., pp. 64-65.

Chapter 16

1. Frank P. Stockbridge, *Yankee Ingenuity in the War* (New York: Harper & Brothers, 1920), p. 222. See also chapter 16, note 26.

2. Ibid., pp. 222-24. Trawlers described in Muhlhauser, *Small Craft*, pp. 250-68.

3. Navy Department, Office of Naval Intelligence, *German Submarines in Questions and Answers* (Washington: Government Printing Office, June, 1918), p. 23.

4. Stockbridge, *Yankee Ingenuity*, p. 226.

5. Ibid., p. 227.

6. Sims, "The Victory at Sea," vol. 39, pp. 355-57.

7. Ibid., pp. 358-60.

8. Ibid., pp. 360-61.

9. Ibid., p. 361.

10. Ibid., p. 553.

11. Ibid., pp. 361-63.

12. Griffin, *History of the Bureau*, p. 24.

13. Hendrick, *Life and Letters*, chapter 22, n.p., see Letter, Ambassador Page to President Wilson, May 4, 1917, and his July 8, 1917 letter to his son.

14. Sims, "The Victory at Sea," vol. 39, p. 369.

15. Ibid., p. 361.

16. Griffin, *History of the Bureau*, p. 36.

17. Ibid., p. 33-34.

18. Nutting, *The Cinderellas of the Fleet*, p. 176. See also Jeffery L. Rodengen, *The Legend of Electric Boat*, pp. 27, 58; also, Todd A. Woofenden, *Hunters of the Steel Sharks: The Submarine Chasers of WWI* (Bowdoinham, ME: Signal Light Books, 2006), p. 13.

19. Griffin, *History of the Bureau*, p. 35.

20. Woofenden, *Hunters of the Steel Sharks*, p. 13.

21. A. B. Feuer, *The US Navy in World War I: Combat in the Sea and Air* (Westport, CT: Praeger Publications, 1999), p. 39.

22. Hilary R. Chambers, *United States Submarine Chasers* (New York: Knickerbocker Press, 1920), pp. v-vi.

23. Woofenden, *Hunters of the Steel Sharks*, pp. 61, 181.

24. John L. Leighton, *SIMSADUS: London* (New York, Henry Holt, 1920), p. 78. Chambers, *United States Submarine Chasers,* chapter 1, describes the vessel's features, including the armament carried on chasers, as does Woofenden, *Hunters of the Steel Sharks*, chapters 1 and 2.

25. Nutting, *Cinderellas of the fleet*, pp. 65-66.

26. https://www.history.navy.mil/research/publications/documentary-histories /wwi/december-1917/captain-richard-h-le.html

https://www.history.navy.mil/research/publications/documentary-histories /wwi/january-1918/captain-richard-h-le.html

https://www.history.navy.mil/research/publications/documentary-histories /wwi/january-1918/vice-admiral-william-13.html

Chapter 17

1. Woofenden, *Hunters of the Steel Sharks*, p. 28.

2. Ibid., p. 28.

3. Ibid., p. 30.

4. Nutting, *The Cinderellas of the Fleet*, p. 85.

5. Sims, "The Victory at Sea," vol. 39, p. 363.

6. Ibid., p. 363.

7. Nutting, *The Cinderellas of the Fleet*, p. 84.

8. Ibid., p. 84.

9. Navy Department, Office of Naval Intelligence, *Antisubmarine Information* (Washington: Government Printing Office, November 1, 1918), p. 37. The overseas service of *SC-151* is in Woofenden, *Hunters of the Steel Sharks*, pp. 13, 82, & 95.

10. Nutting, *The Cinderellas of the Fleet*, p. 85.

11. Sims, "The Victory at Sea," vol. 39, p. 456.

12. Ibid., pp. 457-58.

13. Chambers, *United States Submarine Chasers*, pp. 7-8.

14. Sims, "The Victory at Sea," vol. 39, pp. 457-58.

15. Merritt archive, Department meeting comments, May 8, 1918, p. 6.

16. Sims, "The Victory at Sea," vol. 39, p. 459. The best modern book describing subchaser operations during the war is Todd Woofenden's *Hunters of the Steel Sharks* (Signal Light Books, 2006).

17. Ralph D. Paine, *The First Yale Unit: A Story of Naval Aviation 1916-1919* (Cambridge, MA: Riverside Press, 1925), vol. 1, p. 156.

18. Ibid., p. 57.

Chapter 18

1. Paine, *The First Yale Unit*, vol. 1, p. 31.

2. Ibid., p. 30.

3. Ibid., p. 31.

4. Ibid., p. 25.

5. See Paine, *The first Yale Unit*, vol. 1, for the evolution of the unit in chapter 7, "From the Campus to New London;" and for their early training see chapter 8, "Rolling Down to Palm Beach."

6. Ibid., p. 31.

7. Ibid., p. 195. For information about the Davis gun see Stockbridge, *Yankee Ingenuity*, pp. 302-3.

8. Paine, *The First Yale Unit*, vol. 1, p. 195.

9. Ibid., p. 57.

10. Ibid., p. 156. See also page 57 where Paine gives the following example of what the pilots were told would occur: "Submarine E-1 will leave at 1 P.M. Sarah Ledge 1.40 and trim down. Underway 1.50, course 220 to Bartlet's Reef L.S. [Lightship], then course 260. At 2.20 S.W. of Light Ship, show conning tower and head south for 7½ minutes. At 2:30 go to 60 ft. depth on course 75° and porpoise about every 5 or 10 minutes. At 2.50 come up near Sarah's Ledge."

11. Ibid., p. 156.

12. Ibid., pp. 57-58.

13. Merritt archive, weekly report, September 17, 1917. See also department meeting notes dated May 8, 1918 regarding a test conducted the following spring.

14. Paine, *The First Yale Unit*, vol. 1, pp. 155-56.

15. Merritt archive, memorandum from Commander McDowell to Merritt, August 16, 1918.

16. See Paine, *The First Yale Unit*, for accounts of Ingalls' exploits in New London (vol. 1) and in combat (vol. 2), where he received the British Distinguished Flying Cross and the American Distinguished Service Medal. Paine provides lengthy accounts of the airmen from Yale who served in the Naval Reserve Flying Corps.

17. Paine, *The First Yale Unit*, vol. 2, pp. 361-62.

Chapter 19

1. Griffin, *History of the Bureau*, pp. 68-69.

2. Ibid., p. 69.

3. Merritt archive, daily log, May 16, 1917.

4. Ibid., department meeting notes, April 10, 1918.

5. Ibid., excerpts from a series of progress reports from Merritt to Commander McDowell, from June 1 to 4, 1918.

6. Ibid., copies of telegrams regarding Admiral Sims' request for "screened microphones for use on flying boat."

7. Ibid., test report, July 16, 1918. Admiral Griffin, *History of the Bureau*, pp.63-64, described the British interest in screened microphones.

8. Paine, *The First Yale Unit*, vol. 1, p. 195.

9. Griffin, *History of the Bureau*, p. 69.

10. Bean, "The Naval Experimental Station," p. 5.

11. Richard G. Van Treuren, *Airships vs. Submarines* (Edgewater, FL: Atlantis Productions, 2009), p. 97.

12. Hugh Allen, *The House of Goodyear: Fifty Years of Men and Industry*, (Cleveland, OH: Corday & Gross Co., 1949), p. 269.

13. Roy A.Grossnik, *Kite Balloons to Airships: the Navy's Lighter-than-Air Experience* (Washington: Government Printing Office, n.d.), pp. 5-8, and Hugh Allen, *The House of Goodyear* (Cleveland, OH: Corday & Gross, 1949), p. 269.

14. Allen, *The House of Goodyear*, p. 270.

15. Griffin, *History of the Bureau*, p. 69.

16. Scott, *Naval Consulting Board*, p. 79.

17. Ibid., pp. 78-79.

18. Hayes, "Detection of Submarines," pp. 39-43.

19. Merritt archive, department meeting notes, June 5 and June 12, 1918.

Chapter 20

1. Caryn Hannan, *Wisconsin Biographical Dictionary, 2008-2009 Edition* (Hamburg, MI: State History Publications, 2008), p. 259. Golfing was also a source of recreation for American naval officers when circumstances allowed. See, for example, Thompson, *Take Her Down*, pp. 192-95 and Woofenden, *Hunters of the Steel Sharks*, pp. 130, 131.

2. Article, "Earl Haig 'Plays Himself In': Once 'Field Marshal' in France, Now 'Captain of the Royal and Ancient,' One of the Greatest Honors in Golf" (*The American Golfer*, November, 1920). There were also options for a game of golf in the U.K., with Scotland having several courses, including one near Edinburgh and the Firth of Forth. From Wilson, *Hush*, p. 145: "Everyone was ashore from the wardroom except two . . . They had arranged to play golf, but the fog had shut down too thick on the Forth to make it worth while chancing the trip to the Braid Hills."

3. Kevles, *The Physicists*, p. 122.

4. Mason, "Submarine Detection," 25, 6, p. 99, and 25, 7, pp. 117-18.

5. Ibid., 25, 7, p. 117.

6. Ibid., 25, 5, p. 76.

7. Ibid., 25, 7, p. 118.

8. Sims, "The Victory at Sea," vol. 39, p. 173. Leighton, *SIMSADUS: London*, pp. 23-47, provides an excellent summary of the naval bases at Queenstown and Brest.

9. Kevles, *The Physicists*, p. 122.

10. Mason, "Submarine Detection," 25, 6, pp. 99-102.

11. Ibid., 25, 7, pp. 116-20.

12. Ibid., 25, 7, p. 117.

13. Ibid., 25, 6, p. 100.

14. Ibid., 25, 6, pp. 100-01. See also Hayes, "Detection of Submarines," pp. 16-18, 29-37 for a discussion of the acoustic sensors and progressive compensation. Both references include illustrations of the compensators.

15. The Type "H" compensator developed for Mason's MV-tube for destroyers, and the test results for USS *Jouett* (DD-41) is described in detail in Hayes, "Detection of Submarines," pp. 34-39.

16. Mason, "Submarine Detection," 25, 7, p. 120.

17. Hayes, "Detection of Submarines," pp. 39-44. Hayes described his experience with the U-3 Tube "Eel," a towed, flexible array of twelve in-line hydrophones, and the specialized electrical compensator designed for this listening device.

18. Harvey Hayes "U.S. Navy MV Type of Hydrophone as an Aid and Safeguard to Navigation" in *Proceedings of the American Philosophical Society*, vol. 59, no. 1 (1920), pp. 371-404.

19. Mason, "Submarine Detection," 25, 6, p. 102, and 25, 7, p. 118 for Admiral Sims' quote.

20. Bean, "The Naval Experimental Station," p. 5.

21. Griffin, *History of the Bureau*, pp. 54, 59.

22. Chambers, *United States Submarine Chasers*, pp. 7-9.

23. Woofenden, *Hunters of the Steel Sharks*, p. 82.

24. Chambers, *United States Submarine Chasers*, pp. 2-3.

25. Nutting, *The Cinderellas of the Fleet*, p. 76.

26. Vannevar Bush, *Pieces of the Action* (New York: William Morrow and Company, 1970), p. 71.

27. Hashagen, *U-Boats Westward*, chapter 11, pp. 129-42.

28. Griffin, *History of the Bureau*, pp. 60-61.

29. Information about the trailing wire can be found in Chambers, *United States Submarine Chasers*, p. 5; Nutting, *The Cinderellas of the Fleet*, p. 76; Messimer, *Find and Destroy*, p. 120; and Woofenden, *Hunters of the Steel Sharks*, p. 43.

30. Merritt archive, test plan "Program For 'Thetis' and G-4," August 28th, 1917,

31. Ibid., weekly report to Commander McDowell, September 3, 1917.

32. Chambers, *United States Submarine Chasers*, p. 5.

33. Nutting, *The Cinderellas of the Fleet*, p. 85.

Chapter 21

1. Merritt archive, Naval District Research Section meeting notes, April 10, 1918.

2. Bureau of Standards, *War Work of the Bureau of Standards* (Washington: Government Printing Office, 1921), p. 134.

3. Griffin, *History of the Bureau*, p. 72.

4. Bureau of Standards, *War Work*, p. 135. See Charles F. Thwing, *American Colleges and Universities in the Great War*, p. 123, who credited the scientists for their work on this topic: "Physicists, too, accomplished great results in the art of signaling. In this complex and unique art special use was made of the infra-red and ultra-violet rays, which are invisible."

5. Antonia Colella and Luke Colella, *Now We're Talking* (Bloomington, IN: 1st-Books, 2003), pp. 17-24.

6. Ibid., pp. 20, 23.

7. Kenneth Edwards, *We Dive at Dawn* (Chicago: Reilly & Lee, 1941), pp. 108-9. Edwards included a photograph of a carrier pigeon about to be released from the bridge of a submarine, see facing p. 244.

8. Stockbridge, *Yankee Ingenuity*, p. 235.

9. For information about Reginald Fessenden see: https://www.ieee.ca/millennium/radio/radio_unsung.html

10. Griffin, *History of the Bureau*, pp. 37, 71.

11. Merritt archive, Station Order No. 27, June 12, 1918.

12. Bean, "War-time Naval Radio Instruction," pp. 15-16.

13. Griffin, *History of the Bureau*, p. 71.

14. Bean, "War-time Naval Radio Instruction," p. 16.

15. Griffin, *History of the Bureau*, pp. 99, 128.

16. Hayes, "Detection of Submarines," p. 2

17. Ibid., p. 3.

18. Griffin, *History of the Bureau*, p. 68.

19. Merritt archive, department meeting, June 12, 1918.

20. The apparatus experimented with by Vannevar Bush in New London is described in his autobiography: Bush, *Pieces of the Action*, pp. 71-72. Bush's system was very similar to that being developed by Ernest Merritt.

21. Merritt archive, Test Report, June 30, 1918.

22. Ibid., memorandum to Commander McDowell, August 22, 1918.

23. Ibid., memorandum to Captain Defrees, September 30, 1918.

24. Ibid., memorandum regarding British Mark IV Search Gear, September 30, 1918.

25. Ibid., memorandum to Captain Defrees, September 19, 1918.

26. Ibid., memorandum to Captain Defrees, November 2, 1918.

Chapter 22

1. Thomas, *Raiders of the Deep*, pp. 290, 294.

2. Ibid., pp. 286-87.

3. Ibid., p. 294.

4. Navy Department, *German Submarine Activities*, p. 9.

5. Ibid., p. 9.

6. Ibid., pp. 8-9. See also pp. 143-150 for the recommended plan of defense

7. Thomas, *Raiders of the Deep*, p. 295.

8. Navy Department, *German Submarine Activities*, p. 10.

9. Thomas, *Raiders of the Deep*, pp. 301-02.

10. Ibid., pp. 304-05.

11. Navy Department, *German Submarine Activities*, p. 10.

12. Ibid., pp. 10-11.

13. Ibid., p. 143. The entire document is found on pages 143-151; see also pp. 8-9.

14. Ibid., p. 8.

15. Merritt archive, memorandum, Commander C. S. McDowell to Merritt, March 30, 1918. The B.I.R. is the British Admiralty's "Board of Invention and Research."

16. Ibid., status report, Merritt to McDowell, April 22, 1918.

17. Ibid., memorandum, Merritt to McDowell, May 31, 1918.

18. Navy Department, *German Submarine Activities*, P. 151.

19. Ibid., p. 153.

20. Bean, "Naval Experimental Station," p. 5.

21. Merritt archive, typescript meeting notes, September 1, 1918, p. 3.

22. Commander McDowell, at a meeting of the technical council of the Naval Experimental Station, recommended "to install an X-Tube on the HILDEGARDE [SP-1221], assigned to New London, 1917-1919]. It is also thought desirable to put this on the Fire Island Lightship." Merritt archive, Technical Council Notes, July 28, 1918. It should be remembered that on May 28, *U-151* had been operating off Fire Island, cutting Atlantic cables running out of New York.

23. Navy Department, *German Submarine Activities*, pp. 144-51.

24. Woofenden, *Hunters of the Steel Sharks*, pp. 192-94.

25. Nutting, *Cinderellas of the Fleet*, p. 88.

26. Woofenden, *Hunters of the Steel Sharks*, pp. 192-94.

27. Navy Department, *German Submarine Activities*, p. 117.

28. Ibid., pp. 139-41, for a list of all vessels damaged or sunk.

29. Ibid., pp. 82-91. Testimony by survivors regarding the attack by *U-151* is provided for these vessels.

Chapter 23

1. Sims, "The Victory at Sea," vol. 38, pp. 617-18.

2. Jellicoe, *Crisis of the Naval War*, p. 110. For the British views on convoys, see his chapters 4 and 5.

3. Sims, "The Victory at Sea," vol. 39, p. 161.

4. Ibid., vol. 38, p. 618.

5. Sims and Hendrick, *The Victory at Sea*, p. 349.

6. Sims, "The Victory at Sea," vol. 39, p. 355.

7. Scheer, *Germany's High Sea Fleet*, p. 262

8. Ibid., pp. 273-74.

9. Sims, "The Victory at Sea," vol. 39, p. 170.

10. Sims and Hendrick, *The Victory at Sea*, pp. 358-61.

11. Ibid., pp. 360-61.

12. Ibid., p. 323.

13. Ibid., pp. 322-23.

14. Sims, "The Victory at Sea," vol. 39, p. 355.

15. Scott, *Naval Consulting Board*, p. 107.

16. Navy Department, Office of Naval Intelligence, *Antisubmarine Tactics* (Washington: Government Printing Office, October, 1918), p. 4. See also Muhlhauser, *Small Craft*, p. 257.

17. Scott, *Naval Consulting Board*, p. 107.

18. Hashagen, *U-Boats Westward*, p. 113. Emphasis is Hashagen's.

19. Millholland, *The Splinter Fleet*, p. 207.

20. Ibid., p. 207.

21. Hashagen, *U-Boats Westward*, p. 113.

22. Mason, "Submarine Detection," p. 117.

23. Sims, "The Victory at Sea," vol. 39, pp. 364, 365, 367.

24. Chambers, *United States Submarine Chasers*, pp. 9, 11.

25. Millholland, *The Splinter Fleet*, pp. 50, 51, 53, 57.

26. Chambers, *United States Submarine Chasers*, p. 19.

27. Ibid., p. 21-22.

28. Millholland, *The Splinter Fleet*, p. 63.

29. Ibid., p. 63. The refueling process is also described in Chambers, *United States Submarine Chasers*, p. 23, and Woofenden, *Hunters of the Steel Sharks*, pp. 65-66.

30. Chambers, *United States Submarine Chasers*, pp. 23, 25-26.

31. Millholland, *The Splinter Fleet*, pp. 65-66.

32. Chambers, *United States Submarine Chasers*, p. 26.

33. Ibid., p. 27.

34. Millholland, *The Splinter Fleet*, p. 75.

35. Chambers, *United States Submarine Chasers*, pp. 28-29.

Chapter 24

1. Sims, "The Victory at Sea," vol. 39, p. 352.

2. Ibid., pp. 352-57.

3. Ibid., P. 357.

4. Wilson, *Hush*, p. 33.

5. Navy Department, *Antisubmarine Information*, pp. 38-39.

6. Chambers, *United States Submarine Chasers*, pp. 28-29.

7. Ibid., p. 29.

8. Woofenden, *Hunters of the Steel Sharks*, pp. 183-84, 189.

9. Sims, "The Victory at Sea," vol. 39, p. 370.

10. Woofenden, *Hunters of the Steel Sharks*, pp. 77-78.

11. Ibid., p. 81-83.

12. Sims, "The Victory at Sea," vol. 39, p. 461.

13. Fred George Bankson, *A Sailors Diary During World War I Aboard the Submarine Chaser 177* (Available at http://readytogoebooks.com/jgbooks/Diary-P-1918.html)

14. Gibson and Prendergast, *The German Submarine War*, p. 287.

15. Ibid., p. 268.

16. Ibid., p. 318.

17. Navy Department, *Antisubmarine Information*, pp. 39-42. The report is highly detailed, and includes a "Plot of Operations," depicting the engagement and the positions of the subchasers, although the involvement of *Roebuck* is not shown. This engagement by the subchasers is given in detail, including the report of a possible suicide among the crew, by Admiral Sims, "The Victory at Sea," vol. 39, pp. 465-68.

18. Sims, "The Victory at Sea," vol. 39, p. 461.

19. Ibid., pp. 464-65.

20. Ibid., p. 465.

21. Thompson, *Take Her Down*, pp. 156-57.

22. Ibid., pp. 180-81.

23. Ibid., pp. 188-89.

24. Sims, "The Victory at Sea," vol. 39, p. 470.

25. Ibid., pp. 470-71. The role of American subchaser in the Otranto Barrage is covered in detail in Woofenden, *Hunters of the Steel Sharks*, chapter 5.

26. Navy Department, *Antisubmarine Tactics*, p. 4. Quoting from a German submarine manual, under "Procedure When Pursued With Hydrophones," the first item listed was "A rough sea is the best natural protection."

27. Sims, "The Victory at Sea," vol. 39, p. 471.

28. See Woofenden, *Hunters of the Steel Sharks*, pp. 98-106 for an excellent account of the battle at Durazzo. Note that both Ensign Hilary Chambers in *SC-128* and Chief Ray Millholland in *SC-225*, participated in the bombardment of Durazzo.

29. Gibson and Prendergast, *The German Submarine War*, p. 276.

30. Sims, "The Victory at Sea," vol. 39, p. 476.

31. Nutting, *The Cinderellas of the Fleet*, pp. 91-92.

32. For the post war activities of the chasers, and their return, see Woofenden, *Hunters of the Steel Sharks*, chapters 6 through 9.

Epilogue

1. Thomas, *Raiders of the Deep*, p. 332.

2. Ibid., p. 333.

3. Sims and Hendrick, *The Victory at Sea*, p. 199.

4. Griffin, *History of the Bureau*, p. 73.

5. See Tarrant, *The U-Boat Offensive,* for a comprehensive review of U-boat losses and their causes, although some are still listed as "unknown."

6. Hayes, "Detection of Submarines," p. 46. Hayes' emphasis.

7. Merritt archive, memorandum to Captain Defrees, November 9, 1918.

8. Griffin, *History of the Bureau*, p. 68.

9. Walter Cady, "Piezoelectricity and Ultrasonics." *Sound: Its Uses and Control*, 2, 1, (Jan-Feb 1963), p. 46.

10. Karl F. Graff, "History of Ultrasonics," *Physical Acoustics*, Vol. 15. (New York: Academic Press, 1981), p. 43.

11. Cady, "Piezoelectricity and Ultrasonics," p. 48.

12. Ibid., pp. 48-49.

13. Merritt archive, department meeting notes, June 5, 1918.

14. Ibid., Technical Council meeting notes, July 21, 1918.

15. Ibid., San Pedro Report, August 1, 1918. Original emphasis.

16. Graff, "History of Ultrasonics," p. 43. Graff may have mistakenly referred to Professor Wood having been assigned to a Board of Inventions in Paris; the French Ministry of Inventions had established a principal research facility in Paris, where it was most likely Wood had been working.

17. Cady, "Piezoelectricity and Ultrasonics," p. 49.

18. See Hackmann, *Seek and Strike*, pp. 83-89 for a review of Boyle's work on echolocation.

19. Merritt archive, Technical Council meeting notes, September 1, 1918. This author's emphasis. See also Hackmann, *Seek and Strike*, pp. 89-95 for details regarding American involvement in the development of ultrasonics for submarine detection.

20. Gary E. Weir, "Surviving the Peace: The Advent of American Naval Oceanography 1914-1924," *Naval War College Review*, 1, 4 (Autumn, 1997), p. 88.

21. Manstan, *Cold Warriors*, p. xxiii.

22. Recent books about the Cold War activities at Fort Trumbull in New London can be found in Thaddeus G. Bell, *Probing the Ocean for Submarines* (Los Altos Hills, CA: Peninsula Publishing, 2011), and John Merrill and Lionel D. Wyld, *Meeting the Submarine Challenge* (Washington: Government Printing Office, 1997). There are many Cold War stories that have been published about the civilian and naval veterans of a technological struggle spanning a half century, when a nuclear holocaust was at risk. There are still many more adventures in the memories of these individuals, which have yet to be written—the dedication and commitment of the Cold Warriors during a frightful time must not be forgotten.

BOOKS

Allen, Hugh. *The House of Goodyear*. Cleveland, OH: Corday & Gross Co., 1949.

Barber, Lieutenant Francis M. *Lecture on Submarine Boats and their Application to Torpedo Operations*. Newport, Rhode Island: U.S. Torpedo Station, 1875.

———. *Lecture on the Whitehead Torpedo*. Newport, Rhode Island: U.S. Torpedo Station, 1874.

Barnes, J. S., Lieut. Commander, USN. *Submarine Warfare Offensive and Defensive, Including a Discussion of the Offensive Torpedo System, Its Effects Upon Iron-Clad Ship Systems, and Influence Upon Future Naval Wars*. New York: Van Nostrand, 1869.

Bell, Jack. *Civil War Heavy Explosive Ordnance*. Denton, TX: Univ. of North Texas Press, 2003.

Bell, Thaddeus G. *Probing the Oceans for Submarines*, (second edition, second printing). Los Altos Hills, CA: Peninsula Publishing, 2011.

Bowers, Peter M. *Curtiss Aircraft 1907-1947*. London: Putnam, 1979.

Bridgman, P. W. *Reflections of a Physicist*. New York: Philosophical Library, 1950.

Bureau of Standards. *War Work of the Bureau of Standards*. [Washington: Government Printing Office, 1921], Facsimile edition, Miami: HardPress, n.d.

Bush, Vannevar. *Modern Arms and Free Men*. New York: Simon and Schuster, 1949.

———. *Pieces of the Action*. New York: William Morrow and Company, 1970.

Butler, Gerald W. *Nahant's Naval Secrets*. Nahant, MA: Nahant Historical Society, 2012.

Cady, Walter G. *Piezoelectricity*. New York: McGraw-Hill, 1946.

Chambers, Hilary R., Jr. *United States Submarine Chasers in the Mediterranean, Adriatic and the Attack on Durazzo*. New York: Knickerbocker Press, 1920.

Clark, William B. *When the U-Boats Came to America*. Boston: Little, Brown, and Co., 1929.

Cochrane, Rexmond. *Measures for Progress: A History of the National Bureau of Standards*. Washington, D. C.: Government Printing Office, 1974.

Colella, Antonia and Luke Colella. *Now We're Talking*. Bloomington, IN: 1stBooks, 2003.

Council of National Defense. *First Annual Report for the Fiscal Year Ended June 30, 1817*. Washington, D. C.: n.p., 1917.

Daniels, Josephus. *Our Navy at War*. Washington, D. C.: Pictorial Bureau, 1922.

DeLany, Walter S. *Bayly's Navy*. Washington, D. C.: Naval Historical Foundation, 1980.

Dickenson, H. W. *Robert Fulton Engineer and Artist His Life and Works*. London: John Lane, 1913.

Domville-Fife, Charles. *Submarine Warfare of Today*. Philadelphia: J. B. Lippincott, 1920.

Edwards, Kenneth. *We Dive at Dawn*. Chicago: Reilly & Lee, 1941.

Fay, H. J. W. *Submarine Signal Log*. Portsmouth, RI: Raytheon Company, 1963.

Feuer, A. B. *The US Navy in World War I: Combat in the Sea and the Air*. Westport, CT: Praeger Publications, 1999.

Friedman, Norman. *U.S. Submarines Through 1945*. Annapolis, MD: Naval Institute Press, 1995.

Fulton, Robert. *Torpedo war and Submarine Explosions*. New York: William Elliot, 1810. Facsimile reproduction. Edited by Herman Henkle, Chicago: The Swallow Press, 1971.

Gibson, R. H. and Maurice Prendergast. *The German Submarine War 1914-1918*. London: Constable and Co., 1931.

Gray, George W. *Science at War*. New York: Harper & Brothers, 1943.

Griffin, Robert S. *History of the Bureau of Engineering, Navy Department, During the World War*. [Washington: Government Printing Office, 1922], Facsimile edition, Miami: HardPress Publishing, n.d.

Grossnik, Roy A. *Kite Balloons to Airships: the Navy's Lighter-than-Air Experience*. Washington, D. C.: Government Printing Office, n.d.

Hackmann, Willem. *Seek & Strike: Sonar, anti-submarine warfare and the Royal Navy 1914-54*. London: Her Majesty's Stationery Office, 1984.

Hannan, Caryn, ed. *Wisconsin Biographical Dictionary, 2008-2009 Edition*. Hamburg, MI: State History Publications, LLC, 2008.

Hashagen, Ernst. (Vesey Ross, translator). *U-Boats Westward*. New York: G. P. Putnam's Sons, 1931.

Hayes, Hammond V. *Submarine Signaling: An Address by Hammond V. Hayes, Ph.D., August 30, 1920*. Boston: Submarine Signal Company, n.d.

Hendrick, Burton J. *The Life and Letters of Walter H. Page*. Vols. 1 & 2, Garden City, NY: Doubleday, Page & Co., 1923. (Also available by searching "Diaries, Memorials, Personal Reminiscences" for "Page, Walter" at: http://wwi.lib.byu.edu/index.php/)

Henry, Chris. *Depth Charge!: Royal Navy Mines, Depth Charges and Underwater Weapons, 1914-1945*. South Yorkshire, England: Pen & Sword, 2005.

Horne, Charles F. PhD, ed. *Source Records of the Great War*. Vols. 1-7, National Alumni, 1923.

Hough, Richard. *The Great War At Sea, 1914-1918*. Oxford: Oxford University Press, 1983.

Humphreys, David. *An Essay on the Life of the Honorable Major-General Israel Putnam*. Middletown, CT: Moses H. Woodward, [1788] 1794.

Jane, Fred T. *Fighting Ships*. London: Sampson Low, Marston & Co., 1912.

Jellicoe, John Rushworth, Viscount of Scapa. *The Crisis of the Naval War*. New York: George H. Doran, 1921.

———.*The Grand Fleet 1914-1916: Its Creation, Development and Work*, New York: George H. Doran, 1919.

Kevles, Daniel J. *The Physicists*. New York: Alfred A. Knopf, 1978.

Kipling, Rudyard. *Sea Warfare*, Annapolis: Naval Institute Press, 2002 [C. Herbert Gilliland, editor of the facsimile reprint of *Sea Warfare* originally published London: Macmillan, 1916].

Leighton, John L. *SIMSADUS: London*. New York: Henry Holt, 1920.

London, Peter. *U-Boat Hunters: Cornwall's Air War 1916-19*. [Britain]: Dyllansow Truran, 1999.

Ludendorff, Erich. *My War Memories: 1914-1918*. Vols. 1 & 2. London: Hutchinson & Co., n.d. [c. 1919]

Lundeberg, Philip K. *Samuel Colt's Submarine Battery*. Washington: Smithsonian Institution Press, 1974.

Manstan, Roy. *Cold Warriors: The Navy's Engineering and Diving Support Unit*. Bloomington, IN: Authorhouse, 2014.

Manstan, Roy and Frederick J. Frese. *TURTLE: David Bushnell's Revolutionary Vessel*. Yardley, PA: Westholme, 2010.

Martin, Benjamin. *Philosophia Britannica*. Reading, England: C. Micklewright, 1747.

Merrill, John. *Fort Trumbull and the Submarine*. Avon, CT: Publishing Directions, 2000.

———. *From Submarine Bells to Sonar: Submarine Signal Company (1901-1946)*. Avon, CT: Publishing Directions, 2003.

———. *Submarines, Technology, and History*. Haverford, PA: Infinity Publishing, 2004.

Merrill, John and Lionel D. Wyld. *Meeting the Submarine Challenge: A Short History of the Naval Underwater Systems Center*. Washington: Government Printing Office, 1997.

Messimer, Dwight, *Find and Destroy: Antisubmarine Warfare in World War I*. Annapolis: Naval Institute Press, 2001.

Millholland, Ray. *The Splinter Fleet of the Otranto Barrage*. New York: Reader's League of America, 1936.

Millikan, Robert A. *The Autobiography of Robert A. Millikan*. New York: Prentiss Hall, 1950.

Moore, John, compiler. *Jane's Fighting Ships of World War I*. [facsimile edition of *Jane's Fighting Ships of World War I*. 1919] New York: Military Press, 1990.

Morris, Richard K. *John P. Holland 1841-1914: Inventor of the Modern Submarine*. Annapolis, MD: United States Naval Institute, 1966.

Mowthorpe, Ces. *Battlebags: British Airships of the First World War*. Britain: Wrens Park, 1998.

———. *Sky Sailors: The Story of the World's Airships*. Gloucesterhire, UK: History Press, 2010.

Muhlhauser, George H. P. *Small Craft*. London: John Lane Co., 1920.

National Research Council. *Third Annual Report of the National Research Council*. Washington: Government Printing Office, 1918.

Navy Department, Bureau of Ordnance, *Navy Ordnance Activities: World War 1917-1918*. Washington: Government Printing Office, 1920.

Navy Department, Office of Naval Intelligence. *Antisubmarine Information*. Compilation No. 14. Washington: Government Printing Office, November 1, 1918.

————. *Antisubmarine Tactics*. Publication No. 42. Washington: Government Printing Office, October, 1918.

————. *German Submarines in Question and Answer*. Publication No. 32. Washington: Government Printing Office, June, 1918.

Navy Department, Office of Naval Records and Library, Historical Section. *German Submarine Activities on the Atlantic Coast of the United States and Canada*, Publication Number 1. Washington: Government Printing Office, 1920.

Newbolt, Henry. *Submarine and Anti-Submarine*. New York: Longmans, Green and Co., 1919.

Nolan, Liam and John E. Nolan. *Secret Victory: Ireland and the War at Sea 1914-1918*. Cork, Ireland: Mercier, 2009.

Nutting, William W. *The Cinderellas of the Fleet*. Jersey City, New Jersey: The Standard Motor Construction Co., 1920.

Paine, Ralph D. *The First Yale Unit: A Story of Naval Aviation 1916-1919*. Vols. 1 & 2. Cambridge, MA: Riverside Press, 1925.

Perry, Lawrence. *Our Navy in the War*. New York: Charles Scribner's Sons, 1918.

Price, Alfred, PhD. *Aircraft versus Submarine in Two World Wars*. South Yorkshire, England: Pen and Sword, 2004.

Quarberg, Lincoln A., ed. "Wisconsin Battles the U-Boat Menace" in *The Liberty Badger*. Vol. 34, University of Wisconsin at Madison, 1919. 398-400.

Ragan, Mark. *Submarine Warfare in the Civil War*. Cambridge, MA: Da Capo Press, 2002.

Rodengen, Jeffery L. *The Legend of Electric Boat*. Ft. Lauderdale: Write Stuff Syndicate, 1994.

Roland, Alex. *Underwater Warfare in the Age of Sail*. Bloomington & London: Indiana Univ. Press, 1978.

Scheer, Reinhard. *Germany's High Sea Fleet in the World War*. London: Cassell and Co., 1920.

Scott, Lloyd N. *Naval Consulting Board of the United States*. [Washington: Government Printing Office, 1920], Facsimile edition, Miami: HardPress Publishing, n.d.

Sims, William S. with Burton J. Hendrick. *The Victory at Sea*. New York: Doubleday, Page & Co., 1920.

Stockbridge, Frank P. *Yankee Ingenuity in the War*. New York: Harper & Brothers, 1920.

Submarine Signal Co. *Submarine Signaling*. Boston: Merrymount Press, 1912.

Tarrant, V. E. *The U-Boat Offensive 1914-1945*. Annapolis: Naval Institute Press, 1989.

Taylor, Michael, compiler. *Jane's Fighting Aircraft of World War I*. [adapted from the 1919 edition of *All the World's Aircraft*] London: Random House Group, 2001.

Thomas, Lowell. *Raiders of the Deep*. Garden City, N.Y.: Doubleday, Doran & Co., 1928.

Thompson, T. B. *Take Her Down*, New York: Sheridan House, 1937.

Thwing, Charles F. *The American Colleges and Universities in the Great War*. New York: MacMillan, 1920.

Tobey, Ronald C. *The American Ideology of National Science, 1919-1930*. Pittsburg: Univ. of Pittsburg Press, 1971.

Trench, Martin E., J. P. Sullivan, W. J. Coggeshall, and J. E. McCarthy, compilers, pamphlet. *The Naval Torpedo Station*. Newport, RI: Training Center Press, 1920.

Van Treuren, Richard G. *Airships vs. Submarines*. Edgewater, FL: Atlantis Productions, 2009.

Weir, Gary E. *Building American Submarines 1914-1940*. Washington, D. C.: Naval Historical Center, 1991.

Wells, H. G. *In the Forth Year: Anticipations of a World Peace*. New York: MacMillan, 1918.

————. *The War That Will End War*. New York: Duffield & Company, 1914.

Wilkins, John. *Mathematical Magick: or the Wonders that may be Performed by Mathematical Geometry*. 4th ed. [1st published 1648] London: Ric. Baldwin, 1691.

Wilson, H. W. *Hush or the Hydrophone Service*. London: Mills & Boon, 1920.

Woodward, David R. *Trial by Friendship: Anglo-American Relations, 1917-1918*. Lexington, KY: University Press of Kentucky, 1993.

Woofenden, Todd A. *Hunters of the Steel Sharks: The Submarine Chasers of WWI*. Bowdoinham, ME: Signal Light Books, 2006.

Wright, Helen. *Explorer of the Universe: A Biography of George Ellery Hale*. New York: E. P. Dutton & Co., 1966.

Yerkes, Robert M., ed. *The New World of Science: Its Development During the War*. New York: The Century Co.,1920.

JOURNALS, MISC PERIODICALS, AND MANUSCRIPTS

American Association for International Conciliation. "Documents Regarding the European War Series No. IX, Official Correspondence Between the United States and Germany." *International Conciliation*, 94 (September, 1915).

Article. "Admiral's Incognito Adventures: Secret Mission in England." *Auckland Star*, 50, 137 (June 10, 1919).

Article. "Earl Haig 'Plays Himself In': Once 'Field Marshall' in France, Now 'Captain of the Royal and Ancient,' One of the Greatest Honors in Golf." *The American Golfer* (November, 1920).

Article. "Harvey Hayes, Formerly of Oneonta Submits Design to Government." *Oneonta Daily Star* (December 27, 1917).

Article. "Prof. Hayes Summoned to Leave Swarthmore and Complete Device." *Oneonta Daily Star* (December 28, 1917).

Article. "Sure U-Boats in Gulf of Mexico." *The Day* [of New London, CT] (April 6, 1917).

Article. "Swarthmore Inventor Called By U.S. To Finish U-Boat Device: Prof. H. C. Hayes, College Physicist, Perfecting Device to Defeat Submarine—To Work in Secret Laboratory." unidentified newspaper clipping, c. Dec 1917.

Article. "Whannel Was At Fort Trumbull During World War I." *ECHO*, 11, 8, U.S. Navy Underwater Sound Laboratory, New London, CT. (March 11, 1955).

Bankson, Fred George. *A Sailor's Diary During World War I Aboard the Submarine Chaser 177*. Available at http://readytogoebooks.com/jgbooks/Diary-P-1918.html

Bean, James (Ensign). "War-time Naval Radio Instruction." Stanford, 1920, covers plus sixteen manuscript pages. [Submarine Force Library and Museum archives]

———. "The Naval Experimental Station at New London, Conn." n.d. [c. 1920], covers plus five manuscript pages. [Submarine Force Library and Museum archives]

———. "Notes from the Hydrophone School." Sept. 10 [1918], covers plus sixty-five manuscript pages. [Submarine Force Library and Museum archives]

Bushnell, David. "General Principles and Construction of a Submarine Vessel." *Transactions of the American Philosophical Society* 4 (1799) 303-312.

Cady, Walter. "Piezoelectricity and Ultrasonics." *Sound: Its Uses and Control*, 2, 1, (Jan-Feb 1963) 46-52.

Fay, R. D. "Underwater-Sound Reminiscences: Mostly Binaural." *Sound: Its Uses and Control*, 2, 6, (Nov-Dec 1963) 37-42.

Graff, Karl F. "A History of Ultrasonics." *Physical Acoustics*, Vol. 15, Chapter 1, Warren P. Mason and R. N. Thurston, eds. New York: Academic Press, 1981.

Hayes, Harvey. "Detection of Submarines." *Proceedings of the American Philosophical Society*, 59, 1 (1920) 1-47.

———. "U.S. Navy MV Type of Hydrophone as an Aid and Safeguard to Navigation" in *Proceedings of the American Philosophical Society*. 59, 5 (1920) 371-404.

———. "World War I Submarine Detection." *Sound: Its Uses and Control*, 1, 5 (Sept.-Oct. 1962) 47-48.

Lasky, Marvin. "A Historical Review of Underwater Acoustic Technology 1916-1939 with Emphasis on Undersea Warfare." *U.S. Navy Journal of Underwater Acoustics*, 24, 4 (October 1973) 597-624.

———. "Review of undersea acoustics." *J. Acoustical Society of America*, 61, 2 (February 1977) 283-297.

———. "Review of World War I Acoustic Technology." *U.S. Navy Journal of Underwater Acoustics*, 24, 2 (July 1973) 363-385.

Lemon, Stanley G. "Towed-Array History, 1917-2001." *IEEE Journal of Oceanic Engineering*, 29, 2 (April 2004) 365-373.

Mason, Max. "Submarine Detection by Multiple Unit Hydrophones." *The Wisconsin Engineer*, 25, 5-7 (Feb-Apr, 1921) 75-77, 99-102, 116-120.

MacLeod, Roy M. and E. Kay Andrews. "Scientific Advice in the War at Sea, 1915-1917: the Board of Invention and Research." *Journal of Contemporary History*, 6, 2 (1971) 3-40.

McDowell, C. S. "Naval Research." *United States Naval Institute Proceedings*, 45, 6, (June 1919) 895-908.

Melville, Rear Admiral George W. "The Submarine Boat: Its Value as a Weapon in Naval Warfare." *The Annual Report of the Smithsonian Institution for the Year Ending June 30, 1901*. (Washington: Government Printing Office, 1902) 717-738.

Merritt, Ernest. Cornell archives, ref: 14-22-46 b3, March 23, 1917-December 27, 1918.

Millikan, Robert A. "A New Opportunity in Science." *Science*, 50, 1291 (Sept. 26, 1919).

Naval Torpedo Station. "Notes on Moveable Torpedoes." A series of individual articles, bound together, no date, c. 1875, paginated in sequence, 1-33.

Richardson, E. H., ed. *The Official Bulletin*, [published weekdays] Vol. 1 No. 1-No. 69, Washington D.C.: Committee on Public Information, (May 10-July 31, 1917).

Roosevelt, Theodore. "American Preparedness." *The New York Times Current History: The European War*. Vol. 4, July-September, 1915. New York: New York Times, 1917.

Sims, William S. "The Victory at Sea." Serialized in *The World's Work: A History of our Time*. [Page, Arthur ed.] Vol. 38-39. New York: Doubleday, Page & Co., 1919-1920.

Walding, Richard. "Bragg and Mitchell's Antisubmarine Loop." *Australian Physics*. Vol 46, No 5 (September/October 2009) 140-45.

Weir, Gary E. "Surviving the Peace: The Advent of American Naval Oceanography 1914-1924." *Naval War College Review*, 1, 4, (Autumn, 1997) 84-103.

Wilson, H. A. "The Theory of Receivers for Sound in Water." *The Physical Review: A Journal of Experimental and Theoretical Physics*. 15, 3 (1920) 178-205.

Wizard, William. "Plan For Defending Our Harbor." *Connecticut Courant*, Hartford, CT, September 9, 1807.

Wood, A. B. "Reminiscences of Underwater-Sound Research, 1915-1917." *Sound: Its Uses and Control*, 1, 3, (May-June 1962) 8-17.

Page numbers in boldface refer to illustrations.

222, 226, 242-43, 244, 248, 255, 260, **261**, 262-63, 265. *See also* Y-gun

destroyers, 3, 4, 11, 12, 18, 36, 43, 47-48, **48**, 154, 172, 237; as convoy escorts, 155, 166, 238, 241, 242-44; detection of by U-boats, 51; in a hunting group, 48, 51, 170, 219, 247, 257, 259-60, 263, 264-65, 267, 269; listening devices for, 95, 114, 145, 190, 193, **196**, 197-98, 202, 204, 206-08, 226; at Queenstown (Ireland) naval base, 202-03, 258

Deutschland (German mercantile submarine): in American ports of Baltimore and New London, 18, 64-66, 67, **68**, 288n19; conversion to combatant vessel, *U-155*, 232, 245; *Deutschland*-type submarines, 229, 231; objections to by Allies, 66; possible intelligence gathering mission, 65, 69. *See also U-155*

Ditman, Albert (naval reserve pilot): on flights to (in Curtiss R-6) and experimental work at New London, 176; on experiences with suspected German sympathizers, 176; on tests of listening devices and difficulties, 185

Dole, George S. (Ensign, commanding officer of *SC-93*): on winter conditions in New London, 163

Domville-Fife, Charles (commander of British hydrophone flotilla): on hydrophones, 19; on depth charges (hit or miss), 19; on Motor Launch submarine hunting vessels, 47, 49; operation of hydrophone flotilla, 46, 50-51

Dover Straits: mine fields, 41, 42

drifters (British): as submarine hunting vessel, 27, 30, 36, 40, 46, 47, 49, 259, 267, 285n20

Durazzo, Albanian naval base: attacked 250, 268, 302n28

E-1: crosses Atlantic, 147; mentioned in test plan with aircraft at New London,

297n10(ch.18); with submarine bell, **148**, 212

Eagle (British man-of-war): 1776 attack on by *Turtle*, vii, x

echo-location: described, 52-53; considered for future development, 97, 103, 273, 274-76; sound propagation poorly understood, 277. *See also* supersonics

Edison, Thomas: heads the Naval Consulting Board, 72; on scientific approach to solving submarine problems, 73, 98. *See also* Josephus Daniels

Edwards, Kenneth (British naval lieutenant commander): on submarine communications via carrier pigeon, 217-18

electric eel (listening device): described, 193, 194, 197-98, **199**, 206, 208, 298n17(ch.20); on Curtiss HS-2, **199**; on B-class dirigible, **200**

electromagnetic detection: described, 43, 44, 221; devices for surface vessels actively hunting, 222-24 (test data plot, **225**); secrecy and concerns about German countermeasures, 226. *See also* AD-tube; magnetic indicator loops; Ernest Merritt; Alexander Crichton Mitchell; MK IV (British) Search System

English Channel: declared a war zone, 2, 25; shore stations (acoustic and electromagnetic) in, 40-42, 222, 233; *U-62* pursued in, 51; operations in, 146, 150-51, 167, 211, 244, 263

European scientific mission. *See* scientific mission to America

Fabry, Charles: French delegate on the scientific mission to America, 53, 101-02, 103

Fay, Harold J. W. (of Submarine Signal Company): proposes establishment of experimental station at Nahant,

Massachusetts, 96, 97; provides
listening device to Naval Experimental
Station, 128

Fay, Richard D. (of the Nahant
Experimental Station): on submarine
detector patent, 198

Fessenden, Reginald: develops wireless
radio communication, 219

Fessenden oscillator: for iceberg
detection, 94; tests of for underwater
communications, 94-95

Fire Island Lightship: installation of
X-tube device recommended, 237,
300n22(ch.22)

*The First Yale Unit: A Story of Naval
Aviation 1916-1919* (Paine), 172

Firth of Forth, Scotland, 19, 20,
22-23, 27, 30-33; listener training,
148; shore stations (acoustic and
electromagnetic) established in, 40,
44; *U-21* in, 22; *UB-63* attacked,
262. *See also* Hawkcraig Admiralty
Experimental Station; C. P. Ryan

Fisher, John: chairman of the Board of
Invention and Research, 25-26, 34;
on German superiority, 25; warns
Admiralty of U-boat threat, 25

"fix" (bearing determination): 6, 151,
168-70, **169**, 256-57, 260, 265. *See
also* position plotter

Fleming, J. A. (British scientist), 24

Folkstone, (English Channel), 42, 62

Fort Trumbull: site of Naval
Experimental Station, xi, 7, 111, 118,
142, 278

Fulton, Robert: promotes submarine and
torpedo warfare, 13

G-1: with Y-tube installed, **197**; proposed
for supersonic (echo) detection
system installation, 275

G-2: at Nahant Experimental Station,
126; at the submarine base (February,
1918), **164**; as test vessel at the
Naval Experimental Station, 202,

203; proposed for supersonic (echo)
detection system installation, 275

G-3: as test vessel at the Naval
Experimental Station, 223, 224

G-4: at the submarine base (February,
1918), **164**; as test vessel at New
London, 156, 211-12

General Electric Co. (Nahant
Experimental Station), 95, 97, 98,
109, 111, 112, 125, 150

George, Lloyd (British Prime Minister):
sends the Balfour mission to the U.S.,
92

George Washington (SSBN 598):
submarine warfare at the end of the
twentieth century, **271**

Gerard, James W. (U.S. Ambassador to
Germany), 58, 289n2

German war strategy: submarines, 69,
110, 219, 245. *See also* unrestricted
submarine warfare

*Germany's High Sea Fleet in the World
War* (Scheer), 11, 79

Gibraltar: antisubmarine activities, 239,
250, 253-54, 255, 257, 258, 262-63,
269; convoys, 240-41

Golf, a wartime recreation, 201,
298nn1&2

Goschen, Edward (British ambassador to
Germany), 11

Grand Fleet, The (Britain): described in
The Grand Fleet, 1914-1916 (Jellicoe),
18; at Jutland (Battle of), 12; prepares
for war, 11-12; and *UB-116* at Scapa
Flow (fleet had moved to the Firth of
Forth), 44-45

Granton Pier (Edinburgh): Ryan's early
experimental work at, 26-27, 28, 33,
34, 40, 44. *See also* Alexander Crichton
Mitchell

The Great War: referred to as, xi, 2, 7,
12, 17, 19, 86, 172, 191, 271, 278

Griffin, Robert S. (Chief of the Bureau
of Steam Engineering): on aircraft
for submarine hunting, 181; on

airships for submarine hunting, 193; on electromagnetic detection, 222; on invisible light (infrared) for communication, 216; on listener training, 145; member of the NRC Military Committee, 76, 111; favors New London as a site for an experimental station, 111-112, and promises cooperation from the submarine base, 112; on Pensacola, early submarine detection tests at, 94; on scientific staff, his concerns about understanding naval operational requirements, 144-45; on secrecy, 131, 273; on shore stations, British, 40; on need for submarine chasers, 154, 155; estimate of submarines lost due to use of antisubmarine devices, 272; on supersonics, 53

Griz Nez. *See* Cap Griz Nez

Hale, George Ellery: disagrees with Thomas Edison, 73; with National Academy of Sciences, 73-74; supports President Wilson's change of attitude toward Germany, 74; hosts the scientific mission to America, 101

Halsey, William Clowden: his submarine used in War of 1812, 13, 283n9

Harvard (SP-209): in the war zone, **242**

Harvard Radio School, 146, 147, 220. *See also* James Bean

Harvard Underwater Sound Laboratory (World War II), xi

Hashagen, Ernst (commanding officer, *U-62*): on antisubmarine warfare, xii, 246-47; on evasive techniques and listeners, 210-11; on mine fields, 42-43; on pursuit by British hydrophone flotilla near the English Channel, 51; on silencing, 247; on his U-boat service, 51

Hawkcraig Admiralty Experimental Station: established at Aberdour, 27-28, **41**; BIR scientists at, 34-35;

move from Granton Pier (Edinburgh) to, 26, 27, 34, 44. *See also* listener training (British); C. P. Ryan

Hayes, Harvey C. (Swarthmore College): on the electric eel listening device, 197-98; on electromagnetic detection, 221; at New London, 118-19, **120**, **144**; post-war tests of MV-tube type fathometer, 207, 208; on resonant [hydrophone] receivers, 22-23; on submarine detection, 104-05; on effectiveness of the technologies developed for the war, 272

Hertz, Heinrich: Hertzian waves, 218

High Seas Fleet (Germany); battle of Jutland, 12, 81; prepares for war, 11

Hildegarde (SP-1221): for installation of X-tube device at New London, 300n22(ch.22)

History of the Bureau of Engineering (Griffin), 40, 94, 131, 181, 216

Hogue (British cruiser): sunk by *U-9*, xi, 12, 22, 245

homeland defense against submarines. *See* Chief of Naval Operations

Houghton, S. C. (Lieutenant Commander, Royal Navy Volunteer Reserves): British liaison officer at the Naval Experimental Station, 185, **192**; attended supersonic system tests, 274

Humphreys, David, viii

Hunley: underwater attack, x; use of spar torpedo, 13

Hunters of the Steel Sharks: The Submarine Chasers of WWI (Woofenden), 238, 248, 262

hydrophone, 18, 19, 20, 23, 27, 29-30, 36, 137, 185-87, 193-94, 197, 206, 208, 210, 234, 245, 256, 259; described, 22, 31, 105; resonant and non-resonant, 22-23; tests of (at Nahant and New London), 123-24, 127-28; types (sound receivers) available shown, **106, 196 (inset)**; use

of on U-boats, 46, 51, 153, 211, 246.
See also listening devices (American
and British)

hydrophone flotilla (British): described,
46; limitations during hunting
operations, 19, 50-51; use of trawlers
and drifters and losses, 46-47;
operations with, 247, 262-63, (listener
shown, **264**). *See also* Motor launch

hydrophone schools. *See* listener training
(British and American)

Imperial German Government: on
Lusitania, 55, 58-60; Woodrow
Wilson and declaration of war, 85-86

Imperial German Navy (*Kaiserliche
Marine*): on submarines and U-boat
campaign, xii, 2, 11, 52, 70, 81

infrared (IR) signaling: operational
tests (lightless signaling), 215-17;
devices shown, **217**. *See also* Bureau of
Standards; Robert S. Griffin; Theodore
Case

Ingalls, David (naval reserve pilot): at
New London, 179; service overseas,
180, 297n16

invisible light. *see* infrared (IR) signaling

Jefferson, Thomas: letter from David
Bushnell, vii, viii, ix

Jellicoe, John Rushworth (British First
Lord of the Admiralty): creates the
Admiralty's Anti-Submarine Division
(ASD), 35, 39; on convoys, 240; on
hydrophones, 18; on listener training,
29, 33; on magnetic indicator loops,
43; on concern over U-boats, 18; on
U-boat tactics, 15, 137; with Admiral
William S. Sims, 90, 240

Joffre, Joseph (Commander of allied
forces on the Western Front): in
America (1917), 93.

Jouett (DD-41): as Naval Experimental
Station test vessel, 202,

298n15(ch.20); antisubmarine patrols
along the U.S. coast, 237-38

Jutland, Battle of (also known as the
Battle of the Skagerrak), 12, 245

K-tube (listening device): developed at
Nahant, 109, 128, **129**, 186, 193-94,
206, 234; early tests of in English
Channel, 153; listener shown, **130**;
for subchasers, standard equipment
on, 156, 166, (shown on *SC-19*, **130**),
208, 215, 248, **250**; installed on
submarines, **1**, 148

Kaiserliche Marine. See Imperial German
Navy

Kelly, "Red" (commanding officer of *SC-
124*), 5, 251

Kevles, Daniel: on Thomas Edison, 73;
on Max Mason, 201; on MV-tube
operation, 204

Kipling, Rudyard: on submarine warfare,
1-2

Koenig, Paul (commanding officer
of *Deutschland*): on mercantile
submarines, 64-65

Königin Luise (German minelayer), 11; is
sunk, 11

Körner, Frederick (officer on board
U-151): on arriving off the U.S.
Atlantic coast, 228; as listener
on *U-151*, 230; on mine laying
(Chesapeake and Delaware Bay), 229,
230; on severing transatlantic cables,
231; on submarine warfare, future of,
271

L-8: at the submarine base (February,
1918), **164**.

L-9 (*AL-9*): Atlantic crossing, 147-48,
265; at Bantry Bay (Ireland), **1**, 265-
66; listening device installed, 148;
testing at Nahant and New London,
114-15, 126-27; as U-boat hunter,
266-67. *See also*, T. B. Thompson

listener shown **264**; operating with a destroyer, 48, 51, 257, 259, 263, 267; stationed at, 262; U-boats attacked by, 262-63; underway at sea, **50**

MV-tube (listening device), 109; described, 204, 206; as installed on *G-2* and possibly *Jouett*, 202, **203**; overseas installations, 201; post-war application as fathometer, 208

Nahant Antisubmarine Laboratory, 97. *See* Nahant Experimental Station

Nahant Experimental Station: established as partnership between Submarine Signal Co., General Electric Co. and Western Electric C0., xi, 97, **98**, 111; and the Naval Consulting Board, 102, 103, 105, 222; and the scientific mission to America, 102-03; and the Special Board on Antisubmarine Devices, 99, 111, 121, 131, 136, 143; testing and industrial focus at, 102, 109, 112, 115, 124, 125-130, 137, 147, 153, 165, (with aircraft 176, 186, 193, 194), 202, 203, 214, 234, 235, 248; patent issues, 104, 198. *See also* C-tube; K-tube; *Margaret* (SP-524)

Narada (SP-161): assigned to the Naval Experimental Station, 117; outfitted for testing, 124, 202

Nash, George H.: designs the Nash Fish, 37

Nash Fish, 35-37, **37**, 38, 123

National Academy of Sciences: on the war, 73; with President Wilson, establishes the National Research Council, 73-74

National Research Council (NRC): established, 74, 75-76; military committee of, 91, 111; scientific approach to submarine detection, 102, 105, 110, 118, 222; and the scientific mission to America, 101, 102, 274; and the Special Board on Antisubmarine Devices, 99, 104. *See*

also Ames scientific mission to France; Balfour mission to the U.S.; Council of National Defense; George Ellery Hale; Robert Millikan

Naval Consulting Board (NCB): established and committees formed, 72, 73, 95, 98; Industrial rather than scientific approach, 100, 102-03, 105, 111, 222; and the Special Board on Antisubmarine Devices, 103-04; Special Problems Committee formed (re: "submarine menace"), 95, 96-97. *See also* Council of National Defense; Thomas Edison

Naval Consulting Board of the United States (Scott), 70, 110

Naval Experimental Station (New London): aircraft at, **175**, 176-77, 182-200, (*See* Naval Reserve Flying Corps) chapter 19; foreign visitors at, **192**; funding for, 142, 294nn9&10; industrial support for, 143; listener training at, 145-46, 148; marine railway, **158**; at New London (Fort Trumbull), xi, 3, 4, 44, 99, 102, 105, 109, 110-112, 118, 122-23, 137, 142, **143**, 153, (*also* chapters 17, 19, 20, 21), 232, 234-35, 248, 273; radio telephone school at, 146; scientific attachés, 143; secrecy at, 129, 130-32; staffing (civilian), 7, 119, 142, **144**; staffing (Navy), 7, 142; Station shown (aerial photograph), **140**; Station shown (plan view drawing), **138-139**; subchasers at, 127, 155-57, 163, 238; supersonic (echo) detection, 53, 275, 276; test vessels needed, 116-17, 124; winter conditions 1917-1918, 163-65, 171. *See also* James Bean; Mohican Hotel; *and individual staff*: P. W. Bridgman; H. A. Bumstead; William Guyton Cady; Theodore Case; Harvey C. Hayes; Max Mason; Ernest Merritt; Robert Millikan; M. I. Pupin; H. A. Wilson; John Zeleny

London, 164-65; on the Otranto Barrage, 258, 267; on post-war antisubmarine technology research, 208, 272; screened microphones, requests for overseas testing, 185; on section patrol (converted yachts), 241; on subchasers, 7, 154, 155, 159, 255; on submarine chaser crew inexperience and training, 165; on the subchasers crossing the Atlantic, 250-51, 255; on subchaser hunting tactics, 167-68, 170, 258-59; on *U-53*, the hunt for, 263-65; on difficulties finding and destroying U-boats, 3, 153, 244, 255; on U-boats on U.S. coast, 229-31, 232

sound waves & phase: discussed, 115-16; related to listening devices, 97, 107, 109, 114, 186, 197-98, 204-06, 208. *See also* supersonics

Special Board on Antisubmarine Devices: established and authority expanded (Secretary of the Navy Daniels), 4, 35, 98-99, 104, 111, 114, 118, 121, 122, 223; goals, 227, 248; naval operational requirements and scientific interests, coordination of, 103, 112, 116, 119, 123-24, 126, 136, 138, 142, 144-45, 180, 183, 198, 216; on non-acoustic (electronic) detection, 211, 214, 226; on secrecy, 130-31, 219-20; on supersonics, 53, 273, 275. *See also* Clyde S. McDowell

spies (and German sympathizers), mentioned, 96; concerns about, 131; poster warning of, **132**

The Splinter Fleet of the Otranto Barrage (Millholland), 5, 132, 247

Squier, George O. (Army Chief Signal Officer), 76

Standard Motor Construction Co.: selected to build submarine chaser engines, 155; use on British motor launches, 49, 155-56

Stifinder (Norwegian bark): sunk by *U-152*, 238, **239**

Stirling, Yates Jr. (commanding officer at the submarine base): provides support to Naval Experimental Station staff, 122; operations with the Naval Reserve Flying Corps, 177-79

Stockbridge, Frederick: on Guglielmo Marconi, 218-19. *See also* Charles P. Scott; Richard H. Leigh

subchaser (SC-class) vessels: assigned to U.S. coastal antisubmarine patrols, 237-39; Atlantic crossing, 5, 170, 208, 248, 250-54, **254**, 258; crew requirements, 157; described, 209, and as "vicious-looking little war vessel," 158; hunting group shown, **168**; hunting tactics described, 167-70, 209-10, 215-16, 258; at Nahant, 127; need for, 154-155, 159; at New London, 6, 132, (marine railway, **158**); numbers built, 157; specifications and construction of, 155-56, (shipyards, 156, **157**, 158); training of, 165-66, (realism questioned, 170); winter conditions at New London, 158, 163-65. *See also* deck guns; listening devices; listeners; individual SC-class vessels; *also* Fred George Bankson; Hilary R. Chambers; George S. Dole; William W. Nutting; Ray Millholland; George Wallace

subchaser bases. *See* Bantry Bay (Queenstown, Ireland); Corfu (Greek island of); Plymouth (England)

submarine base, Groton, Connecticut, 4, 111, 112; with aircraft, 176, 177-79; civilian staff at, 118, 122, 131 ,137, 156, 211; listener training at, 145, 147; provides submarines for experimental work, 126, 142, 165, 166, 170-71. *See also* Atlantic Submarine Flotilla submarine bell: patent for submarine communications, 94; on submarines, **148**. *See also* lightships

submarine chasers. *See* subchasers

submarine detection (by sound): issues associated with, 97, 104-05, 256. *See also* listening devices; supersonics

submarine detection (electromagnetic and electronic devices): issues associated with, 43, 97, 210-11, 221-22, 226, 273, 291n9. *See also* electromagnetic detection; trailing wire

Submarine Signal Company, 23, 94-95, 97, 98, 124, 284n7. *See also* Nahant Experimental Station.

submarine silencing (German): vulnerability understood, 4, 110, 244, 245-48, 255. *See also* Ernst Hashagen; Ray Millholland; Office of Naval Intelligence; Lloyd N. Scott

submarine warfare: origins in Connecticut, vii-x

Submarine Warfare of Today (Domville-Fife), 46

submarines, American. *See* individual D-class, E-class, G-class, L-class boats

submarines, British. *See* individual B-class boats

submarines, German: construction of, 64, 245; in Mexican waters, newspaper speculation, 84; numbers available, 4, 17. *See also individual U-boats* (U-type, UB-type, UC-type); *also Deutschland*

supersonics: for active (echo) submarine detection, 52, 97, 274-75, 276; of interest to British scientists, 53; plans for use by France, 54; frequency range considered, 52, 274; Paris conference on (October 1918), 277; topic discussed during scientific mission to America conference, 53, 103, 274; suggested for "secret signaling," 275. *See also* cavitation; *scientists involved*: Walter Guyton

Cady; Paul Langevin; M. I. Pupin; Harris J. Ryan

Sussex (British steamer): torpedoed, 62, **63**, 68, 74, 79, 82

Sutphin, Henry R.: on Electric Boat contract for British Motor Launch class vessels, 47, 286n4(ch.5)

T.A. Scott (American steamer): sinks after accidental collision with Deutschland, 67

Take Her Down (Thompson), 114, 266

Tarlair (British "drifter"): assigned to Hawkcraig, 27, **27**, 30; as a listener training ship, 33, 148

Tesla, Nikola, 218

Thetis (SP-391): assigned to the Naval Experimental Station, 117, **117**, 122; used for listener training, 147; test support, 123-24, 156, 185, 211-12, 223-24

Thomas, Lowell: on the effect U-boats had on the war, 22; interview with Frederick Körner about *U-151*, 228-31, 271-72; interviews with U-boat officers Hans Valentiner and Rudolph Zentner about sinking of *Lusitania*, 57-58;

Thompson, T. B., (*L-9* executive officer): on experimental work at Nahant, 126-27; at New London, 114-15 (refers to civilian staff as "brainy beachcombers"); on Atlantic crossing, 147; U-bout hunting along west coast of England described, 266-67

Thwing, Charles F.: on physics the basis of technology, 99, 143, 291n9; on infrared signaling, 299n4

Ticonderoga (Navy cargo ship): torpedoed and sunk off U.S. coast, 238

The Times of London: article by H. G. Wells, 23-24; on science and the war, 24

torpedo: word coined by Robert Fulton, 13; history of, x, 13-17; torpedo defense, 96; use against U-boats, 4,

18; use by U-boats, 12, 18, 22, 47, 55, 57-59, 62-63 (number carried, 69, 231, 232), 74, 88, 137, **242**, 243, 269; visible track when fired, 3, 47, **48**. *See also* Bliss-Leavitt; Naval Torpedo Station; Schwartzkopff; Whitehead

trailing wire device: described, 210-11, **213**, 222; referred to as "electric fingers," xii; tests of (in the English Channel), 212, 214; tests of (at New London), 211-12; use of, 257-58. *See also* trawling apparatus

training. *See* listener training

trawlers (British), 46-47, 49; as convoy escorts, 240; listener shown, **30**; listening device tests in English Channel, 150, 153; use in U-boat hunting groups, 36, 38, 259, 262, 267

trawling apparatus, 151, 211-12

Trelissick (British steamer): torpedoed and sunk by *UC-72*, **242**

Triple Entente, 2

"trombone" device. *See* Max Mason

Turtle: attack on *Eagle*, vii-viii, x; illustration of by Francis Barber, **vii**; described, viii-x; replica of, viii, 316, **335**. *See also* Bushnell, David

Tynwald, steamship: rescues passengers when *New York* strikes a mine, 89

U-9: attack on *Aboukir*, *Cressy*, and *Hogue*, xi, 12, 245

U-20: attack on *Lusitania*, 47, 55, 57; shown, **56**

U-21, 22

U-22, 51

U-53: (1916) at Newport, Rhode Island, 66, **67**, 69; sinks shipping on return voyage, 66-67; (1918) hunt for while operating near the British Isles, 263-65; returns to Germany, 265

U-59: damaged by mines, 42

U-62, xii, 42, 51, 210-11, 246. *See also* Ernst Hashagen

U-63: on return past Gibraltar at Armistice, 269

U-82: log book entries about attack on convoy, 242-43

U-88: lost in mine field, 57-58

U-117: off American coast, 91, **92**, 232, 239

U-140: off American coast, 232, 239

U-151: off American coast, 227, **228**, 228-31, 234, 237, 238, 271. *See also* Frederick Körner

U-152: off American coast, 232, 238-39, **239**. *See also Stifinder.*

U-155: off American coast, 67, **68**, 232, 239, 245; referred to as a U-cruiser by Reinhard Scheer, 69. *See also Deutschland*

U-156: off American coast, 231, 232

UB-21, 51

UB-29: torpedo attack on *Sussex*, 74

UB-50: torpedo attack on HMS *Britannia* near Gibraltar, 269

UB-63: attacked and sunk by British, 262

UB-71: attacked and sunk by British, 263

UB-116: lost by remotely detonated mines at Scapa Flow (Orkney Islands), 45

UC-49: attacked and sunk by British, 263

UC-72: torpedo attack on British steamer *Trelissick*, 242

UC-78: presumed lost by mines in the Dover Straits, 42

U-boats. *See* submarines, German

U-boats attacked: evidence needed to confirm loss, 151-52; losses, 4; by ramming, 3-4, 18, 47, 48, 93, 228, 241, 244, 266. *See also* depth charge; mine fields (British); individual U-boats listed

U-boat detection avoidance and escape tactics, 167, 210-11, 226; use of oil slick, 151-52, 246-47, 260, 263, 265. *See also* Max Mason; Office of Naval Intelligence; submarine silencing (German)

Garnet Books

Titles with asterisks (*) are also in the Driftless Connecticut Series

*Garnet Poems: An Anthology of
Connecticut Poetry Since 1776**
Dennis Barone, editor

*The Connecticut Prison Association and the
Search for Reformative Justice**
Gordon Bates

*Food for the Dead: On the Trail of
New England's Vampires*
Michael E. Bell

*The Long Journeys Home:
The Repatriations of Henry 'Ōpūkaha'ia
and Albert Afraid of Hawk**
Nick Bellantoni

*The Case of the Piglet's Paternity:
Trials from the New Haven Colony,
1639–1663**
Jon C. Blue

Early Connecticut Silver, 1700–1840
Peter Bohan and Philip Hammerslough

*The Connecticut River: A Photographic Journey
through the Heart of New England*
Al Braden

*Tempest-Tossed: The Spirit of
Isabella Beecher Hooker*
Susan Campbell

*Connecticut's Fife & Drum Tradition**
James Clark

Sunken Garden Poetry, 1992–2011
Brad Davis, editor

*Rare Light: J. Alden Weir in Windham,
Connecticut, 1882–1919**
Anne E. Dawson, editor

*The Old Leather Man: Historical Accounts of a
Connecticut and New York Legend*
Dan W. DeLuca, editor

*Post Roads & Iron Horses: Transportation in
Connecticut from Colonial Times to the Age of
Steam**
Richard DeLuca

*The Log Books: Connecticut's Slave Trade and
Human Memory**
Anne Farrow

*Birding in Connecticut**
Frank Gallo

Dr. Mel's Connecticut Climate Book
Dr. Mel Goldstein

*Hidden in Plain Sight: A Deep Traveler Explores
Connecticut*
David K. Leff

*Maple Sugaring: Keeping It Real in
New England*
David K. Leff

*Becoming Tom Thumb: Charles Stratton,
P. T. Barnum, and the Dawn of American Celebrity**
Eric D. Lehman

*Homegrown Terror: Benedict Arnold and the
Burning of New London**
Eric D. Lehman

*The Traprock Landscapes of
New England**
Peter M. LeTourneau and Robert Pagini

*Westover School: Giving Girls a Place of
Their Own*
Laurie Lisle

Roy Manstan emerging from the replica Turtle *after submerging the vessel at the Mystic Seaport Museum, 2008.* (Courtesy Jerry Roberts)

Born in Georgia and raised in Connecticut, Manstan received a BS degree from Lafayette College, an MS degree from the University of Connecticut, both in mechanical engineering, and an MA in zoology from Connecticut College. He began his career at the U.S. Navy Underwater Sound Laboratory (USN/USL) in 1967. USN/USL became the Naval Underwater Systems

Center (NUSC) in 1970, then the Naval Undersea Warfare Center (NUWC) in 1992, from which he retired in January, 2006. In 1974, he completed Navy SCUBA training at the Submarine Base in Groton, CT, and was a member of the Engineering and Diving Support Unit, becoming its diving officer in 1986. During and after the Cold War, the author led this field engineering/diving team on operations throughout the world—from the Arctic to Africa and the Azores; and to the Orkney Islands, Naples, Bahrain, Oman, Singapore, the Philippines, the Panama Canal, St. Croix, Puerto Rico, Cuba, Bermuda, and nearly every naval base along the U.S. coast. In 2003, Manstan volunteered to assist Frederic Frese, teacher at Old Saybrook [CT] High School, with the design and construction of a working replica of David Bushnell's eighteenth-century submarine *Turtle*. The project culminated with its launch in 2007 and operational testing in 2008. The author continued his volunteer work, helping students build a twenty-first century submarine, which was entered in the 2011 International Human Powered Submarine Races. In 2010, Manstan published, with co-author Fred Frese, *TURTLE: David Bushnell's Revolutionary Vessel*, and in 2013, he published *Cold Warriors: The Navy's Engineering and Diving Support Unit*, the history of his Cold War field engineering team.